Courtesy of the authors

About the Authors

BARRY ROSENBERG is a longtime journalist specializing in aviation, technology, and issues of national defense. He has written for respected industry publications such as *Aviation Week &
Space Technology* for the past twenty years and regularly writes
reports on issues of peace and security for the Carnegie Corporation of New York and others.

CATHERINE MACAULAY has contributed to many publications over the years. Her work has appeared in magazines
ranging from *E/The Environment Magazine* to the *Daily Racing
Forum*.

Coauthors and partners, Rosenberg and Macaulay have
shared their lives with a retinue of cats, dogs, and horses for the
past two decades. They divide their time between Westchester,
New York, and Calabasas, California.

MAVERICKS
OF THE SKY

THE FIRST DARING PILOTS OF THE U.S. AIR MAIL

BARRY ROSENBERG &
CATHERINE MACAULAY

HARPER PERENNIAL

NEW YORK • LONDON • TORONTO • SYDNEY

HARPER ● PERENNIAL

FIRST HARPER PERENNIAL EDITION PUBLISHED 2007.

Designed by Daniel Lagin

The Library of Congress has catalogued the hardcover edition as follows:

Rosenberg, Barry.
   Mavericks of the sky: the first daring pilots of the U.S. Air Mail/Barry Rosenberg & Catherine Macaulay.—1st ed.
      p. cm.
   Includes bibliographical references and index.
   Contents: Fleet—Burleson—Regularly scheduled—Otto—Into the eye—Willoughby—Lipsner—Civil service—Pathfinders—Bellefonte—Stinson—The Star—It's over—Complications—Letters, what letters?—Dear Mr. Praeger—Strike—Wilson—A killer year—Knight.
   ISBN-13: 978-0-06-052949-9
   ISBN-10: 0-06-052949-0
   1. Air pilots—United States—Biography. 2. Airmail service—United States—History. I. Macaulay, Catherine, 1952– II. Title.

TL539.R645 2006
629.13092'273—dc22   2005056143

ISBN: 978-0-06-052950-5 (pbk.)
ISBN-10: 0-06-052950-4 (pbk.)

07   08   09   10   11   ❖/RRD   10   9   8   7   6   5   4   3   2   1

To Margaret

&

Joan and Harold

CONTENTS

viii CONTENTS

MAVERICKS OF THE SKY

CHAPTER 1

FLEET

The 12-cylinder Liberty engine was the biggest, most powerful piece of hardware ever strapped into a wood and canvas biplane. Fashioned into a "V" shape, its combustion cylinders pushed out an enormous 400 horsepower.

The nation's top engine designers had spent a year tweaking the engine, and on May 2, 1918, it was ready for testing in a bomber. The U.S. War Department had pinned a lot of hopes on the power plant. The brute power of the Liberty would let bombers fly at higher and safer altitudes—and carry greater destructive payloads. When the Liberty was fit into the nose of a fighter plane, it would climb faster and maneuver better to attack and evade. Such a formidable addition to America's war-fighting machine would help the country hold its head high among its European allies.

The engine was planned for the de Havilland DH-4 bomber, a British-designed biplane being built in the United States, and flight testing could only be entrusted to the Army's most experienced pilot—Maj. Oscar Brindley. He was the first civilian flight instructor hired by the Army, a legendary pilot whose name was known across the Atlantic. Brindley was joined in the twin-cockpit bomber by Lt. Col. Henry Damm.

The ship was sitting tall on its haunches at McCook Field in

Dayton, Ohio, having been prepped for the pilots with meticulous care. With confidence and ease, Brindley guided the airplane smoothly into the sky. The gas tank was only partially full, and hardware like the twin .30-caliber Lewis machine guns in the rear had been removed so as not to overtax the engine with too much weight. Satisfied with the Liberty's performance at 5,000 feet, Brindley brought the ship back down so the fuel tank could be topped off and the hardware reinstalled. Now at near maximum weight, the airplane took off again. But it seemed to stall before it cleared the small maple trees that bordered the field and crashed to the ground before the eyes of horrified witnesses. Maj. Brindley died instantly, and Lt. Col. Damm passed away on the trip to the hospital.

Army leadership was devastated. What would this mean for the Liberty program? An engine failure like this could set development back months. An immediate investigation was called.

Heavy security greeted Maj. Reuben Hollis Fleet at the gates to McCook the next day. Fences, barbed wire, and armed guards were in place at the Army Signal Corps's main aircraft engineering facility, all designed to shut out the prying eyes of German spies. Fleet's credentials were checked and rechecked, and a call was made to confirm his business there. The major eventually gained entry, and he soon found himself inspecting the wreckage along with base commander Lt. Col. Thurman Bane.

Fleet was eminently qualified to determine the cause of the accident because he had seen his share of crashed machines as the officer in charge of the nation's thirty-four pilot training fields. It was his job to turn thousands of wide-eyed farm kids into tough combat fliers capable of fighting the Hun in the skies over France and Germany.

Scouring every inch of the DH-4, Fleet and Bane soon found the answer. A spark plug had jammed itself between the wing's trailing edge and aileron, making it impossible for Brindley to control the craft. The Liberty wasn't at fault, after all; the program could continue.

The engine still needed a thorough sorting out, though, and a second Liberty-powered DH-4 was standing by at McCook. Bane didn't have to look far to find an experienced pilot, and he ordered Fleet into the air. It was not what the major had expected when he arrived, but there wasn't much he could do except salute and don his pilot leathers. As an instructor, Fleet knew that a pilot could never have too much space to fly in, and McCook, being focused more on ground activities, didn't have the wide open spaces that test flying demanded. The solution was just a few miles away at Wilbur Wright Field, where its 2,000 acres of long grass runway and expansive space had been a center of U.S. military aviation since 1904 when Wilbur and Orville Wright turned it into their base for experimental flying and pilot training. The Army bought the land at the start of World War I and placed much of its aviator, maintenance, and gunnery training among the twenty-four hangars there. On most days, pilot cadets buzzed about in Curtiss JN-4D Jennies and Standard SJ-1 biplanes. Today the skies were clear, Maj. Fleet having them all to himself and his de Havilland.

A couple hours later, Fleet walked out to the flight line at Wright Field, where the plane stood waiting, the Liberty contained within a metal cowling at the nose of the craft. All the senior officers were standing by, interested to see how the engine, and Fleet, checked out. There would be no passenger on this test flight; if there was a problem, Fleet would go down alone.

Stepping onto the wing, the major flung his leg up and over the rim of the front cockpit and dropped himself onto the padded metal seat. It took the might of two men to crank the propeller and start the engine, and a pair of mechanics awaited Fleet's command.

"Contact!"

With that, they threw all their muscle into spinning the prop. The powerplant roared to life, its prop churning the wind into shards of percussion.

Nose into the wind, Fleet throttled up the Liberty, allowing its power to propel him down the grass field, accumulating speed faster and faster until the wheels of the big bomber slowly rose and Fleet was away.

Leveling off at 2,000 feet, the aviator proceeded to push the engine hard, testing the airplane's climbing and banking capabilities under full power. The DH-4 was a proven design, but the difference between her top speed and stall speed was barely 30 miles per hour, a margin so slim that it could make the steadiest pilot wince. The major took the plane through a series of four loops. Then, to everyone's horror, there came the deafening sound of silence.

Suddenly homeless in the sky, the de Havilland nosed over and began falling.

What was Fleet doing? Had the Liberty stalled?

The plane began to drop: 2,000 feet, 1,800 feet, 1,600, 1,400 feet—still Fleet hadn't leveled out. The major's life seemed to hang in the balance.

Then, at just 800 feet above the ground, the engine came to life and Fleet managed to pull the aircraft out of the dive. Upon landing, the major unbuckled his harness, climbed out of his ship, and was summarily dressed down by Lt. Col. Bane. What in heaven's name had he been thinking up there? Fleet knew better than to stall a plane at that altitude. The major had a reputation for safety, and here he'd pulled a fool stunt like this.

The chastising went on until Fleet peeled off his shirt and wrung out the perspiration, remarking that he'd pass up lunch.

Reuben Fleet was born in Montesano, about 75 miles south of Seattle near the Pacific Ocean. In the heavily forested land radiating out from Puget Sound, Fleet had learned the value of self-reliance right from the start. In the woods of Washington Territory in the late 1800s, the path to manhood typically followed three tracks: Indian trader, fur trapper, or lumberjack. Still considered the Wild West of America, the Pacific Northwest branded its own unique mark of independence onto a person's character, and Fleet was no exception. He'd grown up alongside Indians, had a marksman's eye for beaver and bear, and knew the best spots to dip his line for steelhead trout. His father had helped push the Great Northern Railroad into Washington Territory. His mother had crossed the Rocky Mountains in a covered wagon at the age of four.

Tall and erect like the sequoia trees of his home state of Washington, the major had been climbing the ladder of success for some time, his assault made with the sure-footedness of a billy goat. Exuding confidence and somewhat argumentative, Fleet at times could be unyielding in his convictions. Yet people regularly forgave him, both because of his earnest good looks and because he so often turned out to be right.

Everything touched by Fleet in his thirty-one years had turned golden. But now that streak of success looked like it was about to end. His superiors had a new job for him. Henceforth, he'd be working with the U.S. Post Office Department, helping them establish an aerial service to deliver the mail.

Fleet wanted no part of the assignment. May 1918 was the height of World War I. Every available resource was needed to win the war overseas. After a little more than a year of fighting and with the war grinding through soldiers, the Americans needed healthy, young men capable of grabbing the stick of an airplane, taking her up into the sky, and staying aloft without getting lost or shot down within the first twenty minutes.

That's why the whole airmail thing seemed absurd to him. It would be one thing if Army pilots were tasked with flying secret communiqués between government agencies. They weren't. Instead, Army pilots would be shuttling regular mail—birthday greetings, utility bills, and postcards from newlyweds visiting Niagara Falls—across America's skies.

The new assignment was the first real curveball Fleet had ever been thrown in his career, and the project had already worked its way up the chain of command to the desk of the commander in chief. President Woodrow Wilson had personally approved the operation, and like it or not, Maj. Fleet was now in command.

Wilson and his commanders were shocked by how many accidents the Army pilots were having. The country had been at war for just over a year and already dozens of fliers had been killed. Once the pilots left the safe confines of Fleet's flight schools in the United States, they began to die at alarming rates in the skies over France and Germany. Thirty-three American fliers and observers were either killed, injured, or captured in just the months of March, April, and May; and American units had barely even begun combat operations. Many more than that were killed or injured during training.

The problem had less to do with the superior dogfighting skills of aces like Baron Manfred von Richthofen than with the fact that the airmen were simply getting lost. With only a rudimentary compass to navigate by, and facing unfamiliar enemy terrain beneath their wings, they were unable to find their way back to base and eventually ran out of fuel and crashed. They were proficient with the stick and rudder, but they lacked the basic ABCs of cross-country flying.

Fleet certainly recognized the limitations of the Army's training operations, but he wasn't as convinced about *how* the brass in Washington intended to address the problem. Beginning May 15, 1918, pilots of the U.S. Army Signal Corps would begin delivering Uncle Sam's mail in order to gain firsthand experience in the art of navigation. Contact flying—that's what pilots needed, experience at flying over long stretches of unfamiliar territory. And now, with the help of the U.S. Post Office Department, they were about to be given that skill by flying the mail 218 miles between New York and Washington. The idea was to put a green Army pilot on the mail run for a couple months and give him the experience at flying from city to city without slamming into a mountain or riding into a thunderstorm. Theoretically, he'd then be ready to be shipped off to the front. The skills gained along the way might not keep him from being shot down by the Red Baron, but at least a pilot wouldn't die simply because he'd gotten lost in the sky.

But nine days! That's all the time Fleet had to pull this off. Nine lousy, career-ending days to acquire the aircraft, select the pilots, find the airfields, erect the hangars, arrange for spare parts, and assign mechanics and field personnel—in short, organize every detail necessary to get this little project off the ground. That's because Secretary of War Newton Baker hadn't gotten around to telling Fleet about his new assignment until May 6, just a couple days after he returned from Dayton.

Until this moment, Fleet's career had progressed without a hitch. Proud holder of the seventy-fourth set of pilots wings issued by the Signal Corps's Aviation Section, he was considered one of the Army's best flying officers. He was organized and got things done. Married, a graduate of military school, an upstanding citizen of his small town who bought and sold both timber and land, Fleet had already accomplished much in his career. Having been elected to the Washington State House of Representatives at just twenty-eight, he'd almost single-handedly pushed the state into the forefront of aviation a year later, in 1915, by proposing a bill to spend $250,000 on aviation training for the National Guard. Fleet had cleverly chosen that price tag to embarrass the Woodrow Wilson administration, which was spending less than that sum on aviation for the entire country. He punctuated his jab by chartering a plane and sitting in the passenger seat while it flew circles for thirty-five minutes around the capital dome in Olympia.

Officers at the War Department in Washington wondered what all the commotion was about in the wilds of the Evergreen State, better known as the forty-second state in the Union, and they dispatched a colonel to make a report. He didn't know much about aviation when he got to Washington State, but Fleet taught him a thing or two. That same year, Army funding for aviation development was approved for $300,000. A program was put in place to teach two representatives from each state's National Guard how to fly.

Fleet's can-do attitude suited him for military command. Having decided to pursue aviation instead of politics, he arrived in San Diego a week before America declared war on Germany on April 6, 1917. The Army had only seventy-three airplanes at the time, thirty of which were stationed at Rockwell Field where Fleet was headed. By August he had his wings, having earned the difficult Junior Military Aviation designation, reserved for fliers who could land with a dead stick from 3,000 feet and park their plane within a 100-foot circle five out of six times.

With the military desperate for officers, the older and more-mature Fleet quickly found himself with his first command—acting commanding officer of the Eighteenth Aero Squadron, a training and maintenance group based at the Army's Hazelhurst Field on Long Island, New York. Four months later, just as the military's requirement for pilots exploded, Fleet was transferred to the War Department in Washington, D.C., as chief of flight training for the U.S. Army, and executive officer to Col. Henry "Hap" Arnold, the senior officer in charge of all Army aviation.

Fleet was squarely at the epicenter of a new military stratagem called "Airpower." Strategists like Arnold were convinced that military superiority on the battlefield was not to be won by thousands of soldiers charging at the enemy with their fixed bayonets, but rather with airships armed with machine guns and bombs, their squadrons wreaking havoc deep in enemy territory. Arnold had been touting the tactic for some time now, and even President Wilson was intrigued by the concept. Aero ships would lend new meaning to the ancient, military operative of holding the high ground. Airpower would help the Allies gain a victory over Germany; it would help protect democracy overseas; and it that would change the face of war.

The push for the use of airpower overseas was all the more reason eyebrows were raised when word got out that the Army was planning to engage in airmail instead of airpower. President Wilson, the man who had promised to muster every able-bodied American to the war effort, now wanted to divert men and machines away from the battle so he could experiment with delivering cards and letters. Across Capitol Hill and echoing through the buildings of the War Department, telephone wires were burning with the same talk—what was the president thinking?

Within the marbled halls of postal headquarters, located on Pennsylvania Avenue between Eleventh and Twelfth Streets, no such reservations were being voiced. Quite the contrary. Inside the sprawling, redbrick, neoclassical building with its landmark fifteen-story watchtower, postal officials were doing cartwheels. They'd been trying to establish a service like this since 1912. Though dozens of airmail flights had taken place around the world, they'd been little more than stunts—with some barnstorming aviator flying a sack full of mail a dozen or so miles from a local fairground to a nearby post office. Publicity stunts. Nobody, it seemed, had much interest in developing a day-in/day-out scheduled airmail operation, least of all the U.S. Congress.

But a few true believers at the post office had kept plugging away at it, cajoling and politicking for airmail funding until, finally, $100,000 had been wrested from Congress for the fiscal year ending June 30, 1918. The money would launch a rudimentary aerial shuttle service between New York and Washington, with a stopover in Philadelphia. Both northbound and southbound runs would operate six days a week except for Sundays—a full day of prayer being necessary to pull off this little experiment.

The value of the plan was debatable. But to make it all happen in nine days?

No. Impossible, said Fleet.

Newton Baker listened intently as the major presented the waste-of-men-and-machines argument that had been making the rounds in Washington. Baker, the former mayor of Cleveland, was not unsympathetic to Fleet's argument. Just months prior he had signed orders establishing universal military conscription—the draft. His orders had put four million Americans under arms, and he wasn't happy having soldiers do a civilian's job. Baker agreed to arrange a meeting with the postmaster general. Fleet was a persuasive man. Perhaps he could make the postmaster general change his mind, or at least postpone the impossible May 15 deadline.

Just minutes later, Fleet found himself standing before the right honorable Albert Sidney Burleson, the latest in a long line of United States postmaster generals that began with Benjamin Franklin in 1775. Imposing, educated, and proper, A. S. Burleson was a trusted member of President Woodrow Wilson's cabinet and appointed guardian of Uncle Sam's mail.

Fleet had a minute to talk and began with his usual frankness. In the first place, no one had ever organized a regularly scheduled aero mail service before, not anywhere in the world. An undertaking of this scale would require enormous preparation. Just coordinating the mail runs between two major cities—the nation's center of commerce and its center of government—would be a logistical nightmare. Then, there were the airplanes themselves. The handful of used Curtiss JN-4D "Jenny" military trainers assigned to the operation were, for many reasons, wholly inadequate. Built for short, high-altitude reconnaissance missions, their anemic 90-horsepower Curtiss OX5 engines were not powerful enough to haul heavy payloads over long distances. Ninety miles was about their limit without refueling. Not that it mattered; hell, the Jenny wasn't even equipped with a cargo hold. And that was only the beginning.

Nothing was ready. No preparations had been made. None of the airfields had even been acquired. Surely, the postmaster general could understand that targeting the launch of such an operation on May 15 was simply not possible.

Burleson waited for Fleet to finish, then proceeded to dress him down in nothing short of a tirade. If the airfields weren't ready, then the major could bloody well operate out of cow pastures! Having served the Lone Star State of Texas in the U.S. House of Representatives for fourteen years, the postmaster general was not about to change his mind because a lone major in the Army couldn't get the job done. The date would not be changed—not for Fleet, not for anybody shy of President Wilson, and he'd already penciled the date in on his calendar. Besides, the press had been notified. This inaugural event would make top-of-the-fold news in every newspaper in the country. There was even talk about canceling school in Washington so youngsters could come watch history in the making. Major Fleet would do well to mark the date as well. Discussion over, matter closed.

As a military officer, Fleet knew the importance of following commands, no matter how unrealistic they were. First he needed to acquire airships. Even though he was a high-ranking officer, he still didn't have the power to commandeer six airplanes for the airmail. That requisition would come from Air Service Production chief Col. Edward Deeds, whose influence was strong as the leader of the team that had designed the Liberty engine. The Jenny aircraft Fleet needed had to be specially modified for airmail flying. As it stood, the JN-4D came equipped with two cockpits, each with its own set of flight controls. For starters, the front cockpit would have to be replaced with a cargo hold. Then, too, fuel and oil capacities had to be doubled. The Jenny had a range of only 90-some miles, not even close enough to fly the 140 miles between Washington, D.C., and Philadelphia. Finally, and most important, the Jenny's 90-horsepower engine just didn't have enough *oomph* to plow its way through the air with 200 pounds of mail onboard. The engine would have to be replaced with a more powerful one.

And one last thing, Fleet needed the planes to be built and in the air within nine days.

Col. Deeds immediately sent out an SOS to the Curtiss Aero-plane and Motor Corporation of Garden City, Long Island, utter-ing those lip-smacking words that every defense contractor yearns to hear: *We need more planes.*

Curtiss Aeroplane had been churning out so many aero ships for the military that founder Glenn Hammond Curtiss had already amassed a personal fortune of $7 million by 1916 standards. Only thirty-seven years old, the mustachioed, wiry man with the intense gaze had succeeded in making a name for himself, both as an inventor and an adventurer. He was intrigued by speed—getting from point A to point B as fast as humanly possible. Curtiss already owned the world speed record for a motorcycle—137 miles per hour on two wheels. Hungry for action, he was a regular entrant in air derbies around the country, piloting his own designs for prize money. In between the whirl of competition, he'd put his engineer's cap back on and start designing planes. Like the Wright brothers, he'd gone from fixing bicycles straight into tinkering with the mechanics of flight. Aviation was new and exciting and ripe for the taking. Cur-tiss was doing great things for the Navy. The brass wanted a plane capable of taking off and landing on water, and his experiments had led to the first seaplane.

Curtiss set to work on the new job for the Army. Like any aero-nautical engineer trying to improve aircraft performance, he'd have just three parameters at his disposal: speed, range, and maneuver-ability. Improving speed was simple; the Curtiss OX5 would have to go. It would be swapped out for the "Hisso," a sturdy, lightweight, and efficient 150-horsepower engine that was far superior to any-thing else available in the United States. It was Swiss designed and French built by a company called Hispano-Suiza for speedy fighter planes like the Spad. The Wright-Martin Aircraft Company of New Brunswick, New Jersey, a joint venture of the Wright brothers and fellow airplane tinkerer Glenn Martin, was licensed to build it in the United States.

Improving the Jenny's range would prove more difficult, par-ticularly with the addition of the heavier, thirstier Hispano-Suiza engine. Curtiss saw two options: cut the overall weight to the bone, or add fuel capacity. Because the Jennies would be loaded with heavy mail sacks, there was little he could do about weight. Instead, he would combine two 19-gallon gas tanks and two 2.5-gallon oil tanks. The new configuration would give the Jenny enough legs to fly nonstop from Washington to Philadelphia.

While Curtiss was tackling his obstacles, Fleet focused on finding the right airfields. Hazelhurst Field in Mineola, Long Island, would be the logical choice for the northern terminus, but Fleet had no intention of disrupting the pilot training there with the chaos of an airmail service. Another airstrip would have to be found—some open field with good, level ground and no trees anywhere in sight. On the list of hazards most likely to kill a pilot, trees weighed in after fog and mountains. Murphy's Law being what it is, a tree always seemed to be growing in the wrong spot, generally wherever a pilot wanted to set down.

Finding a plot of land that fit that description in New York City would be near impossible. The city had already absorbed much of the available land throughout the five boroughs. But there was another open field not too far away. It was good and level, with plenty of room to land and take off—Belmont Park Race Track. Its huge 1.5-mile oval infield had no trees and would make an ideal airstrip. Belmont was also near Hazelhurst Field, allowing Army personnel to shuttle easily between the two places.

The track's 650 acres of manicured grass and raked dirt had been attracting New York City's finest since its gates first opened in 1905. From their private boxes at the racetrack, wealthy financiers and industrialists like J. P. Morgan, William Vanderbilt, and Harry Payne Whitney cheered on the same horses as the two-dollar Joes in the grandstand. The place was a magnet for people eager to get away from it all, and on weekends, hundreds of newfangled automobiles would make their way to its elegant grounds, creating the first recorded traffic jams in America.

The only drawback was the track's location. Fourteen miles due east on Long Island, Belmont was still a distance from New York City's central post office on Ninth Avenue in midtown Manhattan. The mail would have to be transferred to trains or trucks, adding as much as an hour to its transit time. Still, when all was said and done,

Belmont Park Race Track was the most suitable piece of land for miles around. The fact that it was privately owned wasn't a problem; Fleet had the inside track.

Maj. August Belmont II was not surprised when Maj. Fleet rang him up. The two had been introduced by Maj. Thomas Hitchcock Sr., who was officer in charge of flying at Hazelhurst. Some months earlier Hitchcock had flown Fleet on his first aerial tour of New York City. With airplanes a common denominator, Hitchcock introduced Fleet to his old friend August Belmont, another aviation enthusiast. Some years earlier, Belmont had opened his racetrack for a flying competition between all the great aviators of the day. More than 150,000 people had come to watch the highlight of the event, the $10,000 Statue of Liberty Race, a 33-mile, hell-bent-for-leather aerial race from the green oval to the Green Lady in New York Harbor and back again. When the race was over, American aviator John Moisant emerged the victor, beating out British flyer Claude Graham-White in a time of just over thirty-five minutes.

In his youth, Hitchcock had been one of the first Americans to play organized polo, teaming with, of all people, Belmont's father. The two had whacked away on horseback across the grounds of the Mineola field in 1877, playing the earliest recorded match on Long Island. The circle of Hitchcocks and Belmonts went back forty years, and now it included Reuben Fleet.

Maj. Belmont was at ease living the sportsman's life. Rich and influential, he was a highly visible member of New York's moneyed class—an entrée made possible by his father, a Jewish wunderkind from Prussia, who had gone from sweeping floors at the famed bank of the Rothschilds to teen financier. His ascent quickened after moving to New York City, where he mastered Wall Street, ultimately becoming the U.S. minister to Holland and national chairman of the Democratic Party. Along the way, he'd also managed to snag the estimable hand of the daughter of Commodore Matthew Perry, four years before the famed naval commander sailed his warships into Tokyo's Edo Bay.

As an inheritor of wealth and position, August II immersed himself in the sport of kings. Holding the reins of his Kentucky stud farm in one hand and the leadership of the Jockey Club and the New York Racing Association securely in the other, the son of the floor sweep had become one of horse racing's most prominent figures. Not only did he own and operate a world-renowned racetrack, his stud farm regularly produced top stakes winners. Belmont loved the game. Photos of him in the newspaper society columns regularly showed him at the track talking with trainers, squinting into the sun with a pair of binoculars around his neck. But though Belmont exuded the ease and sophistication of a gentleman content to play the game, beneath that polish lay a man with the instincts and nerve of a Las Vegas gambler. The acknowledged powerhouse of the American turf broke away from the rest when it came to breeding horses that could win. Like the best card players, he seemed to have an instinct for what to keep and what to throw away.

Increasingly, a restlessness had broken the calm exterior of his life. A fire had razed part of his racetrack, some investments hadn't panned out, and with the war raging in Europe, he badly wanted to help. Posters of a white-haired Uncle Sam were appearing everywhere, that craggy finger pointing at every American, demanding them to pony up for the war effort. But at sixty-five years old, and well past his fighting prime, what could he offer?

Belmont did have something, though, that the military wanted—a good eye for horseflesh. Horses had carved out a long, proud history for themselves in the military. Under cannon fire or a spray of arrows, their heaving forms had served humankind throughout the course of warfare. Straining against the blood-gorged earth, horses by the millions had performed their duties reliably, without fanfare, using their mighty strength to move supplies, equipment, and wounded soldiers through fighting fields across the globe. Modern technology may have brought tanks, airplanes, and machine guns to warfare, but the equine soldier remained a viable piece of fighting equipment, its "horsepower" as indisputable as the great heart that drove it. Who better qualified to select and train mounts for the cavalry than someone as knowledgeable as Belmont?

The U.S. Army promptly inducted him into service, commissioning him a major in the Quartermaster Corps. Before leaving for his new assignment, though, the major wanted to tie up some loose ends. For one, he had to sell off most of his yearlings at his stud farm. He hated to do it. One youngster in particular showed real promise. Foaled the year before, the big red yearling had the obvious pedigree to race. But there was something else about him, something different. Despite his instincts, Belmont had gone ahead and sold him along with the others. Given the length of time he'd be away, it seemed prudent to do so. The dispersal sales at Saratoga hadn't gone badly, with the red yearling bringing in a whopping $5,000.

Unfortunately, in that move, Belmont had unwittingly folded the hand of a lifetime. The man whose vision and leadership had influenced an entire industry had let go of the horse whose Olympian records and lap-trouncing speed would come to dominate thoroughbred racing for years to come. He'd sent to auction the very horse his wife had named in honor of the battle he was now preparing to fight—Man o' War.

Of course Maj. Fleet could use the infield at Belmont Raceway as an airmail terminus. And given that this entire operation was part of a pilot training program for the Army, the airmail service was welcome to use the facility free of charge. The only condition was that the pilots couldn't buzz the horses with their planes.

Now Fleet had one airfield down, and two to go. The post office had a line on a farmer's field near Philadelphia in a suburb called Bustleton 15 miles northeast of Center City. The pilots would just have to stay away from the telephone and telegraph wires on the west boundary and avoid the farm road that ran along the south side. But its 130 acres of flat, open pastureland would work well. All in all, it would serve just fine as the Philadelphia aero terminal.

With New York and Philadelphia in hand, Fleet turned his attention to Washington, D.C.—the southern terminus of the airmail route. His first choice for an airfield lay across the Potomac in College Park, Maryland. It had served as an Army aviation school earlier in the decade, and setting up operations there seemed a natural.

But postal officials immediately sniffed *pish posh* at that. College Park wouldn't do. They would never get President Wilson to travel the 9-mile distance to College Park on inaugural day. It was in Maryland, after all. Instead they preferred a place in the heart of the nation's capital. Potomac Park, located just south of the Lincoln Memorial between the Tidal Basin and the Potomac River, was always busy with people. They came to picnic, listen to music from the band shell, or enjoy a rousing game of polo. Yes, that would do nicely. The mail will fly out of Potomac Park. Matter closed.

Fleet was furious with the choice. Not only was the park too small to be an airfield (only 900 feet long by 300 feet wide), it was a polo field. One had only to look at the morass of divots to see the damage that thundering hooves alternately charging and pivoting had done to the ground. How was an airplane expected to take off and land on that? Then there were the trees. The entire park was ringed with them—some of them were 60 feet high. Their canopy might offer park-goers shade from the sun, but they presented an unimaginable hazard for pilots flying in or out of the park, which was bordered by a roadway, allowing cars everywhere. Certainly no aviator or, for that matter, anyone with any common sense at all had selected that site. But a chain of command could not be disputed. Postmaster General Albert Burleson had made the selection, and Fleet would have to live with the choice for now.

Belmont—Bustleton—Potomac Park. With all three airfields in hand, the combined resources of the U.S. Army and the Post Office Department pushed toward the day of May 15, 1918. Corrugated metal hangars were erected, fuel tanks were installed, and spare propellers, engines, and tires were stockpiled. Crews of Army mechanics and field personnel were transferred to the new sites, and administrative clerks and secretaries were marshaled and dispatched to staff the new facilities. Like the giant behemoths they were, each organization lent the weight of its resources fully to the task.

As they worked, Fleet turned to arguably his most important task, selecting the pilots to fly the air routes. He needed six of them, four for the relay team and two as backup. The men he had in mind would be crack fliers, each with plenty of experience on the stick. Ideally, they'd be flight instructors, men capable of flying themselves out of any emergency. As head of all pilot training for the U.S. Army, he could recruit the best.

Postal officials, as usual, had other plans. They'd been doing a little pilot recruiting of their own, with an eye toward paying off some old IOUs. To their way of thinking, 2d Lts. James Clark Edgerton and George Leroy Boyle—both fresh out of flying school— would make ideal airmail pilots. Edgerton's father was purchasing agent for the entire postal department. Appointing his son to the team was a postal nod to the power and position of the man holding the purse strings.

Boyle was chosen for a different reason. His future father-in-law was none other than Judge Charles McChord, the nation's interstate commerce commissioner, and Boyle's selection was a big, wet kiss on the cheek for the judge. Inside postal circles, the very mention of the name McChord drew words of appreciation, because he had saved "parcel post," one of the best ideas the post office ever came up with.

Since it emerged onto the scene in 1913, parcel post had helped grease the wheels for a whole new economy by letting people use the post office to ship goods across state lines. It was in Judge McChord's court that postal department lawyers had broken the monopoly of a handful of private companies that controlled all interstate shipping. As a result, parcel post had become a huge moneymaker for the Uncle. More important, though, it was becoming a vital growth engine for the nation's economy. Thanks to this fast, new way of mailing packages, regular folks could buy and sell anything to anyone living anywhere in the country. With parcel post an apple grower in Wisconsin could peddle his produce to someone living in Baltimore, and all he had to do was mail the box of Red Delicious apples from his local post office. A housewife in Iowa could treat herself to the latest millinery styles coming out of New York and have them delivered by her regular mail carrier right to her door. It was much cheaper than private shippers, and the post office handled tens of thousands of packages: fruit, dry goods, medicine, machine parts, baby chicks even—everyone confident that their package would arrive at its destination intact and on time. Parcel post was helping merge America's fragmented regional markets into a single, nationwide economy.

As far as postal officials were concerned, Edgerton and Boyle were both nonnegotiable currency. Never mind that between them they hadn't enough experience to fly their way out of a wet paper bag. They had other, more valuable, credentials. Not only would each be made members of the inaugural day airmail team, they would be its public face. The honor of piloting the inaugural ship out of Washington would go to the judge's future son-in-law, George Boyle. Upon this greenhorn's unleavened shoulders would be heaped all the heartfelt appreciation and all the unbridled enthusiasm of every last person gathered at Potomac Park—including President Wilson, his wife, and just about every VIP within a 50-mile radius. All eyes would be riveted on him as he climbed into his mail-laden biplane and lifted into the skies—provided of course that the lad managed to clear the trees, which, given his experience, was questionable.

Edgerton, the other rookie pilot, would hold down the second most visible slot on the team—the Bustleton to Potomac Park leg that would be the first airmail flight into Washington, D.C. His arrival was planned for just a couple hours after Boyle's departure, so most of the spectators and reporters would no doubt still be there to witness the historic touchdown—or crack-up.

Fleet was stupefied. Edgerton and Boyle were fledgling fliers, though Edgerton had additional bomber training. With roughly sixty hours worth of stick time in their logbooks, their experience qualified them to stay in the background and keep their mouths shut. Nobody was asking him, though. Postal officials were adamant that Edgerton and Boyle be front and center on inaugural day.

Once again Fleet found himself hamstrung. First Potomac Park, now this. He set about to counterbalance the two greenhorns with four experienced pilots. It was understood that the point of flying the mail was to train inexperienced pilots, but for these early flights Fleet wanted men of experience to get the service running smoothly. He went through his roster of pilots and did some quick picking and choosing.

First Lt. Howard Paul Culver was less than pleased when he received word of his new assignment. Like other airmen training to fly and fight, he wanted to do just that. An assignment overseas was the ticket, a boat to France, maybe a squad under his command.

He'd already packed up his wife and child and come east, hoping to be ordered overseas. Stationed at Hazelhurst Field, he was anxiously awaiting the call when instead he got one from Fleet.

"Can you feature being a mailman when there is a war on," he told his wife. It hardly seemed right, "especially after putting in hundreds of hours training students in combat. Why can't the railroads carry the mail the way they've always done?"

For a pilot eager to do his part in the war, the news smarted. The sting was lessened, though, after Culver met the other members of the team. Lt. Torrey Webb—a graduate of Columbia University—had a degree in mining engineering and a keen interest in the oil business. After enlisting in the Army Signal Corps, his crack piloting skills had caught Fleet's eye during training at Ellington Field.

Second Lt. Stephen Bonsal had graduated from Yale with a degree in journalism, and, until recently, appeared to be following in the footsteps of his father, a well-known war correspondent. But soon, Bonsal traded a writing hack's life for a career in aviation. Lt. Walter Miller rounded out the field. He took to the challenge and likened himself to riders of the pony express—right down to carrying a gun into the cockpit. There were sure to be some valuables in the mail sacks. A downed plane could be easy pickings. There never seemed to be a shortfall of entrepreneurial folks eager to rob a stagecoach, a train, or a mail truck in search of easy money. Miller wasn't about to let that happen. Not on his run.

Fleet's team was now complete, but time was running short. There were only two days until the inaugural flight, and the six modified aero mail planes ordered from Glenn Curtiss had yet to arrive. It would have been nice to look up and see them in the sky over Long Island, the sun glistening off their wings. Instead, they'd come disassembled, packed in crates and stacked atop a delivery truck that rumbled through the gates of Hazelhurst Field on the evening of the thirteenth. Instead of carrying cargo, the Jennies were cargo themselves. Fleet's team had only eighteen hours to uncrate, assemble, service, tune, and flight-check each aircraft.

Like so many frantic parents trying to assemble their children's toys on Christmas Eve, Fleet's crew began a long night's struggle to piece together the half-dozen aircraft. Each pilot was assigned his own team of mechanics and took charge of one crate. A working area for each crew was chalked off on the hangar floor. Tearing into the huge wooden boxes, the pilots and mechanics hunkered down to the work ahead. But each crate they pried open revealed a new nightmare: Control wires were the wrong length, pressure valves and feed pipes were broken. Nothing worked, nothing seemed to fit, the assemblage of parts being wholly defective. All the while, the clock was ticking down toward the inaugural flight.

Three dozen men worked feverishly on the planes all night, and then all through the morning of the fourteenth. Everyone was exhausted, their nerves frayed from the effects of such a protracted struggle. As noon passed on the fourteenth only two Jennies had been assembled. Fleet needed at least four to pull off this relay. One plane had to be positioned at Potomac Park, another at Belmont Park, and two at the transfer hub at the Bustleton field. Bone weary, the men pressed on, the lack of sleep visible in their eyes. They could barely drag their bodies out to the flight line to test the first completed aircraft. It is one thing to piece together all the parts, quite another to have them work in flight. Edgerton was the guinea pig, and he donned his helmet and goggles with trepidation.

"We trundled the ship to the line for gas and oil, a final check," the young pilot noted. "She stood ready at 3 P.M.—four hours before dark. This was the big moment. Would the engine start after all these back-breaking hours?"

It did, in a puff of smoke and a roar of the exhaust.

"Those present were electrified, fatigue forgotten. Elated, happy shouts rang out spontaneously."

They let the motor idle for fifteen minutes to get it good and hot. Then Edgerton was in the air, the power of the Hispano-Suiza reverberating through his body.

"The tail came up with a rush, the run was short and the climb steep."

A quick once-around and he was back on the ground, just as Lt. Culver was taking off to flight-test the second Jenny. It, too, checked out.

A third JN-4H was nearly complete. If all went well, it might conceivably be finished, provided nothing else went wrong. The clock continued to take hold of Fleet's plans and hold them vicelike. It was becoming clear that the fourth Jenny wouldn't be assembled in time. Time for Plan B.

Fleet's orders were simple: Edgerton and Culver would immediately fly the two new Jennies over to Bustleton, where they would spend the night.

"The major came near to taking my ship but reconsidered and took a conventional JN-4H," said Edgerton.

Fleet would then follow them in the unmodified Jenny borrowed from Maj. Hitchcock at Mineola.

Like chess pieces on a board, the planes had to be moved into position, each prepped, ready, and waiting for tomorrow's festivities. On the morning of May 15, Fleet would personally ferry one of the planes to Potomac Park so Boyle would have something to fly when he made his appearance center stage before the president.

In the meantime, Lt. Webb would remain back at the hangar and continue work on the third near-completed Jenny. Lts. Miller and Bonsal would stay with him to help. As soon as the plane was assembled, Webb would fly her the few miles over to the Belmont field and park her there in readiness for the fifteenth.

If Fleet thought that the weather was going to cooperate, then he was wrong on that account, too. Even at midday on May 14, a blanket of fog remained over Long Island, New York City, and the entire Northeast, bringing visibility down to near zero. Fog—just one trip into its soup could turn even the most cavalier aviator into a true believer of flying's high commandment, namely: *Thou Shalt Not Fly Where Thou Canst Not See*, as yon mountain, tree, or church steeple shall rise up through the shroud and smite down thy flying machine. Fog had a way of suffocating a pilot in its mist, turning his ship into a ghost, and leaving him singing in the hallelujah choir. Flying without a line of sight could cause a spatial disorientation in a man's brain, tricking him into believing he was flying straight and level when, in fact, he was diving straight toward the ground. Flying into fog was like putting a revolver to your head, one bullet in the chamber.

With little or no sleep for the past twenty-four hours, Fleet, Culver, and Edgerton all found themselves faced with long flights. With unimpeachable determination, the men picked up their cue from the people of New York City and pressed on. The top of the Woolworth Building might be hardly visible, but commerce waited for no one. Horse-drawn produce carts were pulled down the street, newly transplanted immigrants sold cheese and olive oil from storefronts that welcomed housewives lightly dodging the rush of carriages and automobiles.

Standing inside its closeness, whiteness all around, the major watched as Culver and Edgerton climbed into their open cockpits. A front of cool, moist air off the Atlantic Ocean had collided with a mass of warmer temperatures inland, producing a singularly nonexistent horizon that stretched across the entire airfield. Making the 90-mile flight to Bustleton would require nerve and no small quotient of luck. Time for a preflight instrument check, perhaps no more than a glance given the scant instruments on their panels—a tachometer, an oil pressure gauge, engine temperature indicator, a clock, and a compass.

"Contact!"

The airmen waited as field personnel grabbed hold of each airplane's propeller, then yanked down, the whole of their bodies pressed into the effort. All at once, in a cloud of exhaust, the two Jennies roared to life—their engines collectively reverberating against the pocket of fog that enveloped everyone around. The wash from the props whipped the grass into a frenzy as both biplanes were turned on their tails and nosed into the wind. Fleet stood nearby, barely visible against the fog. As the planes turned, the words U.S. Mail came into view, emblazoned across the length of each fuselage. In addition, red, white, and blue stripes had been painted across both tails, each one complemented by big, bold stars under the wings—testimony to the planes' newfound status as bona fide, commercial carriers of the U.S. Postal Service.

First one plane, then the other took off across the grass, their engines straining as they picked up speed. Faster they moved and stronger they grew, until all at once the bouncing stopped and they lifted into the sky as if puppets on a string, vanishing into the whiteness.

With Edgerton and Culver safely away, Fleet climbed into his airplane and prepared to take off. It would be a bumpy ride today. Fog had a way of taking smooth air and chopping it into a thousand holes, some fully deep enough for a ship to fall through. He'd have to make the trip to Philadelphia without the benefit of any road maps. In all the rush, there simply hadn't been time to acquire any. Not that it mattered. In this soup, a pilot couldn't see the ground well enough to maintain visual bearings anyway. His only hope was to climb above the fog and hold a steady compass course. At least the fuel gauge atop the cowl read "Full." Unlike the two modified JN-4Hs being flown by Culver and Edgerton, though, "full" to his Jenny trainer wouldn't be enough to get him from Long Island to Bustleton without a stop. He'd just have to set down somewhere along the way and refuel.

Contact!

The prop was spun and the plane's power quickly exploded through the pistons. Turning into the wind, Fleet made a quick trip down the grassy strip, and in another instant was airborne. Driving his ship skyward he began climbing into the mist, the masts of the sailboats in New York Harbor dissolving below his wings. He left behind the few remaining landmarks capable of guiding him and continued to climb, uncertain how long or how high he might have to fly before he broke through into the sun.

"I had to go up without an inclinometer or anything to indicate whether I was right side up or not, just the feel of the ship."

His Jenny climbed for 2 miles, and still hadn't cleared the fog. Then, as Fleet passed 11,000 feet, damn near the ceiling of the Jenny, he pushed through the uppermost limits of the weather and into the blue. With visibility back on his side, he had only the face-numbing cold to fight. At this altitude, its bite was ferocious. More than one flier had felt his ears turn into blocks of ice and seen his hands freeze around the control stick as solidly as if they'd been welded there.

Still, Fleet had his horizon line back and that's all he needed. It was a downright magnificent sight. Riding over the summit of the sky, a range of thick fog beneath his wings, technology had ushered him out of the shabby world of mortals and into the realm of the divine. Up here, on Mount Olympus, a man was truly unfettered and free from the strains of life. The chance to trespass across this holy land drove men to the high altar of flight and kept them coming back to its hardships. This was exactly where Fleet planned to stay for as long as humanly possible, which, according to his calculations, would be another seventy-five minutes or so until his fuel reserves ran out.

Just as he expected, his propeller stopped spinning just north of Philadelphia. Instantly, the sound of whirring machinery was replaced by the purifying sound of wind rushing over his wings. With a dead stick in his hand, Fleet nosed his plane back down through the fog. How far its shroud extended was anyone's guess. For all he knew, it might extend clear to the ground. He continued to grope his way down through the void, hoping no mountain, church steeple, or building lay in his path. At 3,000 feet Fleet broke through the whiteness, catching sight of a scene worth feasting upon—an open field. Swooping down onto the pasture, he rolled to a stop and climbed out of his Jenny. With night fast approaching, he'd have to rustle up some fuel, and fast. One could fly over fog with some skill and luck. But the ink of darkness covered a plane's path completely.

Climbing out of the cockpit, Fleet walked across the field, hoping to track down its owner. Luck was with him. The farmer was home and rustled up a 5-gallon milk can with gas. They walked together back to the plane, the farmer no doubt curious to get a look at the contraption parked in his field. But without a funnel or chamois skin to filter the unrefined gas of the day, the siphoning process didn't go smoothly.

"Perhaps three gallons got in the airplane, and darkness was coming," Fleet remembered.

Fleet was anxious to be on his way. But getting his plane airborne by himself wasn't going to be easy. The Jenny required two people to start the engine, one to spin the propeller and the other to adjust the cockpit booster control to maintain engine compression. The airplane's wooden propeller was massive and when it sprang to life, it did so with abundant, often reckless power that could separate a man's limb from his body should he not jump away in time.

Clearly, the wide-eyed farmer standing beside him would be incapable of executing the carefully orchestrated maneuvers that take place between a pilot and his field mechanic.

Fleet had already broken one flying commandment that day, so why not break another—specifically the one that says unless absolutely alone a pilot should not attempt to start an aircraft without assistance. More than once, a pilot had watched helplessly while his machine ran away down the field because he was busy spinning the propeller and not controlling the throttle in the cockpit.

The procedures manual was quite clear on how to start a Jenny, and it outlined a series of carefully delineated steps. First, the mechanic cranks the propeller four or five times to build up a charge in the cylinders. The pilot then opens the compression switch and waits while the propeller is given a quick turn carrying it slightly past the diagonal position. Then the mechanic yells out "off," a signal to the pilot to close the compression switch. At this point, the plane becomes a loaded weapon. Even the slightest touch on the prop is liable to start the engine and send the propeller spinning. When all is ready, the mechanic calls out "contact," an order that is repeated by the pilot. The all-clear signal given, the mechanic gives the propeller a quick downward pull and jumps out of the way as the wooden blade springs to life.

Such was the protocol. Fleet knew there would be no excuses if his aircraft wasn't in place come tomorrow. Hang procedures, he would manage himself. But doing that would require some fancy footwork. Forgoing the usual "contact" declarations, the major took on the job of two.

"One had to pull the prop through to good compression, run around the wing, jump in the cockpit, and crank the booster to start the propeller before losing compression."

Time and time again, he'd spin the prop, run to the cockpit, and adjust the booster control, trying to bring the engine to life. But time and again, the engine sputtered, then died. Four tries turned into five, then six, then seven.

"It took me at least a dozen run-arounds before the engine caught," he said.

At last, with pistons firing, Fleet opened her wide, the sound of his engine shattering the bovine calm of the countryside. Eager to reach Bustleton before dark, he pushed the Jenny forward, letting the power of his Hispano-Suiza engine propel him across the grass. His wheels were riding the field hard, jostling him in his seat. Picking up speed, his ship broke free of the earth and disappeared into the soft milky ocean of sky overhead.

The farmer watched him go, listening to the crescendo of power vanish along with him. To a man bound to till the soil until death puts him under it, the sight of an airplane mounting up on wings, all moorings freed, must have given him pause. Farmers are a notoriously self-reliant lot, suspicious of change. Most sensible folk, particularly the old-timers, considered these flying contraptions a bunch of tomfoolery. But then, the very times they were living in must have seemed downright dizzying to anyone with two open eyes. The Industrial Revolution was sweeping over the quiet rhythms of agrarian life, dragging rural families headlong into the twentieth century. It was a world with different rhythms, more akin to a race than anything. Telephones, automobiles, and now these newfangled flying machines—everything moving at a faster rate—made it harder for everyone to keep up. Many others realized, too, that farming, like much of American industry, was on the verge of a productivity revolution that would be brought about mainly through the same technologies and mechanization that wrought the airplane.

Whatever conclusion the farmer drew from the incident, it no doubt made for some interesting conversation at the local feed store.

Lts. Edgerton and Culver had arrived safely at Bustleton and were keeping a sharp weather eye out for the major, who had yet to appear. They'd both landed some time ago at 5:45 P.M., and, like Fleet, the two had struggled against the fog almost from the moment they left Long Island. Culver had survived a particularly harrowing incident along the way.

Though a crack pilot and comfortable in the air, Culver found that the fog made it near impossible to tell whether he was flying right side up, much less on a heading toward Philadelphia. Compasses were of little help, being slightly more than spinning tops set inside primitive metal casings. They did, however, have the advantage of amusing pilots, who could spend long hours attempting to guess where the needle might spin next: north, south, east, west, and all points in between.

But Culver's homing pigeon instincts had delivered him right side up to Philadelphia, which was made abundantly clear by a close encounter with the famous Quaker William Penn, whose image appeared ghostlike from out of the fog, just inches from the wingtip of Culver's plane. To the list of fog hazards that included mountains, buildings, and trees would now have to be added the 50-foot cast-iron statue of William Penn perched atop City Hall in Center City Philadelphia.

"I could have reached out and shaken hands with him," Culver said of his close encounter with Billy Penn.

No doubt William Penn would have appreciated Culver's efforts to deliver the mail. The colonial leader grasped early on the importance of connecting the colonies through a single postal system—to share news of the colonies up and down the East Coast and add cohesion to life in the New World. Penn had helped establish just such a communications network in the early 1700s.

Culver's brush with death had taken place late afternoon. Here it was nearly nightfall and Fleet had yet to arrive. What they didn't know was that the major was on the ground again, having run out of gas less than 2 miles away. Once again he enlisted the aid of a farmer. Charles Sales was the name of this man, and he sped to the airplane after witnessing the emergency landing. There was much apprehension among the farming community around the Bustleton field about just this very thing; no one wanted an airplane landing on their head. But Sales had no such reservations. Thrilled with the adventure of it all, he was often seen taking in the sights at the new airfield. He issued an open invitation for everyone there to eat a meal or stay overnight at his house while construction proceeded at Bustleton.

Fleet had had enough of flying this day. Leaving the Jenny where it landed, he and Sales drove the few miles to the airfield. Fleet sent

Culver, a 5-gallon can of gas, and a couple men back to the downed plane and ordered him to fly it in.

"We grouped all available autos and had them turn on their lights so Culver could see where to land if darkness interfered."

Fleet might not have thought it possible nine days ago, but on the eve of the inaugural airmail flights, all four Jennies were safe on the ground and where they should be: one at Belmont and three at Bustleton. Fleet would fly one of the planes to Washington at daybreak the following morning.

But the night was far from over. The flights from New York to Philadelphia had taken a physical toll on all three ships. Propellers were damaged and turnbuckles were loosened by wind and strain. It would be a long night for everyone. With the clock still ticking there was no time for lengthy repairs. At this juncture, improvisation was key. A cork served to plug a hole in the fuselage of one of the planes. It was to be that sort of night. Now, if only things would come together as well tomorrow.

CHAPTER 2

BURLESON

Come morning, Fleet awoke to clear skies, all traces of fog having vanished. It was spring in Washington, its fresh impressions evident in the dazzling blue of the sky, the morning glow on white marble buildings, and the fragrance of cherry blossom trees along the Potomac River basin. Though early, throngs of people had already begun arriving at the Polo Grounds. They'd come by car, by horse and buggy, by foot and on bicycle, everyone eager to see the great event.

"They wound down across the Mall, past the monument, on both sides of the White House, converging finally at Potomac Park."

The newspapers had been writing about the occasion for days, whipping up a frenzy of enthusiasm. Local schools had closed, unleashing hordes of wide-eyed kids onto the field, helping to swell the crowd to more than five thousand people. The world's first regularly scheduled aero mail service was about to be inaugurated, and anticipation was running high. A retinue of Army soldiers and military police stood sentry about the grounds, insurance against the actions of overenthusiastic spectators.

Inside a newly built hangar dozens of young Army mechanics tinkered about a handful of parked biplanes. Newspaper reporters and cameramen hovered around as they worked, eager to capture the great event for tomorrow's readers. Scores of politicians, military officers, inventors, explorers, and postal officials milled about, everyone waiting for the men of the hour to arrive—Maj. Fleet by air and President Wilson by motorcade.

Navy secretary Josephus Daniels was there, his attendance underscoring the War Department's approval of the occasion. A convert to the potential of airplanes, he'd already green-lighted a plan to establish the nation's first naval air station in Pensacola, Florida. The waters of the Atlantic were roiling with German U-boats. The "ubiquitous, sneaking submarine" was wreaking havoc on Allied shipping. Daniels was working with airplane manufacturer Glenn Curtiss to develop a flying boat to search the open seas for U-boats and help safeguard the men and matériel sailing to Europe. Joining Daniels was his young assistant secretary of the Navy. Like Daniels, thirty-six-year-old Franklin Delano Roosevelt was a strong proponent of military aviation and was working closely with Curtiss on the Navy's aviation needs.

Arctic explorer Admiral Robert Peary joined the two Navy men at the park. The man who had "nailed the stars and stripes to the North Pole" a decade earlier was a confirmed aviation enthusiast, as was the gentleman standing near him, Alexander Graham Bell. Both remained explorers of a kind, each driven across vastly different landscapes by a common drive and curiosity.

At seventy-one, the tall, rotund Bell was decades past his landmark invention of the telephone, but his mind still raced with the vigor of youth even as his full white beard belied his age. For some time now, Bell had been conducting experiments with flight, trying to understand its dynamics. He'd started with intricately constructed box kites, some large enough to pull a man into the air, before graduating to the Silver Dart, Canada's first homegrown flying machine. It was a flimsy contraption, little more than a mechanized flying kite, its assemblage of bamboo poles covered in fabric barely airworthy. But after it climbed into the skies on February 1909, Canada found itself part of the exclusive club of nations able to boast sustained, mechanized flight.

Bell was ebullient. As one of the plane's codevelopers, the

maiden flight not only vindicated his convictions about flying but also allayed any suspicions his Canadian neighbors might be harboring about the state of his mental health. Locals knew of the great, woolly inventor, and of his sometimes odd behavior. Bell and his wife had been spending summers in Nova Scotia since 1886. People understood how a great genius might want to drink soup through a straw or wander the hills during wild, raging storms. But this nonsense about flying really had local tongues wagging.

The pilot of the Silver Dart, J. A. D. McCurdy, later recalled the great inventor's reaction on the day of its first flight, the man and machine having returned victorious to the island of earth. "He jumped down from his red sleigh, and I shall never forget the pleasure and animation in his face when he said to me 'My boy, put the machine away. Fly tomorrow, or the next day, but today is almost a sacred day. We'll have nothing to mar it!' "

Standing Lilliputian-like inside this circle of American luminaries was Otto Praeger, who at just 5 feet 5 inches topped out somewhere around Bell's chest. But the giant, burly inventor had found a compatriot in the short, balding bureaucrat. For the past year, the two had been corresponding regularly. Like Bell, the second assistant postmaster general understood the power of technology to enhance man's reach. Praeger knew that, if properly nurtured by government, aeronautics could take commerce and stand it on its head. Today's ceremonies were proof that the U.S. Post Office Department was about to invest in its own version of Airpower and it had nothing to do with winning wars.

As the man in charge of all postal transportation, Texas-born-and-bred Praeger was in a position to turn those beliefs into action. Steamships, powerboats, horse-drawn wagons, railroads, electric lines, automobiles, auto-trucks—if it clip-clopped across the plains, chuga-chugged down the railroad tracks, putt-putted across rivers, or rolled down city streets, it fell under his purview.

He'd already seen the handwriting on the wall for horse-drawn mail wagons. The post office had begun operating a fleet of fifty newly purchased trucks, testing them in selected areas, experimenting with their possibilities in delivering Uncle Sam's mail. Though most roads were little more than rutted paths of dirt, improvements were increasingly being made to them, the war having shown the value of good roads in transporting military troops and supplies over long distances. Praeger saw no reason not to put his new trucks on those very same roads. That would get the mail moving faster. Speed had always been the mantra of the U.S. Post Office Department.

Praeger was a complex man, a study in contrasts. He sat behind the wheel of an automobile only under duress and absolutely refused to fly, yet he was one of the federal government's few proponents of both. He was often imperious, willing his decrees on subordinates with an unyielding exactitude, but could just as easily turn on the Texas charm.

As could his boss, Albert Burleson. Today was his shindig. Well-dressed and slender with long white sideburns, the postmaster had been lauded by Thomas Edison as someone "who is doing things." It had taken flattery, cajoling, and every ounce of politicking to attain the victory that had brought them here today, but eventually he and Praeger had succeeded in convincing their colleagues in Congress into appropriating $100,000 to experiment with delivering mail by air.

Until recently, such requests had been met with incredulity and outright laughter. One legislator suggested that postal officials get their heads out of the clouds and "get down to terra firma."

Today, Burleson was having the last laugh. He'd arrived at the polo field this morning anxious to see the president. This was arguably the most important day of the Texan's political career. Attired in his starched high-collar shirt and black suit, his silver hair neatly combed beneath his hat, the postmaster general prided himself on his deportment and his refined manner of dress, the accoutrements of which included a black umbrella that he carried on his arm rain or shine.

At that moment, a caravan of black open-top cars emerged through the trees. It was the president, right on schedule. Almost simultaneously, legions of policemen appeared from out of nowhere and positioned themselves between the crowd and the rutted dirt road upon which the motor cars were traveling slowly, somberly, like a line of hearses winding their way ever closer to the hangar. A buzz began to spread through the crowd. People started clapping, ripples of cheers rising and falling alongside the processional as it moved across the field. One by one, the cars stopped in front of the hangar and a series of doors swung open. Wilson stepped out, dressed in a dark four-button suit and wearing a creased hat.

The president appeared even more somber than usual. A quiet, reflective man by nature, he'd been consumed by affairs of state. The president's work schedule had always been exhausting, causing him to suffer from the maladies of hypertension, particularly headaches, but the responsibilities of war made them even worse. He hadn't wanted to come today, but he knew his appearance would send a clear signal of support—to Burleson and to the future of the aeroplane, both of which he staunchly supported.

Burleson greeted his old friend warmly. The two men had known each other since 1911, the then congressman having worked tirelessly for Wilson's first presidential campaign. In return, Burleson was awarded stewardship over Uncle Sam's communications empire, appointed to a powerful cabinet post in 1913 at the age of fifty. Burleson's ease and comfort in its labyrinthine corridors had made him a valuable asset to Wilson, particularly on legislative affairs. The president was particularly keen to protect Americans from the injustices inflicted upon them by corporate giants—by smashing monopolies, introducing fair labor practices, and protecting children from exploitation. Wilson established the Federal Reserve System to stabilize the nation's currency and enacted the Federal Farm Loan Act so people could obtain the long-term financing necessary to buy into the American Dream. And it was Burleson whom Wilson had personally selected as his liaison between the executive branch and the legislative branch.

Upon greeting, the postmaster general was careful not to bump the president's left hand, which was bandaged and covered with a white glove. Earlier in the week, Wilson had traveled to Fort Rucker in Virginia to inspect the arsenal of fighting equipment there. He'd watched as tanks fired off their shells amid jarring clouds of smoke. Following the display, he'd agreed to a photo op to help punctuate his support for the state-of-the-art weaponry. With camera bulbs flashing, the ever-restrained Wilson posed before a symbol of America's military might—a drab-colored armored tank. Unwittingly, he'd placed his hand on its still-smoking cannon. Instantly, red-hot pain stabbed at him as he realized too late his mistake.

Days later, the hand still throbbed, the pain contributing to his already dark mood, which was exacerbated by his military advisers. Everyone with stars on their shoulder, it seemed, had an opinion about how the war should be fought. But what could prepare anyone for a war being waged with such revolutionary new technology?

As a child growing up in the Civil War–torn South, Wilson had seen for himself the wholesale slaughter that cannons, swords, and cavalry charges had inflicted. But as destructive as those armaments had been, they were downright medieval compared to the draconian weaponry of today. Machine guns, submarines, tanks, and aeroplanes had fast become the tools of modern warfare. At this very moment, Brig. Gen. William "Billy" Mitchell was amassing an armada of nearly fifteen hundred American, British, Italian, and French planes and fliers to be unleashed against Germany in a massive ground and air assault. And there were reports that Germany was preparing a final last-ditch campaign against Allied forces. The battle would surely be one of the bloodiest of an already bloody conflict. Every available airman would be needed for the cause.

How could the president divert men and machines away from the war effort at a time like this? his generals respectfully asked. All the more reason American pilots must be properly trained and skilled, Wilson shot back. If that meant having them suffer the ignominy of hauling birthday cards, bank notes, and condolence notes from one place to another in order to give them enough cross-country flying experience to prepare them for battle, then so be it. His mind made up, his presence at today's event let everyone know where he stood on the matter.

All that remained was for the fliers to assume their rightful positions center stage. The problem was that neither Fleet nor Lt. Boyle was anywhere to be found. Capt. Benjamin Lipsner stood anxiously awaiting Fleet's arrival. As the point man for today's logistics, it was his responsibility to ensure all ran smoothly, that mechanics were on-site, field personnel were standing ready, and sufficient oil, fuel, and parts were available.

Impeccably groomed, with a firm sense of duty, Lipsner had the straight-backed spit-and-polish dash of a red-breasted Canadian mounted policeman. The captain's gaze shifted to the menacing wall of green surrounding the polo field.

"Has anybody ever hit those trees on takeoff, Sergeant?"

"Not yet, sir."

Both knew that there was always a first time.

Fleet, who only nine days ago had what he considered a promising career in the military, had his mind on the wall of green, too. On the north side of Washington, his biplane was winging its way across the sky. It moved slowly, like a lone bird migrating across a vast, magnificent space. Down below lay the familiar grassy public park tucked inside the panorama of marbled edifices and Parthenon-like buildings, its ring of trees a circle of death to fliers. Fleet was steamed. They should have been cut down days ago. He'd attempted to do just that but found himself up against the D.C. Parks Commission. The best he could do was get permission to chop down one lone tree growing smack in the middle of the field. For even that the red tape was choking. Procedures had to be followed, forms filled out, paperwork routed through appropriate channels. Just have a little patience, they said. The job would be done soon enough, say in about three months.

The major had enough.

"I went to the field and ordered mechanics to cut down the tree six inches below the ground, fill over the stump with cinders, tamp it hard and pull the fallen tree outside the area."

The Parks Commission hit the roof. How dare the major circumvent channels? Fleet was ordered to answer for his actions before Secretary of War Baker.

Had the major taken it upon himself to have that tree cut down?

Fleet's blood began to boil. He was far too autocratic to be bullied by a bunch of pencil-pushing park officials. His motto had always been "Nothing short of right is right," and as far as he was concerned he'd done exactly what it took to get the field ready for operations, precisely as he'd been ordered.

His gaze sure and direct, he fixed upon Baker. "I didn't ask for this job, Mr. Secretary. I am in charge of training all army aviators in the United States so if you want me to run this aerial mail job also, leave me alone and I'll run it!"

Baker knew when he was sitting on a keg of dynamite. He relented. "You know your business, Fleet—continue to run it and I'll back you from hell to breakfast!"

Peering over the side of his ship, Fleet could see throngs of people waving up at him, their wild cheers drowned out by the loud clacking of his engine. Milking the moment for all it was worth, the major dropped down low at treetop level and buzzed over the cheering crowd. He banked hard at the far end of the field, circled back and then bang!—parked her down on the grass with a hard jolt, his tail skid bouncing and bumping as he rolled her over to the hangar.

Everyone watched as the major cut the engine and climbed out of the cockpit, clearly tired from the long succession of round-the-clock workdays. He motioned to an Army mechanic, telling him what parts of the ship he wanted checked. If Boyle never showed, Fleet would be making the inaugural day trip himself.

His concern was allayed by a cocksure voice from off to the side. "Never fear because Boyle is here!"

It was the rookie aviator, a broad smile on his face. Satisfied that all was going according to plan, the major proceeded to wade into the crowd. Dressed in full aviator's uniform, the tall, erect officer moved with the certainty of a soldier confident of his destination—even if it was to the gallows. As a military man, he knew the value of a gaze sure and direct.

Wilson stepped forward and congratulated him on the success of the day, now all but assured. Things had gone swimmingly, said the president. So well, in fact, that the postal department planned to extend the airmail route to Boston. Wilson would announce it today, before the press.

Fleet was stupefied. This little intramural operation being staged today was the product of luck, determination, and the sheer grace of God. They'd be lucky to come out of it without anyone getting killed given the hastily constructed planes and the wholesale inexperience some of these pilots brought to the job. But adding service to Boston? The major was tempted to tell the president the whole lousy story. Now was not the time, though. Not with all these smiling faces. Later he would explain everything, in private. He had other priorities at the moment.

And George Boyle was at the top of that list. The rookie appeared confident, relaxed standing beside the mail plane, flashbulbs going off all around him. Until now, Fleet had been successful in keeping the lad tucked away, outside the whirl of preparations, but it was time for him to assume center stage. Standing there, flanked by eager spectators, Boyle cut a handsome figure dressed in aviator's leather pants and jacket. There was nothing in his look or demeanor to betray the wholesale inexperience he brought to the job. A pilot needs instincts and feel. He has to gauge his airspeed from the force of wind passing over his face, be able to separate a climb from a dive by the pitch of the wind in the wires. Question was, did Boyle have the necessary instincts to stay alive up there? His fiancée undoubtedly thought so. She stood beside him, a bouquet of long-stemmed roses cradled in her arms, smiling broadly, her entire countenance radiating a wholesale confidence in her future husband and in the contraption he was about to fly.

Walking up to the aviator, Fleet handed him an oil-skinned map highlighting the way to Philadelphia, the first stop along the northbound route. The Coast and Geodetic Survey had provided maps of every state between here and there, but in truth the maps offered scant navigational value, drawn as they each were to different scales and showing only political divisions and offering nothing of a physical nature by which to identify cities, town, rivers, and harbors. Boyle, like every other mail pilot, would have to rely solely on visual sightings to get him from Washington to Philadelphia.

Fleet strapped the map to the aviator's thigh to keep it from blowing away once he became airborne. At least the weather was favorable. Boyle wouldn't be fighting his way through any pea soup today. Just follow the railroad tracks running north out of Washington and you'll be okay was his only advice.

As if on cue, two black postal department trucks flanked by police motorcycles emerged on the field. They were Ford trucks—the newest, shiniest ones in the fleet. Praeger had arranged it personally. The crowd hushed in expectation as the vehicles pulled up to the hangar and stopped. The drivers hopped out and walked to the loading doors in the back, opening them wide. Two large, canvas sacks bulging with more than six thousand letters could be seen inside. A sack was brought over to the president, who stepped forward and proceeded to set the day's events in motion. Pulling out an envelope from his breast pocket, he inspected it carefully. Addressed to the postmaster of New York City, it had been affixed with a special, 24-cent airmail postage stamp designed just for the occasion. A Curtiss Jenny in flight seemed a fitting emblem for the world's first regularly scheduled airmail service and its first official stamp.

The president raised the letter above his head like some victory laurel, stirring another round of applause. The moment authenticated, Wilson proceeded to deposit the envelope into the sack. Then, with all eyes upon them, the attendants whisked the mailbags over to the waiting plane where Boyle and Fleet stood waiting. Both men watched as the sacks went into the plane's forward cargo hold, then the lid secured with two leather straps. Again, waves of applause sprang up, and for one brief moment it must have seemed that maybe, just maybe, everything might come off without a hitch. The plane looked great on the field—its red, white, and blue paint glistening in the sun. Now, if Boyle could just clear those trees.

Fleet watched as the rookie aviator shook the president's good hand and strode over to the plane, the bulk of his leather flying suit giving him the stiff-legged self-assurance of a ranch hand in chaps about to mount up and ride the range. But just as Boyle prepared to climb into the cockpit, Postmaster Burleson pushed forward, a large bouquet of carnations clasped in his arms. Boyle stopped in his tracks, uncertain of how to handle the unexpected gesture. One bouquet had already been given out today, but that was to his fiancée. The sight of the notoriously terse postmaster general holding a bunch of spring flowers in his arms, trying to pass them over to a man clad all in leather appeared awkward at best.

"The aviator took them helplessly, hardly knowing what to do with them," wrote one newspaper wag. "Finally he put them down on the wing."

Speeches were the norm at events such as this, but perhaps because of Wilson's tight schedule this morning, no one would be ushering in the faith. Instead, wristwatches were handed out. The gesture seemed only fitting. After all, the plane was about to shatter the clock. What was far would grow near. From here on, the concept of that distance wouldn't be perceived in quite the same way.

Without further fanfare, Boyle climbed into the cockpit, pulled his goggles down over his eyes, and yelled, "Contact!"

Upon his order, field mechanics flung the propeller downward. It spun and sputtered for a few moments, then fell into silence.

Undaunted, the aviator raised his arm once more. "Contact!"

Again, the mechanics heaved their shoulders into the prop. Once again, the 150-horsepower engine merely coughed in response. Murmurs began to spread through the crowd. Postal officials stood nearby, anxiously waiting. The president was pressed for time. If this glitch wasn't solved quickly, he might well leave.

This was likely a time for Burleson to invoke his favorite credo—the same one that had served Thomas Jefferson so well throughout his career: *Nil desperandum;* there is no cause for despair; never despair.

Mechanics swarmed over the aircraft like ants on a picnic basket, searching for any outward signs of trouble. As they worked, Fleet mentally sorted through potential problems at lightning speed. He'd gone over the engine just this morning. Everything had checked out.

As everyone frantically scrambled to solve the problem, the president of the United States stood watching, his arms folded tightly across his chest, his bifocaled studiousness hardening into a singular displeasure. Here was the man who had announced to all America that airpower would help to win the war overseas. Now they couldn't even get the plane off the ground.

He turned to his wife, wholly exasperated: "We are losing a lot of valuable time here."

As she had done so many times before, Edith Wilson settled her husband, urging him to be patient just a little longer.

But the scene was rapidly deteriorating. Something had to be done before Wilson bolted completely. On a hunch, Fleet ordered one of his mechanics to check the fuel tank. It was bone dry. The major was livid. His gaze shifted to Lipsner. The empty fuel tank had embarrassed him, and in front of the president no less.

"I had delegated Capt. B. B. Lipsner, detailed at his request to the Aerial Mail Service Production, to have aviation gasoline at the Polo Field in Washington," said Fleet later. "He failed in his mission and didn't have a drop of gasoline there."

All hands ran for the gas cans, but to Fleet's dismay they found every last one empty. It would fall to a lone mechanic to rescue the moment. Walking over to an airplane parked at the hangar, he inserted a hose into its gas tank and proceeded to refuel the old-fashioned way—by sucking it up as the president and a few thousand others looked on. At least by now, Wilson's interest was piqued. He watched intently, not a word of complaint from his lips.

Finally, the siphoning complete and the fuel transferred to Boyle's waiting plane, all was ready. For the third time, Boyle yelled, "Contact." This time, in a belch of smoke, the biplane roared to life. Adjusting his feet on the rudder bar, Boyle eased the throttle forward and guided the nose of the ship into the wind. Green parkland stretching out before him, an embrace of sky overhead, all that remained was to throttle forward.

The roar of his engine echoed across the crowd as his plane charged toward the line of trees up ahead. Plunging and tossing over the uneven field, he drove the Jenny hard, picking up speed. Its wheels lifted and the nose began reaching skyward. Apprehension gripped the crowd—the trees. His wheels rose higher, a few feet at first, then higher still. Opening the throttle, Boyle gunned his way into the sky, his plane just skimming over the branches.

All at once, everyone began to cheer. History had been made—barely, but made all the same. Watching the wire-braced biplane climb into the sunlight, the whir of its prop punctuating his path across a fluid sky, it must have seemed that Icarus had finally succeeded. How long he stayed there remained to be seen. Still, emotions were stirred mightily across the polo field. Even the newspaper wag who had acridly recounted Burleson's awkwardness with the flowers couldn't help but feel the moment in his story for the next day's paper: "The hum of the engine faded and at the margin of the sky Boyle turned back, around the field he came. And scarce distinguishable, his arm came over the side of his perch as he waved farewell."

CHAPTER 3

REGULARLY SCHEDULED SERVICE

Above the fold on the front page of the next morning's *Washington Post*, sandwiched between the story "French Take Hill 44" and "Strong Shellfire on Italian Front," screamed the headline that Praeger and Burleson had worked so hard to achieve: "Aero Mail a Success."

As a former newspaper reporter, Praeger understood the value of story placement, and nobody could deny that the headline spoke volumes. Truth be told, though, the second assistant postmaster was lucky that the *Post* hadn't printed all the details of Boyle's inaugural flight, choosing instead to limit most of the bad news to subheads in the story.

"Capital Plane in Mishap," read the first.

"Lieut. Boyle After Going 30 Miles Forced to Descend in Maryland" went the second, followed by "Loses Way in Misty Sky, Has Engine Troubles and Breaks Propeller in Coming Down."

It seems the rookie pilot had dutifully followed Fleet's orders to parallel the railroad tracks out of town; the problem was, he'd followed them in the wrong direction. The realization hit him eventually, and in need of directions he set down in a field near Waldorf, Maryland. Too late did he grasp his mistake, though, the field being newly plowed. His wheels sank into the brown, earthen gruel, throwing his ship onto its back like a bad gymnast. Boyle emerged unhurt, but the Air Mail Service had dished up its first casualty less than twenty minutes into its inaugural flight.

But what did that matter. The rest of Fleet's team conducted themselves flawlessly that day.

The mustachioed, young Lt. Howard Paul Culver was waiting at Bustleton to fly the second northbound leg when he heard of the rookie's fate. He immediately climbed into his cockpit and drove his plane into the sky. There might not be any Washington mail in that cargo hold, but throngs of people were awaiting the arrival of a U.S. aero mail plane at Belmont field, and Culver did not intend to disappoint.

Ninety miles later, Culver's ship approached the airspace over Long Island. In the distance, two military chase planes were flying lazy circles in the sky, a rendezvous having been arranged by the military brass at nearby Mineola. With his arrival, all three planes joined in a V formation and proceeded to make a slow pass over the racetrack. Shouts rose from the grandstand as the sight of American planes flying as a single fighting unit overhead, its centerpiece a boldly painted mail plane with five-pointed stars under its wings, caused patriotic hearts to race. Who cared that President Wilson's letter and all the other mail from Washington was lying upside down in a Maryland field. It was the feat being honored; it was the daring young flier being cheered.

Lt. Torrey Webb's flight out of Belmont created similar thrills for the thousands of people filling the grandstand and infield in anticipation of the first regularly scheduled airmail flight from New York to Washington. Everyone watched as a whistle-tooting Long Island Railroad train pulled into the station adjacent to the raceway. Onboard were two precious sacks of mail, which were quickly transferred to a waiting flivver that then sped across the expanse of grass to the mail plane, where its clean-shaven leather-jacketed pilot stood waiting.

Webb's new wife stood proudly by and watched her husband help stow the mail in the hopper just forward of the cockpit. Much of the crowd, however, was distracted by the ongoing speeches. One after another, postal officials, politicians, and dignitaries took to the podium to wax lyrical on the state of aviation. Webb found himself growing increasingly anxious. Their eyes were on the future, his were on the clock. Maj. Fleet had given him direct orders to have the ship in the air no later than 11:30. Webb didn't want to disrupt the ceremonies, but he was first and foremost an Army flier. An order is an order.

The prop was spun and the engine thundered to life. Field personnel grabbed hold of the wings to steady the plane as it slowly taxied to the end of the infield, face into the wind.

Someone yelled, "There she goes!" and all heads turned to see Webb barreling down the infield, throttle forward. A children's choir from Queens began to belt out "The Star-Spangled Banner" as Webb's plane swept past the stage, drowning any vestige of oratory from the podium. People cheered and waved their hats as the Jenny continued its charge across the infield until its wheels lifted from the ground, sending the pilot skyward.

Webb leveled off at 4,000 feet, then set a course for Philadelphia, fully 144 pounds of U.S. government mail stowed inside his aircraft. Behind him, the racetrack receded from view, its boundaries merging into the eye-stretching vista around him. The Jenny continued down Long Island toward Manhattan, crossed over New York Harbor, softly rising and falling over the eddies of air. It wasn't long before northern New Jersey passed beneath his wings, thick plumes of smoke rising from its factories and refineries. The gray changed to green as the farms of central Jersey dominated, and the elegant fieldstone towers and buildings of Princeton University offered a welcome marker to the pilot above. For Webb, graduate of another prestigious ivy-covered university, the panoramas of flying were a world away from the subterranean depths he'd been educated to plumb. The passing towns, the schoolyards, the narrow dirt roads were merely etchings on a flat two-dimensional surface over which he was moving, with as many marvels below the surface as there were from nearly a mile up.

The lieutenant touched down in Philadelphia an hour later without cracking up, getting lost, or running out of fuel, ready to pass his mail sacks off to Lt. James Edgerton who, just six minutes later, was airborne, winging his way toward the nation's capital.

Soaring over Delaware and Maryland, he arrived in Washington to find Potomac Park still crowded with people, many of whom had stayed to enjoy a picnic and catch the day's second show. The field, already small, was dangerously hemmed in by the swell of spectators. Edgerton sized up the situation, then chose a landing pattern that would get him down without getting anyone hurt.

"I decided on a southern approach . . . a side slip to kill forward speed . . . no brakes or flaps . . . better slip to the left away from the crowd . . . quick, the right wing tip must just clear the bandstand . . . a twitch on the stick to straighten out . . . stalling speed, down with the tail . . . and a three-point landing."

The florist shops in town did well that day. Edgerton landed both wings up, and waiting for him there was his younger sister, her arms clutching an enormous bouquet of roses, her face warmed by a shy smile. Fleet, too, was on hand to greet the pilot and offer his "well done."

Then, with all due speed, mail sacks were loaded into an idling automobile-truck for quick dispatch to the city's main post office where a platoon of Boy Scouts on bicycles stood ready. Less than a half hour later, all the youngsters had managed to ply their considerable enthusiasm and pedal power into successful delivery of nearly 750 pieces of mail, including one from the Postmaster General Burleson, personally addressed to his good friend Alan Hawley, president of the Aero Club of America, thanking him for his unfailing support throughout the entire protracted effort. Organizations like the Aero Club had been fervent supports of aviation—stirring up the possibilities of everything from airmail to crossing the Atlantic Ocean by airplane.

Make no mistake, said Burleson in his note of thanks to Hawley, the first airmail flight marked "the beginning of an epoch in the development of speedy mail communication."

The experiment had netted the postal department an astounding victory. The inaugural event had been staged magnificently, right down to the Boy Scouts on their bicycles. Uncle Sam's airmail service was the story of the day in all the big city dailies, some newspapers now calling aero mail the "Pony Express with wings."

It had taken pilots Webb and Edgerton just under three and a half hours to fly the 218 miles between New York and Washington. People were staggered that such a distance could be traversed in such a short period of time.

On May 16, the front-page headline in the *New York Times* trumpeted, "200 minutes," proudly mentioning that a copy of the paper of record was inside one of the mailbags.

That's all the time it had taken to travel from the nation's seat of politics to its center of commerce—a far cry from the fifteen hours it had taken pony express riders to traverse the same route just a few decades earlier. The whole enterprise of delivering mail on wing was breathing fresh air into the most mundane of government businesses. These weren't bunioned civil servants in monochrome uniforms delivering mail door-to-door, their shoulders stooped under the weight of heavily laden sacks. These were daredevils in goggles and leather, courageous adventurers just like the pony express riders of old.

But of all the stories that appeared in print on May 16, the one that surely had Praeger smiling inside was in the *Washington Post*. A smart desk editor had cut right to the chase, having penned a concise subhead worthy of a large metropolitan daily. Just three words—that's all. Never had brevity sounded so sweet.

"Beats the Railroads," it read.

The newspaper had dished up a victory worth savoring. Burleson and Praeger had long chafed at the way railroads held sway over mail delivery in America. To them, the barons running the Central Pacific, the Union Pacific, the Northern Pacific, the Southern Pacific, the Santa Fe, and the Great Northern were common sycophants who had been living off the teat of the postal service for decades now, buying influence in the halls of Congress as they levied overinflated rates for carrying Uncle Sam's mail. Burleson made it a priority to cut them down to size and recently he had done just that by changing the railroad's compensation from *weight* carried to *distance* traveled. That change in accounting cut $7 million from the railroad's annual bill of roughly $62 million and stirred up a hornet's nest not seen since the days of Butch Cassidy's Hole in the Wall Gang.

The assault on the traditional pricing structure had made Burleson an enemy to their ranks. They might argue with him, but they couldn't argue with the headlines. Praeger's Jennies had beaten the railroads, and like it or not, the balance of power was shifting away from them and their steam engines, with the airplane destined to become the beneficiary.

There was no question that the inaugural-day press coverage had both Praeger and his boss agrinning. The next week would prove torturous, however, as successive failures ended up on the front pages of the dailies every morning and afternoon. They read like scenes from a disaster movie.

New York, May 16—Lt. Stephen Bonsal, having found himself on the sidelines for the inaugural flights, is determined to pilot the morning's mail out of Belmont even with the region covered entirely in fog. Under gray-laden skies, he eases himself into the cockpit and with a spin of the prop, the engine revs to life and he is airborne heading for Philadelphia. But trouble comes swiftly. The soup closes in around him, smothering his ship in a blinding whiteout. Bonsal presses on until the gauge on his instrument panel warns him he is nearly out of fuel. Descending below the fog bank, he catches sight of open pasture and prepares to land. But as he makes his approach, he sees a herd of horses grazing contentedly. He comes down low and buzzes the field in an attempt to scatter the horses. But these plugs aren't the twitchy thoroughbreds at Belmont and are oblivious to the plane bearing down upon them. His engine about to quit, Bonsal has no choice but to land. Swerving to miss the herd, he plows into a fence, breaking the propeller. Bonsal walks away unhurt, but the mail is going nowhere fast.

It is nearly 6 P.M. before Bonsal's mail sacks are collected and forwarded to Bustleton. Though darkness is only two hours away, Lt. Walter Miller departs with all due dispatch, even though he has never flown the route to Washington. Thirty minutes later, even he is back on the ground at Bustleton, citing engine trouble and approaching darkness.

Facing a big zero for the day, the rookie Edgerton volunteers to fly the run. The eager military aviator has flown the route twice already and, besides, he's got his good-luck charm—Jenny #38274, the plane he'd personally assembled just two days before. He is in the air at 6:33, his left hand pushing the throttle for maximum speed, his eyes on the horizon and the setting sun.

Word of the flight filters down to Washington, and an expectant crowd gathers at Potomac Park—many, no doubt, coming to see the pilot break his neck. But where Bonsal and Miller failed, this third attempt proves lucky for Edgerton, as he lands safely in darkness at 8:42 P.M., the polo field awash in the headlights of parked cars that Maj. Fleet had secured to illuminate the way.

Washington, D.C., May 17—Lt. Boyle is up at bat again. Despite his misadventure on inaugural day, Fleet decides to give the greenhorn another chance, hoping the young flier might have developed a little more homing pigeon than he exhibited before. As a precaution, the major flies wingman to ensure that the lad reaches his destination. Everything goes smoothly at first. The compass headings appear accurate, and by all accounts both planes are on a direct heading for Bustleton, Pennsylvania. At this rate, it's conceivable that Boyle might actually make it to his destination.

Less than 50 miles into the trip, however, Fleet begins experiencing problems with his throttle. Unable to continue, he maneuvers his plane toward Boyle. Flying wingtip to wingtip, Fleet signals his problem as best he can.

Will the young pilot be able to go on without him?

Boyle yells over the roar of the engines: "I'm OK."

But he wasn't. Before long, Boyle finds himself lost over the Atlantic Ocean. Burning up his fuel, he sputters his way to the mouth of the Chesapeake, where he sets down to reconnoiter. He's not that far off course; with good weather and minimal headwinds, he can still reach Philadelphia in two hours, maybe less. He takes off, only to become lost again. Another three hours pass, and the letters marked "aero mail' in his cargo hold have yet to arrive at their destination. By now, Boyle's Jenny is running on fumes. Down below, he spies a verdant stretch of parkland nestled among the stately mansions of Philadelphia's Main Line. He's only about 25 miles from Bustleton. Just a quick landing, some fuel in the tank, and he'll be back on his way. Pushing the stick forward, Boyle aims the nose of his plane downward, unwittingly setting in motion a most dramatic entrance upon the upper crust of the venerable Philadelphia Country Club.

Upon seeing an airplane about to drop down upon their heads, everyone scatters. Watching the chaos unfold beneath his wings, Boyle begins working the rudder bar for all its worth, desperate to avoid the people running in all directions. Unlike the horses Bonsal unsuccessfully tried to spook two days prior, this crowd is running for their lives. Boyle's dodging skills prove first-rate, however, and he lands without hitting anyone, though the effort sends his ship plowing into a fence and breaks the wing.

Fleet had seen enough. Boyle's days as a flying mailman are over. Postal officials plead to give the lad one more chance.

"The request is denied," Fleet shoots back, and, with the blessing of Secretary of War Newton Baker, Boyle is promptly removed from the duty roster and packed off to flying school for further training.

Washington, D.C., May 18—At last, some measure of success. On the fourth day of airmail operations, all four mail runs come off without mishap.

The moment is memorialized by the *Washington Post*, which declares somewhat ingenuously: "Lieuts. Miller, Bonsal and Culver, Flying, Have No Accidents."

This was not what Praeger had in mind. One day out of four without a pilot getting lost, arriving three hours late, or cracking up does not approximate anything like Regularly . . . Scheduled . . . Service—as in every day, day in and day out.

Things had gone bad—even bordering on the pathetic after Praeger hears that a dog is killed at one of the fields.

"Unused to the sight and roar of an airplane, the dog viciously attacked the whirling propeller of the plane, with the result that the dog was decapitated and the tip of the propeller was splintered."

The only saving grace is that the newspapers didn't find out. No such luck with the Air Mail's first postage stamp.

To commemorate the inaugural flight, Burleson had ordered the special printing of a 24-cent aero mail stamp. The two-toned stamp, depicting a blue Jenny centered inside a red border, should have rolled off the press easily enough, copper-plate printing having remained virtually unchanged since Rembrandt worked an etching needle three hundred years prior. But a printer's devil struck on Burleson's watch as nine sheets of the new airmail stamps came off the presses with the blue Jenny upside down. Eight of the nine were found and quickly destroyed, but a single sheet of one hundred misprinted stamps found its way into a teller's drawer at the post office on New York Avenue in Washington, D.C. It was there, on the morning of May 14, that a bookish but eager twenty-nine-year-old stamp collector named William Robey went to acquire the new aero mail stamps.

When the teller pulled out the sheet of inverted Jennies and handed it to him, Robey surely went bug-eyed. Breathless and faint, he quickly asked to see the teller's other sheets, but they were all printed normally. His prize in hand, he went rushing to the other post offices in town hoping to catch lightning a second time, but his sheet was the only that had managed to escape.

Robey knew immediately that he had hit the jackpot, and he couldn't help telling his friends and fellow stamp collectors. Word of his find spread like wildfire among the stamp community, and within hours a pair of postal inspectors had tracked him down at work. They tried to strong-arm him into giving back the sheet, but as Robey had purchased it legally, he remained steadfast. His backbone paid off. Within the week, the philatelist had sold the sheet of stamps for $15,000. The legend of the Inverted Jenny was born.

It was a dispirited Praeger who penned a note to his brother: "Dear Wally, at this particular junction of putting in this new service, with aviators losing their way in the fog and machines crashing into fences, I don't know whether I am standing on my ear or my feet."

*   *   *

What was the problem here? Praeger expected there would be set-backs en route, which is precisely why he'd taken pains to prepare, if not for every eventuality, then at least for the really big headaches. They had the planes and the pilots, plus a dependable leader in Maj. Fleet. Emergency landing fields had been established, and reserve planes were stationed across the route. Everything had been carefully coordinated with railroad timetables.

Airmail arriving at Bustleton by 12:30 P.M., for example, would make the 3:00 train to Wilmington, the 3:30 to Camden, the 4:40 to Harrisburg, and the 4:32 to Atlantic City. Similarly, mail arriving at Belmont by midafternoon was timed to make the 5:30 train out of Grand Central Station to Boston, and the 5:31 to Cleveland and Chicago. There should have been enough time to make those outbound trains even factoring in the extra hour it took to transfer the mail from the airfields to the railroad stations downtown.

It worked on paper. In practice, it was nothing for a plane to be delayed two or three hours due to mechanical troubles or weather. The result was missed train connections and an entire day's worth of flights going for naught. Who was going to pay extra postage for an airmail letter that doesn't get there any faster than regular mail?

The operation was quickly proving to be more than Praeger had bargained for. The JN-4H Jenny aircraft, in particular, were bedeviled by troubles, and real dogs when it came to holding up under the daily strain of cross-country flying. Army mechanics were burning the midnight oil trying to fix one set of problems only to find the same ships back in the hangar the next day with completely different troubles.

Machines break. Schedules suffer. Praeger accepted all that. After all, it had been only fifteen years since the world's first controlled, powered flight at Kitty Hawk. The mechanical problems would be sorted out eventually.

After two weeks of flying, however, it was clear that the service faced a far greater problem—weather. The air itself had become a translucent, physical enemy that resisted quantifiable analysis.

A cumulous cloud could spawn a storm from out of nowhere and hunt down an unsuspecting pilot in a single, horrifying charge. Sudden changes in air temperature could result in an updraft that was violent enough to send a ship on an express ride to hell. Cross-winds were heaving planes sideways, throwing them miles off course. Weather currents seemed in a constant state of flux. In the uncharted territory of changing winds and varying air pressures and temperatures, pilots were riding the sky through a series of narrow escapes and lucky moments.

Praeger had a simple solution to the bad weather plaguing pilots on their mail runs—plow through the stuff.

The Army, though, wasn't allowing him to touch the flying end of things. That was their domain. From the start, the brass had been reluctant to maintain any sort of continuous flying schedule. In the military, a pilot was considered master of his own destiny, he alone capable of deciding when it was safe to fly. On both sides of the war, it was agreed that Old Man Weather was not to be ruled. Flying through foul air, even in the pursuit of the enemy, was hardly worth the price of a man's life. Even that ace of all fliers, the Red Baron, agreed that the arena of the sky was no place to stage a dogfight when the weather closed in. "Nothing is more disagreeable for flying men than to have to go through a thunderstorm," he said.

As far as the pilots were concerned, bad weather was a legitimate reason to spend the morning playing cards with the mechanics in the hangar instead of fighting a craft through the sky. That attitude was reflected in the postal department's carefully recorded, but dismal, performance stats. Seven flights were canceled completely in the first fourteen days of operation. Combined with constant delays, the airmail had become an operational nightmare reflecting a mere 78 percent on-time success rate.

When one thought of aviation, the words *excitement, danger, thrills,* and *adventure* came to mind, not *efficiency* and *reliability.* And Praeger knew that the percentages would only worsen as summer turned to fall and thunderstorms rolled across the East. The harsh depths of winter would follow, along with it cold, snow, and ice, the likes of which would hamper flying even further. Only 100 percent performance would convince the public that sending a letter by air was just as safe and reliable as sending it by train. It was also the ammunition Praeger needed to quell dissent within Congress, which seemed to take up a vote every few weeks to kill airmail.

The Army Signal Corps wasn't helping any. As far as it was concerned, the mail was getting through well enough. Why couldn't Praeger content himself with completing three-quarters of the scheduled flights on the board?

What they failed to grasp, however, was that Praeger refused to relinquish control over the flying. As things stood, it was the Army controlling the flying schedule, not him, and that he could never, would never, accept. To the second assistant's way of thinking, the military had agreed to provide him with planes and pilots enough to fly them. That did not entitle them to impose their personal views about how and when it was safe to fly. This was an operational decision, one that belonged fully to his department. He would choose what air routes to lay down, he would coordinate delivery schedules. In turn, the pilots would see that every mail sack reached its destination on time, rain or shine, six days a week. Airmail wasn't going to fail because the Army didn't have the stomach for flying in the fog.

At least Praeger still had his greatest ally, Postmaster General Burleson, who also agreed that a part-time air-delivery service was unacceptable to the federal government. Still, in private, Burleson had initially expressed his doubts about supporting airmail. Airplanes were so new, so unproven. No technology, no matter how promising, could afford to be subsidized if it couldn't stand on its own feet. Burleson, for one, would not be involved in "establishing a plaything."

Praeger remembered the conversation clearly.

"It was a misty, dreary morning, the kind that Washington is accustomed to in the winter months, when Postmaster General Burleson sent word that he wanted to see me. He was standing at a window when I entered, looking out at the slushy street and the descending mist. I did not think that this summons meant anything more than that the postmaster general was getting restless and probably would ask whether I thought that the bass might be induced to bite down in some of the lower branches of the Potomac river."

That's not what was on Burleson's mind.

"Do you think that airplanes could operate in this kind of weather?" he asked Praeger. "You know, we have a lot of it in the winter months."

From the postmaster's office both men could see the Capitol Building a half-mile away, but the view of the dome was murky and the thick clouds hung only 400 feet above the ground. Praeger admitted that the only airplane operations he had observed closely were in 1909 when Orville Wright demonstrated his airplane to the Army at Fort Myer, Virginia, and the aviator never even flew that high.

"Shucks, we have come a long way since those flights," Burleson responded. "You make a study of this thing. I tell you what, if I am convinced that the airplane can operate dependably in any kind of weather—of course, no worse than this—I will put the air mail in the postal service.

"But mark this," and he raised a forefinger like a lawyer cautioning a witness, "I don't want to put in the service, and then have to take it out. If we can start a real honest to goodness airmail route that is going to be a fixture in the postal service, I can get all the money we need to keep it going."

CHAPTER 4

OTTO

Together, they made for an odd pair—Albert Sidney Burleson, the tall, well-dressed politician, and Otto Praeger, a short, stout, cigar-chewing son of German immigrants whose signature style consisted of rumpled suits and pockets bulging with notepads and odd snippets of paper.

Unlike Burleson, who had learned of the world from behind the protective veil of wealth, Praeger's parents had come to America riding a wave of immigration that brought tens of thousands of Germans to Texas in the mid-1800s. They settled in Victoria, Texas, near the Gulf of Mexico, where Praeger was born in 1871, the third of four children. At eight, his family moved to San Antonio, with its fertile valley and good fresh water. It was a time of change for the mission town, brought about by the arrival of the Southern Pacific in 1883. With the railroad came a flow of humanity to mix with the gunfighters, cowpunchers, and Mexican laborers, and San Antonio's saloon halls rattled with gamblers and dancing girls in ruffled petticoats.

Still, not everyone came riding in on the rails. Some folks still preferred traveling the old-fashioned way—by stagecoach, which routinely came wheeling through town, dust flying. It was an 80-mile, bone-jarring distance between San Antonio and Austin, with a crusty sort known only as "Shorty" on the reins. Old Shorty swore he drove the most frequently robbed stage in West Texas. His poor passengers lost a fortune, but he always managed it so they walked away with their skins.

Hungry for adventure, young Otto found Shorty to be a source of tantalizing stories. He heard the lessons of self-reliance retold a hundred different ways, and he understood that without connections or money it would fall to him to underwrite his own curiosity about the world. Unmoved by math, bored by "literary fossils" like Beowulf, and uninspired by an education that introduced students to the inner realms of H_2O by "applying a match to a test tube full of hydrogen to see a drop of water form," Otto went searching for something to pour his energies into. But where to find it? The thought of blowing across a western prairie like good old Shorty wasn't exactly his idea of an intellectually stimulating career. Neither was he cut out to be a shopkeeper like his dad, who scratched out a living behind the counter of a hardware store.

There was, however, one subject that spun his six-shooter—current events. Now that trains were speeding newspapers across the country, anyone willing to plunk down a penny could gaze beyond their backyard onto the larger world stage. Otto would hungrily devour every word written about the Spanish-American War being played out on the front pages of the nation's daily papers. No longer did he have to wait for some shred of news to sift its way down from the outside world. He was reading about the American Navy confronting Spain half a world away almost as it happened.

Journalism would be Praeger's ticket to that adventure. He was willing to start at the bottom, as an office boy or even a printer's devil, anything to appease his insatiable appetite for the world around him. Fortunately, newspapers were springing up everywhere. Since the invention of the Linotype machine in 1886 publishing had never been so easy. Anyone with a hankering to speak his mind could set up shop and relay the events of the day as he saw fit.

In 1888, Otto landed a job as a cub reporter for his hometown paper, the *San Antonio Express*. The editor liked his grit and self-confidence. The fact that he spoke two other languages—German and Spanish—was also a valuable commodity. Otto entered the fourth estate filled with coltish high spirits and the arrogance of youth, ready to show everyone what he could do. What he received instead was a verbal thrashing for his feeble attempts at writing.

"Take this mess and boil it down to fifty words of plain English," snapped the editor. "Who the hell cares about the bloom on the honeysuckle vine or what the cat was doing on the rug."

Undaunted, Otto kept showing up each day, learning his craft as he continued to develop his innate talents of critical inquiry. But through it all, he never stopped vowing that when at last his genius was recognized and he found his way to the top, his first order of business would be to fire that *%#@&^ editor.

Though a novice at the game, the determined Praeger received a few choice assignments. He got to shadow a candidate running for the U.S. Senate and traveled to Mexico to cover the trial of an American train conductor accused of killing a Mexican fare jumper by throwing him from a train. When the well of stories ran dry, he relied on the steady stream of old frontier scouts and heroes of the Indian wars who passed through town with their Wild West shows.

"I saw Dr. W. F. Carver kill 100 live pigeons on the wing with never a miss, and watched Kit Carson wing ever so many bats in darting flight. Pawnee Bill's yelling Indians, year after year, rode bareback after a wildly tearing stage coach, but his shooting cowboys always arrived in the nick of time to save the lone woman passenger and her child. Buffalo Bill rode a white charger at the head of his Wild West show, season upon season, until his long black locks silvered, and his statuesque form sat stiff and formal on his mount."

Praeger learned the trade from a cast of itinerant reporters and editors who traveled the expanding frontiers of the nation. They were a restless group, all eager to explore local politics, local saloons, and local women, underwriting their tours with the periodic stint at newspapers like the *San Antonio Express*, bragging that they had "worked with Dana on the *Sun*." A few months' pay banging out stories and then *pfft*—off they'd go on another wild binge, followed by a new locale and a fresh stint on yet another newspaper the next state over. Author-to-be Mark Twain earned his journalistic chops that way, bouncing between papers like the *Territorial*

Enterprise in Virginia City, Nevada, and the *Sacramento Union* in California.

Young Praeger rubbed shoulders with scores of such reporters, receiving a gin-laced education about the principles of journalism and the almighty challenge of keeping the reader interested. At the age of twenty-one, Praeger convinced his editor to send him on a 1,800-mile bicycle trip across Mexico. Armed with a revolver and equipped with a couple dozen pencils and a new bicycle, he set off on what he expected would be the adventure of a lifetime. His paper even planned to syndicate his dispatches to other newspapers. But Mexico in 1892 was not what he expected.

In contrast to America with its bold national confidence inspired by scientific and industrial revolutions, this was a country standing still, ground to a halt by the weight of its own poverty. In this harsh, unforgiving land, workers toiled in the fields for a few pesos and children died from dysentery due to lack of running water. Day after day Praeger pedaled his way through the dust and small adobe villages, seeking adventure and stories of inspiration. Trouble was, nothing much was happening—no kidnappings, no train robberies, no revolutions. His astute powers of observation had netted him little. From Mexico City to Mazatlan the eager reporter searched for action and local color, but instead was confronted with the same hopeless gaze in a thousand different faces. He sat by the light of a campfire each night writing his stories, trying to find the right words to enliven a social and political landscape as dry as a bone. He'd seen the Pacific Ocean for the very first time, its blue expanse unfathomable, though from a reporting standpoint, wholly colorless.

"I know that I disappointed my editor and all my friends, except my immediate family," he said, "because I did not have a brush with Yaqui Indians, or at least shoot it out with a gang of bandits."

But he did have that great "rattlesnake" story. His editor had written him personally, asking for more of the same. But how many times did a guy want to pedal down an old abandoned road, weaving a path through a crowd of coiled rattlesnakes sunning themselves, alternately firing shots into their midst while ringing the bell on his bike to scare them off? Clearly, the whole Mexican adventure had paled under the daily struggle of traveling over rocky, primitive trails, heat suffocating every breath, the only respite being the occasional postcard village that emerged from the dense cactus like some mouthwatering Shangri-la.

"Could I have realized the proportion of toil and discomfort to the total sum of delightful experiences, I would have ventured upon the undertaking with dread, rather than with joyful anticipation."

After three months alone, Praeger returned home, his dreams chastened, but wiser for the experience. During his sojourn, he had seen the word *opportunity* erased from the vocabulary of citizens, witnessed firsthand the stagnation of a people. It contrasted sharply with his home country, which could barely contain its people's ingenuity.

More determined than ever to make something of himself, the young Texas reporter searched for a place to put his sizable energies. No longer content covering local fires and murders, he enrolled at the University of Texas. While there he met Annie Hardestry, a Cajun girl from Louisiana. They married and a son was born that same year. Otto pressed on with his studies and worked part-time as a court reporter. But making ends meet proved difficult, and after two years he ended his university schooling and rejoined the *San Antonio Express*. Now considered one of the paper's more experienced reporters, he was garnering the best assignments and even wrote an occasional editorial piece. A restlessness itched him, though. He wanted to be more than just an observer of events. He yearned to participate in the sociological and technological changes roiling the country—even in San Antonio.

A new mayor had just been elected on a reform platform, and he had big plans for the city. Narrow roads would be widened, and dirt streets paved with asphalt. A civic center would be erected and parks established throughout the city. The only thing holding back the process was an internal government squabble over the position of city clerk, a key job since its holder would be issuing all the permits for the work. Praeger's reportorial instincts were piqued; maybe there was a bigger story here than he thought.

"Who is going to be your clerk?" he inquired, pencil at the ready.

"Why, it is going to be you," the new mayor replied and leaned back in his chair to enjoy the look on the reporter's face.

Praeger took the job and threw himself into the fray. It wasn't long before the sounds of new construction began echoing across San Antonio. Problems followed, though, as the new reform administration, convinced of its mandate for civic reform, had been naive to think they could implement its ideas without political consensus. Praeger later recalled:

"The old political ring, capitalizing on the disconnect of the older burgers of the city, for whom the improvements had come too fast and proved too radical, booted the reform administration out of office, and me back to my old position on the morning newspaper."

Back inside the newsroom, Praeger was promoted to city editor, then to news editor. He aspired to be managing editor or even editor in chief but was blocked by the men in those slots. By now a second son had been born to Praeger, and he decided to go hunting farther afield. Next stop—Washington, D.C. His growing family in tow, he left Texas behind. His new title: "Washington correspondent."

He was now an esteemed member of the D.C. press corps, the best of the best. His colleagues weren't itinerant newspapermen filing stories on their way out of town. These were the top reporters from all the big metropolitan dailies, the wire services, and the foreign press—scribes who had spent years honing their craft and building relationships. He took his place among them, with a view on the greatest show on Earth.

He was there to watch Theodore Roosevelt make his mark on the political stage. TR was high on his list of solid statesmen, having taken liberalism and endowed it with a largeness that only a man of his robust personage could. The former Rough Rider strived to curb the vast political influence that industrial America had wielded under former president William McKinley. Roosevelt used the long-dormant Sherman Act to break up business monopolies. He strengthened the regulatory powers of the Interstate Commerce Commission, and though he was wary of overregulation, he made industry titans play by the rules with legislation like the Pure Food and Drug Act. His other legacy to America was his love for the

American landscape, and he used the power of the Oval Office to protect vast tracks of wild, pristine lands, including Yellowstone and Yosemite National Parks.

From his station in the press gallery Praeger watched approvingly as government used the might of its political power to enhance the lives of its citizens. It was an attitude that became integral to his reporting, which he was now doing for the *Dallas News*, considered the most influential journal in the Southwest. Liberal and Democratic, it offered him the platform he needed for his reform-minded coverage of D.C. politics.

But progressiveness all but evaporated in 1909 with the election of Republican William Howard Taft as president. An enormous 300-pound walrus of a man, Taft had once been Roosevelt's protégé and served as his secretary of war. While Taft showed himself to be a strong advocate of antitrust laws during his four years in office, he dismantled many of TR's checks and balances on business and showed little regard for the environment. Unhappy with the direction of the country, Roosevelt ended his short political retirement and tossed his safari hat into the ring for the election of 1912.

Republicans, Democrats, and Bull Moosers were pulling out all the stops for the election, with party luminaries doing their best to curry favor among the important newspaper correspondents.

It was on such a quest that Texas representative Albert Sidney Burleson showed up at Room 45 in the Washington Post Building, the cramped, little office of Otto Praeger. As the most important newspaper reporter on the most influential newspaper in Texas, Praeger was in a position to do the congressman some good. Burleson was backing a Democratic candidate by the name of Woodrow Wilson—a man of high-minded ideals and progressive thinking. He was convinced that this candidate could do great things for the country.

"One night while the campaign was at fever heat, Burleson and two other campaign orators just in from a speaking trip called on me to catch up on the latest political gossip," remembered Praeger. "While we were in animated conversation, the Western Union operator who was stationed at the office, suddenly called out: 'Flash! Roosevelt shot in Milwaukee.'"

For an instant there was dead silence, with only the sound of the news ticker in the background.

"Roosevelt grappled with the man," announced the operator.

"Like hell, he did," excitedly yelled one of the visitors. "The blankety-blank, he shot himself to create sympathy."

"Never mind if he did," said Burleson, "we've got to get hold of headquarters and see to it that Roosevelt gets a message of sympathy from Wilson!"

The details of the assassination attempt came out the next morning. A deranged man got off a close-range shot at the former president, and he was only saved because the bullet was slowed by first striking a sheaf of paper he was holding in front of him. The next morning, sure enough, every newspaper in the country carried a solicitous message to Theodore Roosevelt from his critic, Woodrow Wilson, and an equally warm message from his dear friend William Taft.

Roosevelt's popularity spiked for a time after the attempt on his life, but it wasn't enough to carry the election. Not only did he lose, but his feud with Taft split the Republican Party vote and served up the White House to the stern-looking Democrat. Wilson carried the nation with only about 42 percent of the electorate, though his 6.3 million votes was more than enough to beat Roosevelt (4.1 million) and Taft (3.5 million). The progressive liberals were back in power.

At the time of Woodrow Wilson's inauguration in January 1913, America and the world were in the midst of a technological revolution that was geologic in proportion. Basically from the time of Adam and Eve to the early 1800s, people had essentially three modes of transportation: foot power, hoof power, and wind power. It had been three thousand years since civilization had been blessed with a new mode of transportation. Then suddenly, within a hundred-year period, the gods of motivation unleashed four new marvels onto the world—the steam locomotive (1803), the bicycle (1817), the gasoline-powered automobile (1885), and the airplane (1903).

Each would change society in its own way, but for three of the four their full impact would only be realized when they were taken

up by the Post Office Department. The steam locomotive was heralded at the time of its invention, but the question lingered: what
was anyone to do with a contraption that weighed tons and only
ran on special iron rails, of which there weren't any? Thirty years
after its creation, there were only 23 miles of train track in the entire United States. What the locomotive needed was a raison d'être,
which the post office gave it with the first contracts to carry mail.
With that, the railroads laid more track, and by 1837, 1,500 miles
of track criss-crossed New York, Pennsylvania, and the Northeast—two-thirds of it carrying the mail. By 1900, the four corners
of America were connected by 186,000 miles of track.

In 1913, Postmaster General Burleson found himself standing
at the same crossroads as Postmaster General Amos Kendal had
seventy-five years earlier with the railroad, albeit with a different
technology—the auto-truck. Burleson wanted to rid his department
of horses and saw trucks as the way to do it. The post office was
heavily invested in equine flesh and maintained vast stables of the
slow, messy animals. While there were already five hundred thousand automobiles registered in the United States, there were just
as many horse-drawn carriages on the same narrow streets. It was
Burleson's plan to introduce postal trucks to the District of Columbia and then, if successful, roll them out nationwide.

Only one obstacle stood in his way. The postmaster position
for D.C. was changing hands from the Republicans to the Democrats and the president's new secretary of state, William Jennings
Bryan, had already called dibs on the D.C. job for a friend. Like
everyone else in town, Bryan was dragging around a ball and chain
of relatives, and, being that the postal department was a traditional
repository for political favors, he felt confident in promising the job
away.

The post office was legendary for its patronage, the practice of
which had been ongoing since the 1700s; it even earned the scorn
of Thomas Jefferson, who once remarked "I view (the post office) as
a source of boundless patronage to the executive jobbing to members of Congress and their friends and a bottomless abyss of public
money."

Burleson felt similarly. The nation's postal system was his domain now and he was not about to have it passed around the president's cabinet like some candy jar. Besides, he needed a man of intelligence and drive to shepherd the reforms he planned to implement. He would never be able to conduct his auto-truck experiment with some political lackey in the job.

Still, dislodging Bryan from his position wouldn't be easy. The man was a two-time congressman from Nebraska and a three-time candidate for president. He had polish, political savvy, and more powerful connections than even Burleson.

There was only one thing to do. He would fight patronage with patronage. He wouldn't insult the secretary by appointing a man of superior qualifications. He'd find a candidate as equally unqualified as Bryan's man, someone whose lack of credentials made him just as unsuitable for the position. Such a person would be appointed not by merit, but by partisanship—in keeping with the spirit of things. That way, the secretary of state would not be offended. Burleson knew of just the man, but he had to be approached indirectly. The last thing he needed was some news reporter picking up on the scent and sparking a feud between him and Bryan.

Working through back channels, Burleson approached another of Wilson's cabinet appointees—Secretary of the Navy Josephus Daniels. Tall, good-looking, and driven, Daniels was owner and publisher of the influential *News & Observer* of Raleigh, North Carolina. The paper served as a pulpit for political discourse of all kinds—so long as it was liberal and Democratic. Unlike many of his newspaper colleagues, Daniels was an inveterate teetotaler, and he preached temperance from his editorial pages. As secretary of the Navy, Daniels would not permit anything stronger than coffee on naval ships, leading sarcastic sailors to toast him with a "Cup of Joe."

It was only natural that Burleson approach Daniels for help, knowing that his choice for the D.C. postmaster job also had printer's ink in his veins.

Shortly thereafter, someone came knocking on the door of Room 45 at the *Washington Post*. Praeger wasn't surprised to see his friend and colleague Thomas Pence standing there. The two had known each other for some years now, Pence being the Washington correspondent for the *News & Observer*. What surprised him, however, was the message his colleague was carrying via Josephus Daniels on behalf of Albert Burleson. The emissary told him about Burleson's predicament.

"Now, the way out, it seems to me," said Pence, "is for Burleson to recommend someone for the place, asking for the appointment on personal grounds. They must be really personal grounds, like some old friend, or fishing or hunting buddy."

Praeger knew a trial balloon when he saw it. This was classic Burleson. One had only to glance at Burleson's family tree to hear the war cry in Albert Sidney's genes. Arrows did little to dissuade him. This Scot was born for the fight.

How many times had he sat in the press gallery looking down to the floor of the House and seen the shrewd political negotiator masterfully arguing his cause. The years had earned the white-haired silver-tongued orator a reputation as someone who stood foursquare to every wind that blew, particularly when they threatened to topple his hard-held convictions. Negotiate, glad-hand, make concessions, engage in some good old cloakroom political wrangling, yes. But roll over—never. He was inflamed at the way government often played the role of handmaiden to special interests, an opinion shared by the president—also a fellow Scot—who had come to office eager to empower Americans, not merely to protect the vested interests of its powerful elite. Burleson might be criticized for the insensitive way he thrust his ideals of thrift into postal policies, but he was nothing if not aware of the duty that government had to serve the majority of its people. He fought against the special interests in Congress and, now, with the power of the new Democratic administration behind him, he intended to do the same at the postal department.

Burleson thought equally well of Praeger. To his mind, the correspondent would make an ideal postmaster for the nation's capital. Praeger's nine years of experience covering the Hill had given him an understanding of how the game was played. He had a wide circle of contacts, many influential members of the media. Though fiercely independent, Praeger was also reform-minded and a staunch party advocate, a man who never sought praise or credit for himself. People genuinely liked him and respected his scrupulous honesty. The idea of lying or cheating even on the most inconsequential matters was absolutely verboten to him. In this tenacious Texan, Burleson had found a man of similar ideals, someone capable of translating his values of thrift and efficiency into postal policy, their lives and convictions rooted as they were in the good Texas soil.

More important, the Washington correspondent was wholly unqualified for the job. He had spent some time as San Antonio city clerk, but his experience in running a public agency was nonexistent, precisely what Burleson needed to make him salable to Secretary of State Bryan.

Back in Room 45, the journalist considered the matter. Should he accept Burleson's offer he knew everything would change. He wouldn't simply be reporting the news, he'd be making it. But the camaraderie of working alongside his colleagues from around the world would vanish. He most likely would end up in adversarial relationships with reporters he used to call friends. Many of the perks would disappear, too. No longer would his calendar be filled with dates and invitations to every important social and political function. He'd have to turn away the goodies that regularly showed up at his office, all meant to influence his news coverage: claret from San Francisco, oysters from Norfolk, oranges from San Augustine, even tamales from San Antonio, the old homestead.

Although Praeger considered most politicians puny, petty, or just plain stupid, he held the process in high regard. The arguments, concessions, and political maneuverings being hammered out daily on the floor of Congress were the very process by which American democracy was forged, the uneasy alliance between individual rights and capitalism always in debate.

And Burleson was a powerful cabinet official. Riding coattails like that could give a person a stratospheric nosebleed.

Beyond all that, Praeger understood his fellow Texan on a fundamental level. The postmaster general might be the older well-to-do congressman and Praeger the low-paid reporter dressed in cheap suits, but theirs was a connection that went deeper than existing hierarchies. These two were conjoined twins when it came to their belief in the party to steer a right and true course in government.

The progressive liberals were back in power, and politicians like Burleson were being invited to make a difference.

"Well, if it will solve the problem," Praeger informed Pence, "why not go back and tell Burleson you have found the man."

Just like that, his long career in journalism came to an end.

The idea for motorizing mail deliveries was the brainchild of Burleson's predecessor, Frank Hitchcock, who realized early on that, properly developed, self-propelled vehicles could run back-to-back shifts, sixteen hours a day, fully six hours longer than the old gray mare. Not only that, they required no oats to keep them moving nor did they mess up the roads with their foul-smelling fly-infested dung piles. During his term from 1909 to 1913, Hitchcock had hired private companies to establish experimental automobile routes in cities like Minneapolis, Milwaukee, Baltimore, and Boston. The setup was haphazard, though, with little coordination and even less oversight of the private companies hired to manage, operate, and maintain the vehicles. Fraud ran rampant, the federal government continually socked with inflated fees for everything from tires to fuel.

Burleson would learn from that mistake. Only by bringing operations in-house could a truck service be put on sound fiscal ground. It simply cost Uncle Sam too much money to outsource motor deliveries to private contractors. Thrift and economy were the crux of Burleson's postal policy. Spending no more taxpayers' money than that collected was common sense to him. He vowed that he would kill the experiment if it ran in the red. He was not about to dip into the U.S. Treasury to foot the bill for postal overruns. Yet that remained a concept downright alien to just about everyone else, bucking nearly a hundred and fifty years of postal thinking. When it came to delivering letters, the American people didn't care how much it cost so long as they got their mail.

By October 1914, Burleson had the congressional funding he needed to create the first federally owned and operated automobile/auto-truck network to carry Uncle Sam's mail. Washington, D.C., would be the test market, and the man in charge would be its new postmaster general.

Praeger was all over the challenge like a dog on a bone. He'd come to the job with little management experience, but his keen powers of observation, honed over two decades of reporting, along with the journalist's mantra—who, what, where, when, and why—helped him grasp the totality of a situation and to know instinctively what questions needed answers. The reporter's love for details, nay, the reporter's need for details, would serve Otto well in the minutiae of guiding a citywide transportation system. Auto-cars and auto-trucks would have to be chosen, drivers and mechanics hired, supply chains established, and refueling and maintenance facilities constructed. And, of course, every expense would be recorded in detailed ledgers so Burleson knew exactly what each dollar was buying.

The new operation wasn't trouble-free, but postal trucks were soon a fixture on the city streets. The job was getting done and, more important, it was operating within budget, as were all other functions of the D.C. post office. By the end of Praeger's first fiscal year he'd posted an extremely rare budget surplus of $103,000, or, as he liked to say, he saved the city $300 a day for every day he was there.

Burleson was impressed. So much so that only a year and a half after handing Praeger the keys to the Washington job, he offered him another—that of second assistant postmaster general for the United States. As the man responsible for the transportation of both domestic and international mail, Praeger would find himself stepping into the postmaster general's inner circle, one ear away from President Wilson. He would be venturing deeper inside the federal government than he'd ever gone as a newspaper reporter.

Praeger's staff presented him with a bound collection of Charles Dickens during a little party on his last day in the D.C. job. It was a nice moment, made more so by Burleson's presence. The postmaster general presented Otto with an inscribed silver cup. Enjoy the day, he said, tomorrow you'll begin to roll out auto-truck service nationwide.

On September 1, 1915, Otto Praeger, the man who picked his way around town by bicycle, taxi, or bus—anything to avoid driving— sat down at his new desk and went to work bringing motorized mail deliveries to the nation. What he'd achieved in one relatively small city he would now re-create tenfold.

Before long, fleets of green trucks, all striped in black and red accents, were introduced to the streets of Detroit, St. Louis, and Philadelphia, their rich, gold letters—U.S. MAIL—visible for all to see. The color scheme had come directly from Burleson, who not only demanded economy from his service, but also uniformity. Everything needed to look up-to-date, modern, in sync, and homogeneous, from the mailboxes on the street corners to the canvas and leather sacks the mailmen slung over their shoulders.

Praeger, however, was beginning to encounter isolated but bitter opposition from a handful of congressmen who resented the invasion of their districts by motor vehicles. Chicago was a particularly tough town to crack. Its mail delivery contractors and their two hundred horse-drawn wagons dug in for a fight. Their champion was the distinguished twelve-time Republican congressman from Chicago, Martin Madden. Soon, Praeger found himself before a House committee on postal affairs, Congressman Madden dismissing the post office's push into Chicago as wrongheaded. Anyone who knew anything about the city knew that a horse-drawn mail wagon could navigate the congested downtown Loop district faster than an automobile. Even a wheelbarrow could be pushed through the city faster than an automobile, laughed Madden.

Opposition to the plan sprang up within the department itself, from the "Civil Service barnacles," as Praeger called them, people who held on to the status quo like it was a life raft floating adrift in a sea of change.

The second assistant would handle the opposition the best way he knew how—in print. There would be a race to determine who was right, and the Chicago press played it up to the hilt. When it was all over, it was Praeger's vehicles that had traversed the inner business district in half the time of the horse-drawn mail wagons.

The victory over Madden had the short, rotund Praeger doing a two-step and, perhaps, just a little crowing.

"It was not necessary to have tests made between the wheel barrow and the automobile," he boasted. "The tests between automobile and horse wagons were impressive enough."

By mid-1917, a fleet of 225 government-owned trucks was operating in Chicago. America's first, federal motor vehicle service was beginning to roll. And what of the postal department's civil service barnacles?

"I soon had them shifted to places where their general negative attitude could no longer block our progress."

Just months on the job, the team of Burleson and Praeger had beaten back detractors and impressed their will on the Post Office Department, from personnel to accounting to operations. Their satisfaction was tempered, however, by behind-the-scene issues. Mail trucks might be rolling in a half-dozen U.S. cities, but most of the vehicles were castoffs that Praeger had pried away from the U.S. Army; heavy and abused during military service, they struggled on crowded city streets. The overworked machines were becoming a maintenance nightmare, overwhelming repair shops with overheated engines, split tires, and bent axles.

Mechanizing delivery, for all its speed and efficiency, was exposing glaring holes in the whole mail-delivery system. The success of parcel post had already overwhelmed the antiquated hand-sorted mail delivery system by dumping tens of thousands of new parcels into it. Auto-trucks just exacerbated the problem by speeding that deluge to each post office, where, inside, tired, overworked civil servants were tearing their hair out trying to keep pace with the growing workload.

Praeger countered with a plan to establish the first long-distance city-to-city truck route just to move packages. He put specially built heavy-duty auto-trucks on the 40 miles between Washington, D.C., and Baltimore. To reduce breakdowns, the route was set up as a relay, with trucks traveling a mere dozen miles before passing off the cargo to another truck.

It was a good plan in theory, another thing altogether in practice. Roads at the time were deplorable. They would fan out from a city center, go a few miles, and then just end. It could take half a day to drive a dozen miles between two towns. Few roads were even graded, let alone covered in gravel or brick. And even those that were deemed "improved" didn't connect to anything. It was hellish when it rained. Downpours would send mail trucks sliding off the muddy trails, and it wasn't uncommon to see drivers hunting the woods for a big tree branch to pry loose mail trucks stuck up to their axles in the quagmire.

It was evident to Burleson and Praeger that city-to-city truck service would have to wait for better infrastructure. As a result, the postal department's plans for mail delivery by auto-truck would remain modest through mid-1918, with Praeger concentrating on intracity vehicle delivery and short hops to and from neighboring cities and towns. For long-distance delivery, he and Burleson had another machine in mind.

CHAPTER 5

INTO THE EYE

Fleet was impatient for a new assignment. Here it was June and the Army had yet to get him back into the war. Newton Baker had sworn that once the airmail's fledgling six-plane six-pilot squadron was put on its feet, the major would receive his transfer. Well, aero mail was standing, listing slightly but standing nonetheless. It was time for a new challenge.

He got more than he expected. His reassignment would have to wait. Praeger intended to open an airmail route between New York and Boston, and Fleet was tasked with making it happen. The major thought it a bad idea in mid-May and hadn't changed his mind since. The Army was also dead set against the plan. At least four more planes and pilots would be needed, and there was simply no way men and machines could be allocated to such an expansion—at least until after the war was over.

Praeger expected the flak and had a response prepared. Additional air routes would gain military aviators even more long-distance flying experience. Considering all the German submarines being spotted off the eastern seaboard, such skills were needed to hunt down the U-boats. The second assistant also asked officials from the Aero Club to do some undercover work. They unearthed more than enough ships sitting idly on the ground to spare a few for the airmail.

And so, on June 3, in the spirit of *Liberté*, *Fraternité*, and *Égalité*, a French army officer assigned to the Army Signal Corps was selected for the honor of piloting the inaugural flight. A throng of military officers, invited guests, and newspapermen stood watching at the Army's Mineola Field as Lt. Gustave Vanel and his mechanic bounced across the wet grass, forty-four hundred letters stowed inside their cargo hold. But no sooner did the French aviator become airborne than a control cable snapped on his plane, causing a wingtip to drop and scrape the ground. Control lost, the plane crashed onto its back. Though both pilot and mechanic survived, the French-American public relations effort did not.

Three days later, the postal department was ready to try it again—this time with an American pilot in the cockpit. The clean-shaven, ever-reliable Lt. Torrey Webb had already proven himself a valued member of Fleet's team, having flown the mail nearly a dozen times without incident. He would scout the air path to Boston.

Among his fellow pilots, Webb had become a bit of a celebrity, appearing in aviation magazine ads for Resistal goggles, which were guaranteed not to "destroy, reduce, distort or impair the vision in any way." There he was in *Aerial Age Weekly* staring resolutely over the cockpit of a mail plane, his Resistal goggles snugly affixed to his helmet. "Upon the eyes of these pilots depend the delivery and safety of the mail," read the advertising copy.

It was only fitting that Webb wear them on his trip to Boston. Throttling his ship across the grassy infield at Belmont, he took off, his mechanic perched uncomfortably atop the four thousand letters filling the forward compartment. But as Webb climbed into the clouds, it was clear that he couldn't see a bloody thing, Resistal goggles or not. It wasn't a question of finding the best air route to Boston. Given the visibility, Webb would be struggling to find Boston at all. He might as well be sticking his head over a steaming kettle for all he could see. Still, the stalwart flier and his brave but uncomfortable mechanic pressed on.

At last, three and a half hours later, having managed to grope his way into Boston, Webb descended onto the racetrack at Franklin Park Aviation Field located just outside the city. It would have been a ceremonious landing save for one little divot on the field that caught his wheels at touchdown and flipped the ship onto its back. Both pilot and mechanic were flung into the dirt and were lucky to escape unharmed.

The airplane took some damage and would need several days of repairs, leaving Webb to sit back and scratch his head, ruminating on his misfortune. This wasn't what he had bargained for, risking life and limb to fly a couple bags of mail around for the post office. Perhaps on the return flight the weather might be more forgiving, allowing him to scout out emergency landing fields for Praeger.

That wasn't the case, however, and Webb instead spent three hair-raising hours in the air flying back to New York: "Visibility was zero—zero and I just skimmed over the telephone poles all the way into Belmont Park. After that, I had had it and I made up my mind to get out of the Army as quickly as possible."

Torrey Webb was packing it in. The man with a degree in mining engineering had seen quite enough of the sky. He'd tough it out until his discharge papers came in 1919, and then he was done.

Three attempts had been made to fly from New York to Boston. The Frenchman crashed on takeoff, Webb crashed on landing, and a third effort also failed. Praeger recognized a bad thing when he saw one. Airmail flights to Boston would stop immediately.

Webb wasn't the only one who was leaving. By mid-June, a much-relieved Fleet found himself heading to San Antonio for a course in advanced flying. Then, following a brief stop at Mather Field in Sacramento, California, as officer in charge of flying, he and his good friend Maj. Belmont would be steaming off to Europe aboard a troop ship.

Praeger was left back in Washington without an officer in charge, but there was little he could do. The major possessed the discipline, verve, and connections to get airmail up and flying. Under his command, the men were beginning to work as a team, developing an espirit de corps even. Camaraderie was about the only thing that the airmail had going for it. Now Praeger was faced with losing that.

Not long after, Maj. Charles Willoughby appeared at Praeger's door. Stout, with severe features and a gaze at once level and penetrating, he had served in the American Expeditionary Force in Europe for more than a year. Like most combat pilots, he rode the skies with one hand on the control stick, the other firmly in control of his own destiny. He was used to exercising authority as commander of the Army's largest flying school outside the United States, in Chateauroux, France. Before that, he'd served as adjutant to Maj. Carl "Tooey" Spaatz at the Army pilot training school in Issoudun, France. Willoughby and Spaatz were of German heritage, and both were willful officers whose lockstep approach to commanding earned them the nickname "The Prussians."

Willoughby and Praeger began to butt heads straightaway. Like Fleet, the new officer in charge lived by the airmen's creed—never fly in tortured skies, even in pursuit of the enemy. He argued that an aviator couldn't fly where he couldn't see, just as Fleet had argued before him. With only rudimentary navigational equipment and no real understanding of meteorology, pilots could hardly outwit the sky.

But the deskbound bureaucrat had his own code of authority. When it came to the U.S. Air Mail, Regularly Scheduled Service ruled. Experts at the National Advisory Committee on Aeronautics backed up his position. They claimed that daily operation of an aero mail delivery service was possible regardless of weather conditions.

Rubbing his closely shaved head, Praeger was forced to rethink his plans. He convened a team of experts to confront the overwhelming obstacles facing the airmail service. The chief routinely surrounded himself with the best minds in engineering, aviation, and even in the military, authorities whose opinions he respected, people like aeronautical engineer Archibald Black; Gen. Billy Mitchell, commander of U.S. air forces in Europe; Canadian-born Lt. Col. Harold Hartney, a flying ace with seven confirmed kills, who commanded the Signal Corps's First Pursuit Group; as well as civilian advisers like Hawley. Together, the group provided the experience and imagination to put airmail under the microscope and determine what was going wrong, and, more important, why.

Beyond the faulty equipment, the rutted fields, the scant few personnel, the hopelessly shy inventories of spare parts, and the sorely lacking appropriations lurked a larger, underlying dilemma—

a proper vocabulary with which pilots, ground personnel, and administrators could readily communicate.

"Define your terms" was not only the mandate for ancient Greek debate, it was the wherewithal by which fliers could understand one another in this new arena of the sky. It wasn't enough to know that there were clouds aloft. Pilots needed to know what types of clouds they would encounter, for each signaled a different weather condition. Specificity was imperative. Thanks to fliers like Charles Willard, one of the first people taught to fly by Glenn Curtiss, terms like "air pocket" had been coined, when, following a nightmarish flight in 1910, he said that "the air was full of air pockets, as a Swiss cheese is full of holes." But much more was needed.

One imperative was to develop radio communications so vital data could be shared between the ground and the air. There was also general consensus that airships should be equipped with not one, but two motors—one as backup in the event the other engine quit, which they routinely did. Paramount of all was the need to establish weather stations so that atmospheric conditions could be observed and measured.

It wasn't enough to say that winds were blowing northwest. Did surface winds at Belmont flow northwesterly all the way to D.C., or did they shift to the southwest above 3,000 feet somewhere over Pennsylvania? Mail pilots had to be alerted to such changes if they were to make the best time between New York and Washington. Praeger's advisers recommended that observation towers be installed at designated points along the route so weather patterns could be observed, measured, and relayed to the pilots.

In Praeger's mind one issue superseded all others, though. Could an airman successfully pilot a ship through angry skies, lightning flashing about? Nothing wreaked havoc with a day's flying schedule more than an approaching thunderstorm. Praeger knew how the military would respond to that question, but he believed that with time and proper study the elements could be mastered. Impatient to put the hypothesis to the test, he put out feelers. He was looking for someone to fling himself into the atmosphere and look at things from the inside out. Raw data, that's what was needed, hard science by which they could begin piecing together the puzzle. The effects of high wind, rain, violent updrafts, and lightning upon a cloth-covered airship were as yet unknown. How would a ship handle in a thunderstorm? Would it be able to survive the explosion of air, and, if so, what structural stresses would such a force inflict? For what Praeger wanted, someone would have to step forward and volunteer.

I'm your man, said Lt. James Edgerton.

Almost from the start, the Nebraska-born, Denver-bred, straight-out-of-the-chute military aviator had become the chief's go-to guy, pushing mail planes to their limits, trying to answer some of his own aeronautical questions. Though only twenty-two, Edgerton was a natural for experimentation. Smart, inquisitive, and able to think fast on his feet, he was hungry for answers to this new medium. He knew only too well what Army policy was regarding the elements. Flying what was considered fair-weather aircraft, any brush with a thunderstorm was considered a brush with death. The War Department had instructed pilots to set down whenever the weather closed in.

"There were supposed to be mysterious and terrifying down currents which would deposit a pilot on the ground amidst a mass of wreckage," said Edgerton. "I was trained, in fact brain-washed, to land at the approach of bad weather."

On a blistering hot day in June, Edgerton had the opportunity to choose between his training and his curiosity. He was flying at 6,000 feet south of Philadelphia on his way to Washington when he caught sight of some isolated cumulus cloud formations.

Like other pilots, he read the mood of the sky through the countenance of its clouds. Delicate trails of cirrus clouds give a green light to a flier, telling him there's smooth sailing ahead. A wide, horizontal formation of stratus clouds, though not as elegant a repose, still indicate the sky's even humor. *Nimbus* is the Latin word for rain, and these low, flat, gray clouds bring precipitation. But with a ceiling of only about 6,500 feet, it doesn't take a pilot long to climb through them into bright blue skies. It is when nimbus clouds begin to rise up and stretch to 10,000-plus feet that they are renamed the dreaded cumulonimbus. A pilot spying such a mountain of cloud on the horizon always went the opposite way.

Edgerton gave the squall a wide berth and pressed on. He knew that turning back would mar his stellar flying record. A running tally was kept on every pilot's flying performance: their number of uncompleted runs, their forced landings and set-downs, be they caused by mechanical problems, weather-related incidents, or, God forbid, pilot error. Edgerton took pride in his unblemished record and intended to keep it that way.

He threaded his way south past Wilmington, Delaware, one eye on the bruised and angry clouds stretching across the horizon. It was clear that there would be no going around this nimbus of the cumulo type. The sky had slammed shut from the north clear to the southeast. The only way to reach Washington was to plow straight through. Still, Edgerton held out hope. Perhaps, farther on, things might break.

By the time he reached Havre de Grace he was facing a wall of black and three simple options: turn back, set down in the nearest field, or proceed—and hope like hell he got through. Already, the plane was pitching badly. That he could handle. He didn't know what lay ahead, but, cocksure with confidence, he knew he had to find out. Taking his plane through this thunderstorm could yield valuable information. Like Praeger, he understood that air mail could not limit itself to sunny skies.

With that, Edgerton picked up the gauntlet thrown down by the chief. He would fly the greatest experiment of all. His decision made, he plunged into the front of the storm. Almost immediately, his plane began to heave and roll: "Torrents of rain found me out . . . in sheets upon my face and goggles, down my neck, a puddle at my seat . . . a world of water."

Fighting to keep hold of the stick, he nosed his ship down, searching for better weather below. Perhaps he could duck through some hole in the clouds, if only to get his bearings. But air proved no kinder at lower altitudes, as convection currents bashed him about. Pulling back on the stick, Edgerton fought his way back up through the darkness, winds thrashing his ship, sending him alternately sliding, then heaving across the sky.

"One instant the plane was a tremendous elevator, leaping skyward hundreds of feet. Promptly the bottom seemed to drop out, the dizzy fall to cover hundreds of feet. Attacked by solid waves of air, the plane reared, slithered and bucked."

He could feel his thighs quivering from the strain of trying to maintain a steady pressure on the rudder bar. The compass was worthless, its dial spinning inside its casing.

Grabbing the stick with both hands, he climbed higher, his plane alternately dragging right, then surging left as he struggled to escape the whirling cauldron of wildly fluctuating temperatures and air pressures all slamming into the plane "like hammer blows." But up or down, no matter where he went, he found himself inextricably lost, worse than lost. He was being tortured inside a maddened swirl of air, its darkness broken only by the terrifying flashes of lightning stabbing at his ship. The propeller was still spinning, the struts and wires not yet busted from the strain. Question was, how much battering could a small, cloth-covered, wood biplane take? Edgerton the pilot was evolving into Edgerton the scientist, mentally recording the effects around him.

Slowly, a realization began to take hold. He couldn't muscle his plane through. He had to ease up, let his ship react to the storm on its own. Fighting his every instinct, he let go of the controls, just a little. To his relief, the ship began riding the waves in fluid succession.

"I supplied what I hoped was intelligent direction. I gave in somewhat to my enemy, and in turn, he gave in somewhat to me."

But his relief was short-lived. His engine was vibrating loudly—too loudly. He recognized the sound immediately. It was his propeller beginning to splinter, throwing off the balance of his motor. He throttled back, hoping to ease the strain. He wondered about his position, as hail began to pelt the plane from all directions, its driving force stinging his face, his arms, every part of his body.

Then, up ahead, like the dawn of a new day, streaks of daylight appeared on the horizon. The muscles in Edgerton's body must have loosened just a little. At this point, he had only to lean back inside the cockpit and ride out the last of the drama to emerge a free man. At last, the tirades of the storm behind him, Edgerton emerged into daylight. Peering over the side of his ship, the young pilot searched the landscape below. To his amazement, he saw that the storm had deposited him almost directly on course. It looked like he'd make it and nearly on time. His stellar record would remain intact after all.

Suddenly, a small slice of propeller flew past the cockpit. Edgerton quickly checked his altimeter—10,000 feet—plenty of glide room to make a safe landing should he need to kill his motor. Cutting back on the throttle, he descended into the familiar, marbled cityscape of Washington, D.C., aiming directly toward the tight perimeter of trees that was Potomac Park. This would have to be the landing of all landings. He wasn't sure whether the aircraft would survive for a go-around.

Below, an anxious group of spectators stood in the rain, their collective gaze transfixed on the wounded biplane descending from the sky. Word of Edgerton's plight had traveled fast. Back at Havre de Grace, people had seen his ship disappear into the void, setting party lines ringing across two states. The storm had been fierce. Signs of destruction were everywhere. Trees had been torn from their roots. Heaven help the young flier, they said.

It was a textbook landing. The ship floated down through the trees, coming to rest on the small, cramped field like the battered eagle it was. Immediately, ground crews came rushing over to where Edgerton sat boardlike inside the cockpit, his cramped thigh muscles racked in pain. Gently, he was helped from his ship, the skeleton of which bore little resemblance to that which had carried him into the storm earlier. The Jenny's fabric wings had been shredded by the wind. Its propeller was splintered, and wires connecting the upper and lower wings dangled loosely.

But a great weight had been lifted from Edgerton's shoulders. Like a mountaineer, he'd scaled the summit of his fears and returned home, spent, but victorious, no longer a servant of the sky. The chief would be happy to hear it could be done.

CHAPTER 6

WILLOUGHBY

Edgerton, the all-American boy with the self-assured smile, kept right on pulling his flying helmet down over his head and climbing into the cockpit for Praeger. He had already taken a Jenny up to the unheard height of 15,300 feet over Laurel, Maryland, searching for the answers to another mystery. Experts believed that wind resistance would decrease at such altitude, making transit across the skies faster. Unknown, however, was how a ship's power plant would perform in such thin, oxygen-deprived air.

Edgerton's observations would be made in detail and in real time, one hand on the stick and the other writing on a pad in his lap—his handwriting wavering across the page from the vibrations of the ship. His experiment not only corroborated existing theories, it added one of his own. At that altitude, it was damnably cold.

Weather-related or mechanical in origin, Edgerton tackled every flying challenge with equal fascination. One that had him particularly vexed was how to suppress engine fire before it brought down the plane. Fire was an aviator's worst nightmare and was often caused by carburetor backfire that sprayed hot gasoline about the engine compartment. Parachutes not yet being available, a pilot found himself married to his cloth-covered biplane for the duration of the flight. If it went down singed, so, too, did he.

It's not that airplanes weren't equipped with fire extinguishers. The problem was that they were mounted near the pilot's right hand, and the engine was too far away for the spray to reach. Edgerton's answer was a long pipe with holes drilled in one end that could deliver pyrene fluid from the extinguisher directly into the engine compartment.

So excited was Edgerton about his new system that he shot off letters to Praeger and Maj. Willoughby outlining in detail the plans for his new system. From postal headquarters, he received a commendation. From his superior officer, he was slapped down for not following the chain of command.

"In the future, however, you will submit all reports of that kind to this office directly instead of through the Post Office department."

Despite such stabs at military protocol, Willoughby's power over his airmail command was slipping—though for all the wrong reasons. The climate in America was openly hostile toward Germans. To be the slightest bit Teutonic during the Great War was to be ridiculed. Snippets and barbs such as "You can tell by the price a girl pays for her shoes or her hat just how much she loves Germany" appeared freely in publications around the country, including the house organ for the postal department—R.F.D. News—the rural-free-delivery voice of the mail carrier.

The war was heightening everyone's prejudice, and not solely in the United States. England's reigning monarch, King George V, thought it wise to change the family name from Saxe-Coburg-Gotha to Windsor in the hope of downplaying his German ancestry.

One look at Willoughby was enough to understand his problem in such a climate. It wasn't simply that he was German. It was that he was so terribly highbrow German. He spoke near perfect English, but with a foreign flavor. He sported a gold signet ring with a coat of arms and could be seen reading with a monocle in one eye. The officer was, in fact, an aristocrat, the son of a German baron, Adolf Tscheppe-Weidenbach. It wasn't until he immigrated to America that the eighteen-year-old Bavarian blue blood assumed the maiden name of his mother, Emmy Willoughby of Baltimore.

Even his distinguished career with the U.S. Army was subject to innuendo. Fellow aviators looked askance at the manner of his flight training, claiming that he had learned to fly from the French in fast-pursuit aircraft like the Spad and Nieuport—while most American fliers plodded through the sky in underpowered Jennies—so he could land behind German lines, impart military secrets, and return before anyone noticed.

Willoughby was flabbergasted at such a notion. A Benedict Arnold he wasn't. But suspicions ran high in a climate of distrust sweeping across America. And the postal department was there in the thick of things. The agency wielded enormous power during the 1910s, and its influence touched nearly every government agency. It helped to organize the military draft and ran campaigns to conserve food and fuel. It distributed mail for war agencies and sold government bonds. It handled the registration of enemy aliens and alien property for the Department of Justice, and it was the primary agency responsible for the execution of the Espionage Act and the Trading with the Enemy Act.

When President Wilson's government invoked its wartime powers to take over the country's telephone and telegraph services, in effect nationalizing companies like Western Union, the nation's entire network of communications was handed over to the Post Office Department. The only form of communication in wartime America that wasn't controlled by Postmaster General Burleson was carrier pigeon.

The silver-haired Texan gladly became the long arm of Uncle Sam—a reach he was not above extending into every American's mailbox. Working in lockstep with him was his fishing buddy Otto Praeger. The second assistant was recently named chairman of the president's National Censorship Board, a job for which he could no doubt thank Burleson. At the height of its work censoring all U.S. mail, all telegrams, and all radio communications, the board employed seventeen hundred people around the world and spent $3 million annually.

Burleson and Praeger were wielding their powers of censorship in no uncertain terms. In fact, they considered it their duty as southern Democrats and patriotic Americans to purify the mails of any seditious material.

A pamphlet on the hardship of India under British rule . . .

banned! A peace plan from Pope Benedict XV that argued that the moral force of right trumped the material force of arms . . . deemed unacceptable for delivery through the U.S. mails.

Any letter, document, poem, article, or book that differed from the Wilson administration's position on the war could potentially be barred from delivery by authority of the U.S. Post Office Department. Publish a Socialist newspaper like the *New York Call* or the *Milwaukee Leader* and forget about mailing it anywhere. Those days, the act of licking a postage stamp and placing it on an envelope containing words deemed seditious by Uncle Sam was enough to land a person in jail.

If the postal department was the siphon through which many of the government's homeland-based security programs were conveyed, then Burleson and Praeger were the vessels of its power. Their authority came by way of the Espionage Act, passed by Congress in 1917, followed in 1918 by the revival of the Sedition Act, which aimed to control dissent against the government.

Two thousand Americans were prosecuted either for dissent, arguing against the draft, or belonging to certain (i.e., the wrong) political groups. Speaking out against U.S. war policies was dangerous to one's health, as perennial Socialist Party presidential candidate Eugene Debs learned when he was sentenced to ten years in jail for preaching "America out of Europe!" Refrain from playing the "The Star-Spangled Banner" before an evening's orchestral performance could land a man in jail, as longtime conductor of the Boston Symphony Orchestra Carl Muck found out.

Former president Theodore Roosevelt repeatedly charged Burleson with blatant misuse of power, openly attacking the administration for its clamp on freedom of speech. This wasn't about maintaining a unified front during troubled times, he argued. This was party politics, plain and simple. In his view, the postmaster general was stepping all over civil liberties, censuring certain newspapers that weren't inside Wilson's political camp.

Burleson wasn't listening. He was too powerful and too much the ideologue to stray far from the administration's view. Besides, the country was of one mind when it came to defeating the Hun.

Anyone deviating from that position was considered a threat to national security.

His command over the nation's communications apparatus made him a very unpopular person. He had a drawer full of death threats, including one promising to blow up the post office building. Burleson ignored them all. He'd been an object of derision since taking his cabinet post. He had a long list of enemies: labor officials, postal employees, railroad executives. But he liked the fact that he knew who they all were. He believed that the caliber of one's detractors helped a man define himself.

While Burleson's enemies were vocal and conspicuous, Maj. Willoughby's enemies whispered behind his back. Not that it didn't concern Praeger. He, too, had German blood in his veins, though he must have known that his close friendship with Albert Burleson made him as unimpeachable as Caesar's wife. He had yet to see proof that his officer in charge was disloyal in any way. Besides, relations between the two had softened ever since the major's "German" problem had surfaced. He was now much more willing to support the postal point of view, particularly the second assistant's fly-in-all-weather dictum. Possibly believing that Praeger and the postal department might help him reclaim his reputation, Willoughby issued a new set of memos to his Army pilots, making it clear that there was only one boss of the airmail, and he didn't have stripes on his sleeve.

"Hereafter, orders suspending or interrupting flights from any station will be issued by the officer in charge of the Aerial Mail Service at Washington or by the 2nd Assistant Postmaster General, Mr. Otto Praeger, Washington, D.C. only. Pilots are not to call Washington unless the weather is absolutely impossible."

From that moment on, there was no question who controlled the flying. Willoughby instructed pilots to fly by compass whenever fog or clouds hampered visibility. To help in that effort Edgerton, Webb, Culver, and Bonsal were each given flight logs and told to fill them with compass readings and visual landmarks taken at five-minute intervals. Such notations would let an aviator fly blind in the fog and still know exactly where he was—theoretically.

Willoughby didn't stop there. He revised the air routes between New York and Washington, overlaying them atop the existing train lines between the two cities. Everyone knew that when skies thickened, an aviator could always drop down out of the soup and follow the one landmark that would lead him to safety—the railroad. Those steel tracks, affectionately called "the iron compass," could always be counted on to guide an aviator into the nearest town where he could set down, get his bearings, and warm his bones with a steaming cup of coffee. It was such an accepted practice that some fliers joked they knew the names of every whistle-stop along the way.

Despite Willoughby's about-face, the growing controversy over his allegiance continued to escalate. In an effort to fend off his detractors, the major penned a series of long letters to Praeger and Burleson aimed at legitimizing his position. Yes, he'd openly espoused his views on German values and work ethic while a professor of language and literature at Racine College in Wisconsin. But that had been years ago, before the war. He had openly admired the German army and its military efficiency, but so did plenty of other people at the time. He'd committed no crime; he was as much a patriot as anyone. After all, he'd been quick to recant those opinions following Germany's invasion of Belgium and the sinking of the *Lusitania* in May 1915, with the loss of nearly twelve hundred civilian lives. One had only to look at his record. He had fought for his country. He'd been willing to die for her if necessary.

Willoughby wasn't the only military officer facing prejudice because of his heritage. America's flying ace Eddie Rickenbacker had endured his share of troubles simply because of his German-sounding name. Back in 1914, when he was winning fame as a race-car driver, the press wrongly reported that he was actually "Baron Edward Von Rickenbacher, a Prussian nobleman" who'd left his home in Germany to show his cold, resolute papa that he could handle affairs himself.

The story was pure fabrication, but it sounded good in print. In truth, the baby-faced racer had been born in Columbus, Ohio, of Swiss immigrant parents. Upon arriving in America, his family had chosen to change its name from Rickenbacher with an *h* to the more American-sounding Rickenbacker with a *k*. But when Rickenbacker enlisted in the Army and tried to sign up for pilot training, he found out just how much difference a single letter could make in a man's life.

Counterintelligence had been sifting through every last detail of his life, searching for any hint of traitorous behavior. Even his favorite racecar, built by two German brothers named Duesenberg, drew questions.

The Army turned Rickenbacker down for pilot training, as well as every member of his Maxwell Special racing team. He tried to change its mind. As a rule, his kind accepted risk readily and were skilled at powering high-performance machinery. They had catlike reflexes, routinely made quick levelheaded judgments, and, in short, possessed all the skills needed to be crack military pilots.

The Army Signal Corps refused him flatly.

"We don't believe that it would be wise for a pilot to have any knowledge of engines and mechanics," it responded. "Airplane engines are always breaking down, and a man who knew a great deal about engines would know if his engine wasn't functioning correctly and be hesitant about going into combat."

Still, just because the Signal Corps didn't fancy his services didn't mean he couldn't go overseas and do what he did best—drive an automobile. With his reputation as a top racer, the now sergeant first class got himself assigned as staff driver to military officials like General John Pershing, the dapper commander of the American Expeditionary Force. Gen. Billy Mitchell requested him specifically whenever he was in France. Mitchell liked Rickenbacker and considered him a regular guy. Upon hearing of his troubles, the general made some inquiries, and the cloud of doubt hanging over Rickenbacker's head quickly lifted. Soon, Rickenbacker would find himself in flight school, promoted to the rank of lieutenant, on his way to becoming a flying ace.

As the summer progressed, it became clear that Reuben Fleet's replacement had lost the hearts and minds of the combat pilots flying for him. Men will dodge bullets and brave gunfire for their commanders, provided they've earned the men's respect. But the German-born Willoughby could not escape his heritage. Nor did his postal-friendly flying policy likely endear him to his men. He was floundering and despite the letters penned to Praeger and Burleson—four, five, six single-spaced pages of gut-wrenching pleas and regrets for past opinions—there was little either man could do. Accusations of disloyalty were nothing to trifle with. Clearly, this was a matter for the War Department.

The military went through its motions, but when all was said and done, nobody could prove Willoughby of being anything less than a loyal soldier. Even so, he was given new orders in July and, much to Praeger's chagrin, sent packing.

The chief was annoyed. Willoughby was efficient and that's precisely what he wanted—from the army, from his staff, from his planes, and, most important, from his pilots. Appealing directly to Secretary of War Baker, he requested that Willoughby be allowed to remain. Praeger called his work with the fledgling service critical. Just ten days, that's all he was asking so that a smooth transition could take place.

But Willoughby's predicament had risen too far up the chain of command. The military wanted him sidelined from the action, and airmail, being a high-profile program, fell too heavily under the glare of the spotlight. Within forty-eight hours, the major found himself aboard a train heading west to Kelly Field, San Antonio. The day in court he'd so fervently sought to clear his name never materialized.

Airmail had been in operation for less than three months and had already gone through two military leaders. Following Willoughby's reassignment to Texas, the brass named a lowly second lieutenant with no aviation experience as officer in charge of airmail. By assigning such a low-ranking officer, the Army made it clear it had lost interest.

But Praeger was not about to let the Army's indifference poison the operation. Anxious to install his own people into the flying end of things, he went looking for someone more suitable. No longer would he butt wills with headstrong military fliers or babysit officers battling their own personal problems. He wanted someone he could trust, a man he could rely on to get the job done.

The man he wanted was already on the team, Capt. Benjamin

Lipsner. Right from the start, he had been eager to help, generously lending his experience in automotive engineering and mechanical maintenance. Fleet blamed him for the empty fuel tank incident on May 15, but it was minor compared to the many near disasters of the last month. Lipsner's record was good enough for Praeger.

Lipsner had also proved his worth in helping to keep the Army's mechanized forces rolling. Gen. Pershing commanded an arsenal of tracked vehicles, trucks, four-doors, and motorcycles, all dependent on petroleum products. The general estimated he needed 5 million gallons of lubricant to keep the tank treads and rubber wheels turning, and Lipsner, as an authority on fuel and lubrication systems, was part of the team working to develop alternate sources to meet that demand (which was equivalent to the entire nation's consumption for three years).

In addition, the college-educated Lipsner was a whiz at organization. He had already created a record-keeping system for the airmail and was preparing to establish a scheduled maintenance program for the airplanes and engines. Qualified as his background was, Lipsner offered another equally important enticement. He was not a pilot.

Straightaway, the chief sat down and penned a letter to Newton Baker. If the Army could spare the use of its captain, aero mail would be greatly appreciative.

Secretary Newton Baker denied the request. However, should Capt. Lipsner wish to resign his commission there would be no objection from the War Department. Lipsner submitted his resignation almost before the ink was dry on Baker's response.

The new job must have seemed like the fulfillment of some eternal dream. As a kid growing up in Chicago, Lipsner would hang out at Checkerboard Field just for the chance to be around planes. He learned a few things from the local pilots and mechanics, and they even let him taxi the planes back and forth. But when he was older and it came to earning a living, it had become apparent that being a pilot was far too dangerous an occupation to support a married man with financial obligations. Now, here he was years later, finally parlaying his talents into what he so dearly loved—aviation. He couldn't wait to get started.

*   *   *

It was becoming increasingly clear, however, that the airmail partnership between the Army and the postal department was faltering. Cooperation between the two organizations had never been the best and was characterized by more of a big brother–little brother relationship than any real, equal partnership. This was despite the fact that the U.S. Post Office Department employed a force of more than three hundred thousand people, greater in size than America's standing army. About all the two organizations had in common was that Uncle Sam signed both their paychecks.

Right from the start, the military had been against anyone save itself handling the flying game. Gen. Billy Mitchell, in particular, opposed any aviation venture that wasn't under strict military control. Aero ships were weapons of war; as such, they rightfully belonged under the control of the military. Besides, what did the postal department know about airplanes? It was in the business of delivering mail.

Agreed, said Praeger. But when it came to delivering that mail, Praeger knew that when the wooden prop was cranked and the engine roared to life, there was no faster way to do that job.

As the days rolled on, it was clear that any hope of marshaling the behemoth forces of the U.S. Post Office Department and the U.S. Army behind airmail was futile and that their efforts were devolving into a behind-the-scenes struggle for control. With immense relief on both sides, the squabbling brothers agreed to fly their separate ways. On Saturday, August 10, 1918, after three months and 30,000 miles of flying the mail between Washington and New York, the U.S. Army folded its tents and pulled out of the experiment.

Despite their disagreements, however, the Army had taught the U.S. Post Office Department how to fly. Pilots Edgerton, Culver, Webb, Bonsal, and Miller had applied themselves fully to the task in true military fashion. Wrestling bad weather, lousy airfields, and poorly maintained machinery and lacking any proper equipment, they'd succeeded in handing Praeger the beginnings of a regularly scheduled service—the world's first—and the chief was not unappreciative. "There are no surer or more courageous fliers in France than the five Army officers who put the Air Mail Service on the map through their work in fog, rain and hail," Praeger said of his Army fliers.

With those words, a chapter in aviation history closed. Another was about to open.

CHAPTER 7

LIPSNER

Lipsner's first order of business was to hire pilots for the country's first *civilian-run* airmail service. He needed serious-minded men—top aviators able to plow through fog, wind, and driving rain over great distances, day in and day out. Ideally, candidates would have a minimum of five hundred flying hours, some of it in cross-country flying. They would also need to possess a certain mechanical acumen along with a rudimentary understanding of radio and navigational operations. Beyond that, this was America, the sky was open.

It didn't take long for word to spread to the barnstormers, test pilots, and military instructors that Uncle Sam was looking for candidates. Lipsner sold bucket-seat roadsters for the National Motor Vehicle Company of Indianapolis and knew his share of racers.

"National had the first car that would hit sixty in second gear," he boasted. "I was National's top salesman and demonstrator for some time, and that also made me an instructor, since I had to teach practically everyone who bought a car in those days how to drive."

One of the young men he'd taught was Eddie Gardner. Even back then, the fellow midwesterner had made an impression on him. Relaxed and confident, Gardner had a take-the-world attitude that resonated with men and appealed to ladies. The humdrum of life wasn't for him. Being near the nexus of speed counted, taking risks—that's what made him feel alive and dynamic. He'd graduated from chauffeuring cars to racing even faster ones, and it was no surprise that this modest, unassuming daredevil would eventually climb his way into the cockpit.

Despite a prematurely receding hairline and relatively advanced age of thirty, Gardner wore the fresh, carefree appearance of youth on his sleeve. Adventure was what mattered, and these days there was no greater freedom than flying. He was already an elder states-man among pilots, with 1,450 flying hours in his logbook. Despite his undisputed skill on the stick, he had earned the nickname "Tur-key Bird" for his one defining flying attribute—wobbly takeoffs and landings that made his airplane look like a turkey in flight. Not one to be made fun of, but not able to shake the nickname, Gardner ac-cepted the ribbing but insisted his fellow fliers shorten the moniker to "turk bird," and from henceforth, he was Turk Bird.

Lipsner hired him straightaway.

Unlike the daredevil Gardner, reliability was the hallmark of twenty-six-year-old Robert Shank. A full head shorter than most people, he had the sturdy, compact build of a gymnast, and he had come to fly-ing purely by chance. In 1915, he'd been working the fairs around the country with a friend when he saw a barnstorming pilot give a thrill to a crowd in Fargo, North Dakota. The flier was experienc-ing some engine trouble and Shank took a look.

"The magneto on his three-cylinder Anzani engine wasn't work-ing properly," said Shank. "I had some experience with engines in the automobile and motorcycle business and helped him fix it."

Later, the barnstormer made a few circles around the fair-ground, and the engine, famous for powering Louis Bleriot's flight across the English Channel in 1909, performed hummingly. For five such performances, the organizers paid the pilot the relative fortune of $2,000.

Imagine, a man actually getting paid to own the skies. It seemed like a ticket to the good life—warm smiles from pretty girls, friendly farmers willing to trade a home-cooked meal and a night in the hayloft for the price of a good flying story. On the surface, barnstorming seemed easy enough. All anyone needed was a hankering to see the country over the side of an open cockpit, and some good old-fashioned showmanship. Military aviators were getting a lot of coverage in newspapers and on the radio, and everyone was curious to see for themselves what these machines could do. At air meets or in some open farmer's field, folks thirsty for amusement stood wide-eyed, necks craned skyward, mouths open as a cloth-covered biplane went buzzing overhead.

Only Shank didn't know the first thing about flying, nor could he possibly scrape together the roughly $8,000 it cost to buy a Curtiss Jenny. But Shank did have a buddy who shared his desire, and together the two found the $1,900 it took to buy a garage-built biplane sight unseen from the Chicago Air Works Company. Delivered a few days later by horse-drawn wagon to Ashburn Field south of Chicago, the two wannabe pilots stood there mutely before their new moneymaker. A flying school operated out of the field, but neither could afford the cost of lessons. Shank later reminisced, "So I got a room at a boardinghouse where the pilots all stayed and sat down to figure out what I was going to do with a plane I couldn't fly."

As luck would have it, the record-setting Eddie Stinson was staying there, too. Everyone loved Stinson. There was no friendlier soul or anyone as talented at grasping the mechanical constructs of flight. He seemed to have an innate sense of what made it all tick. Taking pity on their plight, Stinson ushered Shank and his buddy over to the airfield, and less than three hours later, he had them both soloing.

With the summer fair season approaching, Shank stood primed to start raking in the greenbacks. A talent agency was already booking him to perform around the Midwest. But the new barnstormer hadn't been on the road very long before Stinson asked him to work at the family's aviation school. The weather was warm and the flying easy in San Antonio, Texas, where the down-home Stinson School of Flying was turning out both American and Canadian pilots for the military. Stinson's teenage sister Marjorie handled most of the flight training, while he acted primarily as head mechanic and his mother handled the business side of things. His other sister, Katherine, put in an appearance every now and then, but she was too busy to spend much time there. From London to the Orient, Katherine Stinson the aviatrix was an international celebrity; her dippy-twists and skywriting feats, with flares attached to her wings, put her in demand the world over. Her performance fees kept the family's flying school aloft.

Shank agreed to move to Texas. Barnstorming wasn't paying as much as he had hoped, and Stinson was offering him a steady paycheck and a chance to keep on flying.

"But then the war came along and the Army needed flying instructors at Kelly Field in San Antonio, I went to work there at $300 a month."

And now Shank wanted in on the Uncle Sam's Air Mail Service. Base salary for airmail pilots was $3,000, which was a darn good wage considering letter carriers made just $1,000 a year. Having garnered fully twelve hundred hours in the air, Shank received Lipsner's good seal of approval, his spot on the team assured.

Still, the roster wasn't fully complete. For his next hire, Lipsner turned to an old flying stalwart—Maurice Newton. Behind the thinning hair, the wire-rimmed eyeglasses, and the overall, bookish appearance, the forty-year-old Brooklyn native had the reputation of being a solid, dependable flier. In the air, he was the real deal. He'd been a test pilot for one of aviation's most respected instrument companies, Sperry Gyroscope, and lived long enough to be able to ink the word *pilot* onto his life insurance application—something that usually sent actuaries into cardiac arrest.

His levelheadedness and ability to think clearly under pressure had kept him alive in the saddle. Discipline and reliability were his strong suits, so when it came time for him to move on from Sperry, there would be no barnstorming for him, no flying airplanes through barns and such for the local yokels. A nice, steady job flying mail back and forth sounded just right. With eleven hundred hours in the air, Lipsner signed Newton on, despite his grandfatherly age.

Theoretically, that left one remaining spot on the team. But in truth, Praeger had already filled the vacancy. At twenty-five years of age, Max Miller had already found his way onto the postal payroll working as a $600-a-year airplane mechanic. He had written the chief earlier requesting a job flying the mail along with a salary of $3,600 a year. But at the time, there were no vacancies at any price, airmail being flown by military pilots. Still, Praeger had liked what he'd seen on the application letter. Max had logged more than a thousand hours on the stick, two hundred of them flying cross-country. And he had another attribute that qualified him for the team. Miller was willing to fly in all weather.

"I have carefully considered the risks involved caused by bad weather conditions and I would be willing to do my best under those circumstances and would be ready to go out at any time required," he wrote.

Praeger didn't need to hear any more. He assured Miller that if he signed on as a mechanic, he'd guarantee him a spot on the A team as soon as the new service went civil. Max jumped at the chance. For all the poetry of flying, he also loved getting his hands into machinery. At the same time he was looking for some stability. He'd been living his life in fragments. He tried carving out a life of adventure riding with the U.S. Seventh Cavalry in the Philippines, patrolling the Mexican border for a California Army unit, and plying the skies as a civilian flight instructor at Rockwell Field.

Born in Oslo, Norway, the blond blue-eyed Max Ulf Moeller had years ago abandoned his homeland in search of a future wholly removed from his native, upper-middle-class origins. Not content to work his way across an ocean just to be a farmer in some dull midwestern town the way his brother Ulf had done, Max came to America seeking a new life, one bound only by the limits of his imagination. With the airmail, he found his calling.

The full complement of fliers hired, everyone had only to take the oath of office to make their entrée into Praeger's club complete. Each man would vow to accept the same lousy odds and fly whenever called upon, rain or shine, so help him God. That, and promising to hand over any valuables entrusted to them for delivery, would entitle them to a steady paycheck twice a month drawn on the department's "Power Boat and Aeroplane Services" funds.

Equipment remained the airmail's glaring weakness. It hadn't taken long for Praeger to realize that aeroplanes having a top speed of only 90 miles an hour were severely handicapped by headwinds. The Curtiss JN-4H was a tough little bird, but it lacked speed and range, and its 150-horsepower engine didn't have enough power to push through the weather. It was obvious what was needed—more range, more power, more capacity. In short, more airplane.

Praeger had foreseen this moment some time earlier, and on faith that the Air Mail Service would still be in business, he had placed an order with Standard Aircraft Company in Elizabeth, New Jersey, for a half-dozen new aircraft. These wouldn't be hand-me-down Jennies from the Army. These would be machines designed to carry more mail, fly it faster, break down less often, and be easier and safer to fly.

The new ship was the Standard JR-1B biplane, and though upon first glance it resembled the Curtiss Jenny, it offered a top speed of 100 miles per hour, a climb rate of 6,000 feet in ten minutes, a strengthened fuel tank for safety, and a payload capacity of 300 pounds.

The specs placed, all postal officials needed to do was await the rollout. There was only one problem—time. Praeger couldn't resist cranking out press releases informing the media of the unveiling ceremony set for August 6. The pace at Standard Aero had become frenzied, its five thousand plus army of engineers, craftsmen, clerks, and water boys working three back-to-back shifts trying to assemble the postal department's planes while keeping pace with the military's demand for new aircraft. Every airplane manufacturer was working overtime, Uncle Sam having thrown millions of dollars at them in the name of air defense. Even so, the War Industries Board was scrambling to find ways to step up production. They directed auto manufacturers to reduce their pleasure-car production outputs by 75 percent in order to free up their production lines for much needed combat planes. Even furniture manufacturers were being pressed into service, their existing wood-turning facilities reconfigured into ones capable of producing a plane's wooden parts. The U. S. Army Signal Corps was sending regiments of troops into the forests, searching for spruce and other hardwoods with which to construct fuselages.

The construction of their new aircraft was a golden opportunity for postal department mechanics and riggers to observe the design and construction of each airplane. Know how something is built and you understand how to fix it when it breaks. Like expectant fathers, Praeger's men hovered over the shoulders of factory workers, offering suggestions, pitching in. The engineers at Standard Aircraft might be good with a slide rule, but it would be the postal pilots and mechanics who would keep those planes airborne. They wanted to know the where and why of every bolt and every turnbuckle installed on the JR-1Bs. The group made similar pests of themselves down the road in New Brunswick, New Jersey, where employees of the Wright-Martin Corporation were furiously building Hispano-Suiza power plants under license from the French company of the same name. The 150-horsepower engines, which were powering everything from luxury automobiles to Louis Bleriot's Spad fighter plane, would be serving as the mils for the Standards.

It had been a long time since anyone had a day out of the office, so Praeger made August 6 a special day for all. Standard's president, Harry Mingle, was putting on a big celebratory spread for lunch and there would be a tour of the factory beforehand.

The "committee" that would accept the airplanes was led by the second assistant, who wanted to see firsthand what his money had bought. With him were his new airmail superintendent, Benjamin Lipsner, and pilots Eddie Gardner and Max Miller. Praeger's chief clerk, Geoge Conner, came along, too, as did the superintendent of railway adjustments, J. B. Corridon, and the postal department purchasing agent J. A. Edgerton. His son, Lt. James Edgerton, was there, too, on special loan from the Army. It was Edgerton a few days earlier who had flown the check flights on the Standards.

Praeger and his team stood posing for reporters and photographers. It was a rather staid-looking lineup with some of the men dressed in dark suits and ties, others sporting a brighter cloth as befitting summertime. But darkly attired or in white, all the VIPs wore their white, wide-brimmed skimmers to shield them from the blistering sun. That is, except aviation booster Henry Woodhouse of the Aerial League of America. The short Italian immigrant stood proudly alongside the others, impeccably dressed, his thick crop of hair parted down the middle for all to see, it being far too warm to wear his trademark wool cap. Even Praeger looked good. Not a single wrinkle creased his suit, no wads of paper filled his pockets. His shoes were positively mirrors. He was wearing a broad smile on his face. But then, he had much to smile about, having worked for this moment for some time. By nature, Praeger was not a patient man. But that was behind him. Commercial aviation was at its "zero hour."

These JR-1Bs were the first nonmilitary airplanes ever sold to the U.S. government. Given proper incentives, other orders would follow to more airplane manufacturers. Praeger was helping to kick-start a fledgling industry. He knew the U.S. government wouldn't be in the airmail delivery business forever. Such practices weren't in keeping with public policy. It was only a matter of time before operations were contracted out to the private sector. But an industry must first be created for that to happen. All the big aircraft manufacturers were salivating over their military contracts, but properly nurtured, this new commercial application for the airplane could extend well beyond the life of the war.

With the shop floors walked, and lunch eaten, it was time for speeches at a grandstand set up on Standard's flying field. Hundreds of Standard factory workers filled the rows. Following a tour of the factory, it was time for Praeger to take his turn at the podium. He thanked the Army Signal Corps for its flying lessons but announced that the moment had come for a separation of church and state. It was time for Uncle Sam's civil arm to take hold of the stick.

Next up, Lipsner. The new superintendent was stylishly turned out in a form-fitting Army uniform minus insignia, his commission having already been resigned. The former captain for whom planes had always meant so much was only too aware of the chance fate had bestowed upon him. Standing before the crowd, he proceeded to usher in the faithful.

"Transportation through the air is a practical mechanical proposition," he declared. "The utility of the aero plane as a medium of commercial transport is established. We pass from poetry to mathematics."

Everyone applauded. Lipsner's oratory had been nothing shy of eloquent. Woodhouse of the Aerial League of America waxed lyrical about the future of aviation. So, too, did Alan Hawley of the Aero Club. Giving podium time to aeronautical experts like Woodhouse and Hawley was a smart move by Praeger. Both men were staunch supporters of aero mail, and traveled the country with their own bully pulpits from which they gave voice to the cause. They worked tirelessly in the chambers of Congress, pressing legislators to support funding for aeronautics. They were also talented journalists and regularly wrote elegant arguments supporting aviation, as well as technical pieces on the latest technologies. Published by their respective organizations, their articles were widely read by anyone who had anything to do with airplanes.

All the speeches that day came from the heart. Finally, after what must have seemed like an eternity in the afternoon sun, the ceremony graduated to presentations. Hawley gave Praeger and the entire airmail team commemorative wristwatches while miniature American flags were meted out by Mingle. Finally, the moment everyone had been waiting for arrived. Everyone stood watching as Eddie Gardner took his turn center stage.

The former racecar driver climbed into the cockpit of one of the new JR-1Bs and buckled himself in. Then, throttling up, he punched her into the sky like a kid taking off in his dad's automobile.

Lipsner watched, horrified. Surely, Gardner realized the importance of the occasion. He wouldn't, he couldn't. And yet, he surely was. Filled with the high spirits of the occasion, the daredevil pilot was working the air like a trapeze artist, putting the Standard through a series of ribald maneuvers that were more suited to a barnstorming show than a careful display of mechanical ability. Below, the crowd was standing elbow-to-elbow, their *oohs* and *aahs* punctuating the air as if they were at a fireworks display on the Fourth of July. And to think Gardner hadn't even checked out the plane beforehand. In fact, he'd never flown a Standard until today. Yet plane and pilot were flying like one.

Rather, plane and pilot were both pressed to the limit, the fusion of which resulted in pure artistry. Up there, Gardner was a natural, drawn to flying like a moth to a flame. A split-second loss of concentration or a wrong judgment could spell failure and even death to a test pilot. All five senses had to be focused on each precise maneuver. But in that open cockpit, fear becomes excitement, and the dull succession of minutes and seconds that stretch themselves over one's daily existence transcend into undiluted exhilaration. Racing across the sky, the power of the engine in his ears, a man became more than the sum of his parts. Up there, Gardner wasn't just some farmer's kid from Plainfield, Illinois. He was the master of the world, journeying across the face of eternity.

The flying postman landed to thundering applause and Mingle's open delight at the performance of his plane. The demonstration had been extraordinary. The aerobatics positively lit up the crowd. Lipsner, though, wasn't nearly so impressed. In fact, he was downright steamed. He had just finished predicting that airmail would become a laboratory for aviation where "the spirit of adventure is curbed down to the exactitude of routine performance." And here Gardner pulls a cheap stunt like this. This was to have been a demonstration of a mail plane. What if he'd crashed? What kind of publicity would that have generated?

The new superintendent proceeded to give Gardner a thorough shellacking. The rules were simple. As long as it was Uncle Sam's signature on the checks, fidelity to duty, not individual showmanship, would be the order of the day.

Chastised, Gardner vowed to amend his ways. But transitioning from flight jockey to dutiful postal carrier wasn't going to be easy for the carefree bachelor. And yet that's precisely what Uncle Sam expected of him. On that score, the rules were clear.

"As a pilot in the Air Mail Service, you represent the Post Office Department and as such a representative, you will be courteous and will act the part of a gentleman at all times."

Beginning today, Shank, Newton, Miller, Gardner, and the relief pilot L. Leroy Langley would all be expected to faithfully execute their allotted duties with a smile on their face and a song in their heart, while making every attempt to push the mail on through. On paper, Gardner's days stretching the limits were over. But given the odds stacked against him and the others, they were only just beginning.

*   *   *

In Gardner's defense, everyone's spirits had been running high that day. Miller and Edgerton undoubtedly appreciated the flair Gardner had shown, cut as they were from the same scarf. During their factory tour, they all acted like kids in a candy shop, excitedly kicking the tires of all the planes lined up on the field wingtip to wingtip. Everyone liked their new planes sure enough, but one other aircraft being built in the Standard factory took their breath away. It was the Handley-Page bomber, named after its English designer, thirty-three-year-old Frederick Handley-Page. The behemoth ship stood fully 22 feet off the ground, its massive 100-foot top wing dwarfing just about every other plane in existence. The British had been flying swarms of them against Germany, and Standard had just started building them for the U.S. Army, which had ordered fifteen hundred of a type. Powered by twin 400-horsepower Liberty engines, these planes featured a simple but brilliant slotted wing design to help channel air over the wing and reduce deadly stalls—one of the greatest fears of any pilot.

Given the excitement over Gardner's performance and the vision of a ship before them, it didn't take an oracle to predict that one of these pilots would be jumping into the cockpit of a Handley-Page, slipping a set of goggles over his eyes, and yelling "contact!"

Max Miller got the call. The tall Norwegian loved to fly. All he needed was a pair of wings, a control stick, and an engine for some thrust and he was suddenly a Viking king in Valhalla. Max may not have ever piloted one of these bombers before, but, like Gardner, there was no question that he had instinct and that indefinable feel for the air's mass and movement.

Everyone watched as he coaxed the colossal bomber into the air. It was a thing to behold, its twin motors offering incredible lift even fully loaded. Lipsner imagined the tonnage of mail they could carry and made a mental note to talk to Praeger about its prospects.

Soon, the plane landed sedately back onto the field. A simple, straightforward demonstration of the ship's flying capabilities was what Lipsner wanted and exactly what Max delivered.

The ceremonies were drawing to a close, but the day's flying was not yet complete. Two of the Standard JR-1B aircraft were readied and loaded with mailbags filled with letters from the usual assortment of dignitaries and politicians. Then, with all due fanfare, both planes were dispatched into the sky—destination Philadelphia, Pennsylvania. Slowly, the hum of their engines faded and the two planes began making their way across the fleecy clouds, following a course already chartered by Praeger and Burleson. History would show them arriving at their destination in forty minutes—a new record and a good start for Uncle Sam.

CHAPTER 8

CIVIL SERVICE

Come Monday morning August 12, 1918, the first day of civil operations, Max Miller reported for duty to the airfield at College Park, Maryland, the new home of the U.S. Air Mail Service. In the week that operations were suspended for the transition, flying was switched from the cramped Potomac Park in a long-overdue move. The Washington field was a death trap.

Its tight perimeter thwarted expansion, and the 60-foot ring of trees forced pilots to depart like human cannonballs. The pilot would line up the Jenny at the far end of the field, nose into the wind. Then he would throttle up the engine while ground personnel held back on the wings, their arms and backs straining amid the engine's growling whine, until at last, fully revved, they would let go and the Jenny would go hurling across the grass, propelled as if by some giant, rubber band. If the winds were right, the pilot would clear the treetops. If not, he'd be hauling the mail to Bustleton with branches in his undercarriage.

Landings were equally leafy, particularly in summer when the trees would trap heat inside the field, turning Potomac Park into a cauldron of rising air currents. Pilots quickly learned to sideslip their way into the box, knifing in so close to treetop level that they'd often clip them. Despite the challenges, Praeger continued loading ships to the gunnels, trying to determine by trial and error the maximum cargo-carrying capacity of a Jenny.

"His trial and our error," lamented Edgerton.

Day after day, mail ships descended from the skies like pregnant elephants groaning from their heavy payloads.

Things would be different his morning, however. By contrast, they'd have 160 tantalizingly flat acres in a sleepy suburb located east of the capital from which to mosey in and out of the sky, mail sacks in tow. The field had already earned its share of distinctions beginning in 1907 when it became the Army's first aviation training facility. Wilbur Wright tested the Wright Flyer there for the Army and set a world-record flying pass of 46 miles per hour in 1909. Operations quieted down after 1912 when the Army relocated pilot training to Rockwell Field in San Diego.

Now that was about to change; history was once again about to be made at College Park. In honor of the occasion, a clean, new Standard JR-1B stood ready on the flight line. It had been painted light gray instead of the regular, military green, and it was embellished with three vertical stripes on the tail and an illustration of a mail pouch below the cockpit. A proud numeral "1" graced the fuselage, identifying it and its pilot as the number one tandem in the service. Miller had an additional honor bestowed on him. Round metal badges with the insignia U.S. AIR MAIL SERVICE had been made up, and, like his plane, his badge was stamped #1. Proudly pinned to his leather jacket, the badge was visible proof of his sworn oath to protect and defend Uncle Sam's mail.

The new job came with two golden rules. Number one: Should a pilot be forced down en route, he must hightail it to the nearest telegraph office and ring up the station manager so that arrangements could be made to move that mail. Number two: Under no circumstances was a pilot to let those mail sacks out of his sight. Break rule number two and none of the others mattered.

Over the years, there's never been a shortage of thieves ready and willing to relieve a mail carrier of his sacks. Whether in pursuit of securities, money orders, or just plain easy cash, bad guys have been robbing delivery men since the beginning of time. A downed airplane would be an even more inviting target than a stagecoach or a train.

People entrusted their letters to the U.S. Post Office Department on the belief that they would be delivered without fail—not barring some robbery. Most of the letters carried didn't have any material value, but their contents mattered to each recipient—a soldier's mother standing tired and strained at the washboard, anxious to hear word from her son. These letters represented the bonds by which a people scattered across a vast, geographic continent consoled, shared, promoted, and supported one another. As far as the Uncle was concerned, all letters were sacrosanct.

If the bad guys didn't respect the badge, then there was always the .45 automatic some of the men packed inside their cockpit.

Miller cut a handsome figure in his leathers, but then he looked good in all his outfits—whether he was astride a cavalry horse or on a motorcycle working the Mexican border. His Nordic good looks, breezy manner, and easy smile gave him an air of nonchalance, as if it were all so effortless. He exhibited the same grace in the air, and, anxious to get away this morning, he gunned his ship across the smooth field and was airborne. A new page had been turned just like that.

Flying northward to Philadelphia, it wasn't long before Baltimore came into view, its bustling maze of streets, factories, and neatly bricked buildings soon giving way to a patchwork of undulating farmland, only to be pulled up short at Wilmington, with its tidy downtown, followed a few minutes later by the metropolis of Philadelphia and its tight grid of city streets fanning out in all directions. Such neat reflections of human industry appeared insignificant from such a lofty perspective. One saw through all manner of human pretense at 2,000 feet. The grand edifices that impressed from ground level were insignificant from above. Flying at the pale intersection of clouds and sky, the sun marking all things, Max might be aware of his earthbound brethren, but he could hardly be considered one of them. He had become *Civis Aerius Sum*—a citizen of the air.

Miller landed his plane without incident at Bustleton Field at 1 P.M., where the sacks of mail were transferred to Maurice Newton, who departed for Belmont, Long Island, thirteen minutes later. Pilot and ship arrived intact at 2:15 P.M. The southbound team of pilots, Shank and Gardner, fared equally well. Day one done and civil aero mail was batting 1.000. Only 364 more days to be flown just like that—excluding Sundays, of course.

This is where Ben Lipsner came in. His job was to establish maintenance protocols and coordinate flying schedules at not one but three airfields. Praeger wanted detailed records kept of every accident, every forced landing, every incident. Repairs were to be documented in order to learn what worked and what didn't—with the goal of keeping the ships in the air longer. To track planes at a glance, Lipsner drew up a flight board, using pegs to identify the whereabouts of every mail plane in the service. He devised a way to communicate basic weather conditions through symbols. An "X" on the board meant a pilot would be facing rain today; a simple "+" designated clear skies and smooth sailing.

The new superintendent was throwing all his organizational experience and fervor into getting the service up and running. Shuttling between College Park, Bustleton, and Belmont; managing pilots, mechanics, riggers, and personnel; and ensuring the supply chain was fed with fuel, oil, plugs, and parts was a demanding and time-consuming task. It was clear that Lipsner was no deskbound pencil pusher. Quite the opposite, rarely could he be found at his desk, much to the chagrin of those Washington bureaucrats seeking patronage jobs for their nephews and friends. Surely if the captain were working he would be found in his office, backslapping and glad-handing like everybody else. Many of those asking for favors didn't even support airmail. Still others were looking to see what personal benefits they might derive from the whole business, while more were hanging back, waiting to see which way the winds blew before assuming their self-righteous stand one way or the other.

Lipsner's organizational skills might be first-rate, but clearly, he was no politician. Despite the distraction, the month of August proved to be the best yet. There was good weather for the entire thirty-one days, and performance percentages reached a near flawless 99 percent. No trips had been defaulted, and only two forced landings marred an otherwise perfect scoreboard. It was stacking up to be a good summer.

Praeger was understandably pleased with the number of successful flights, but was troubled by other statistics. The Washington–New York runs were taking nearly five hours to complete. Flying at 75 to 85 miles per hour, aircraft were making good time aloft. But tack on ground handling time, drive time to transport the mail from the airfields to the post offices, and the inevitable delay for one thing or another, and letters stamped "airmail" weren't arriving any faster than it took to transport them by train. Praeger's highly touted aero mail service was, at best, duplicating a train service that had already proved itself to be fast, efficient, and less costly to operate. How was he supposed to justify a service on a cost-benefit ratio when it lost money and offered no appreciable time savings compared to rail?

Despite all the press coverage, businessmen weren't exactly jumping on the bandwagon. To make matters worse, airmail was a manpower- and hardware-intensive operation. It was hemorrhaging red ink under the cost of maintaining its dozen airplanes, pilot salaries, mechanics' wages, and all the other costs of government bureaucracy. Airmail stamps had cost 24 cents, a veritable fortune when letters could be sent by regular post for just three pennies. Praeger had knocked down the price, but even then mail planes were rarely operating at capacity. A letter stamped "airmail" was no longer the coveted souvenir it had been earlier; few were willing to spend the extra change on the service, regardless of how intrigued people were with these dashing young couriers of the air.

"Every city wanted the air mail service," Praeger said, "but educating the communities to pay a higher rate of postage for air mail than ordinary mail was somewhat difficult."

The pilots might be writing the book on the science and technology of aviation, but the tangible benefits weren't obvious to a public expected to pay more for postage, or to members of Congress being asked to fund a costly operation while there was a war going on. What the new service needed was an *aha* moment; something to convince the American public of its relevance to business, as in *aha, so that's why we should care about airmail!*

Crossing mountains and bridging distances was key to the growth of America, and Praeger felt it vital to find longer routes upon which to paint his canvas. It would be there that the airplane would shine, flying serenely over mountains and cities while trains were forced to crawl slowly through mountain passes and inner-city railroad crossings.

The value of connecting geographically distant cities carried as much import for Praeger today as it did for Postmaster General Benjamin Franklin in colonial times. When Franklin proposed connecting Philadelphia and Boston with a weekly mail run in 1760, many people thought he was daft to think such a distance could be crossed so quickly.

Praeger was hearing similar scoffs for his plan—a transcontinental super skyway. The New York–Washington route was small stuff, a working laboratory to understand what the airplane was capable of doing over longer distances.

"There is no guess work about it," Praeger declared. "It is just as feasible to operate a mail line from the Atlantic coast to the Pacific coast in relays of 200 to 250 miles as it is to operate a single line of 250 miles with the certainty with which the aerial mail has been operated between New York and Washington."

Chicago, as the nation's second-largest city, was a natural hub for the airmail's push westward. The Windy City on Lake Michigan was a riotous place, home to the great American stockyards, and the heart of industry in the Midwest. Many of the most important train lines fed into Chicago, including the Twentieth Century Limited out of Manhattan's Grand Central Station, which took twenty hours to make the trip. Chicago's strategic location in the center of the country was ideal for extending the tentacles of airmail south to St. Louis, north to Milwaukee and Minneapolis, and west through Cheyenne and Salt Lake City, all the way to San Francisco. In time, service could even be launched to South America by way of Key West, Havana, and the West Indies.

That was for the future. For now, establishing the major trunkline to Chicago had to be the priority. Praeger sharpened his pencil and crunched the numbers. The distance on the ground between New York and Chicago was about 1,000 miles by train. By air, that number could be reduced to 710 miles as the crow flies. An airplane making 90 miles per hour forward momentum would cut transit time to only nine or ten hours, even with downtime. An aircraft could leave New York at 6 A.M. and arrive in Chicago at 3 P.M., just in time to connect with afternoon rush deliveries. Who knows how much the financial markets could make by shuffling invest-ments back and forth that much quicker, saving as much as a day's interest on financial paper. Praeger was even convinced the post of-fice could also turn a profit on the longer route. It would be the *aha* moment that would get everyone to stand up and take notice.

Postmaster General Burleson had presented Praeger's plan to Congress, and with it an appropriation request for $1.5 million. Laughter could be heard echoing in the marbled corridors. Burleson had to be kidding. Talk under the dome was centered on whether or not to continue the service at all.

Congress wasn't the only unhappy party. The military was coldly indignant to Praeger's plan. He had promised to keep a lid on any expansion while war raged. Now, just weeks after their disengage-ment, he was going back on his word and pushing for enlargement of the service. But that agreement had been made weeks ago. The equation had changed since the U.S. Army pulled out its pilots. The survival of airmail was dependent on widening the network. Praeger would not concede that point; better to give up one's cigars.

Burleson paid a call on Secretary of War Newton Baker to discuss the matter. Wasn't keeping America strong economically important to the war effort, too? After all, the whole point of air-mail was to help fuel the economy. America was emerging from its simple agrarian roots. Local businesses were growing, pressing into ever-widening markets, pushing for larger economies of scale. Never had the swift exchange of goods and information been more important.

"There is a gain to commerce operating at high pressure under war conditions which would fully justify the use of the compara-tively small additional equipment needed," argued Burleson.

Baker agreed with the logic, but the thought of the postal de-partment reneging on its promise lay like bad field rations in the stomachs of many Army officers, particularly those still convinced that all flying operations should be kept under strict military con-trol. Little brother couldn't agree less. The sky overhead was open territory, and not the exclusive domain of the military. Still, knowing how the military was quick to pounce on anyone making the slightest demand on wartime resources, Praeger had his department issue a new press release designed to appease the opposition.

"Mechanical difficulties no longer stand in the way of an immediate far-reaching expansion of the air mail," it stated, "but no extension of that service will be undertaken without due regard for the war demands on our aircraft industry and personnel. Therefore its extension at this time will be gradual and always in fullest harmony with those charged with responsibility for the conduct of the war."

It was pure fabrication on Praeger's part. But the second assistant, being the adroit tactician he was, knew how to play the game. The situation temporarily diffused, he assigned his superintendent the task of moving the mail westward. Carving out a route between New York and Chicago would be daunting by anyone's standards. The service would be venturing beyond the easy flying on the East Coast and would have to cross an actual mountain range—the Alleghenies. It was a dangerous stretch of territory, where the rugged and heavily forested hills made it nearly impossible to find a safe place to land in an emergency. Storm clouds and fog regularly settled in the valleys and obscured the tops of the mountains—not a good thing when a pilot's descending blind. The route was also three times the distance of the New York–Washington run, spanning four states—New York, Pennsylvania, Ohio, and Illinois. Refueling stops would have to be found and emergency landing fields located.

Max Miller, with his homing-pigeon instincts, was dispatched to scout out central Pennsylvania, and he found a suitable landing place in Lock Haven, Pennsylvania, on the eastern base of the Alleghenies, about 215 miles from Belmont. Continuing west and across the mountains, the next stop would be Cleveland, 206 miles away, followed by a refueling stop 152 miles later in the small town of Bryan, Ohio. From there it was 178 more miles to Chicago.

Lipsner plunged forward with preparations for the flight—a challenge compounded by daily operations between New York and Washington. Praeger had dubbed the experiment the "Pathfinder" flight, and Lipsner selected Miller, the airmail's best explorer, as the lead pilot. To make things interesting, though, Lipsner would make the trip to Chicago a race between Miller and Eddie Gardner.

Gardner was the perfect foil for Miller. As friends and friendly rivals, Lipsner knew that they would push themselves to the limit— not because Praeger wanted them to, but because both would want to get to Chicago first. And to make the race a true experiment, each pilot would be flying a different aircraft to see how the designs stacked up over the grueling run. Miller would fly the gray number one Standard with the 150-horsepower Hispano-Suiza engine. Gardner would man a Liberty-powered Curtiss R4, four of which were now in the postal fleet courtesy of the Army.

The Standard was to be stuffed with mail. The R4 would be packing Eddie Radel, the air service's newly hired head mechanic. Easygoing and confident in his wrench-turning skills, it was his job to oversee aero mail's staff of mechanics and riggers. He had been Katherine Stinson's personal mechanic, and Lipsner held him and his talents in high esteem.

"Here was a young man with more experience in the art of aviation mechanics than anyone else I was able to find. He was beloved by all the pilots as well as the mechanical staff. When Radel said a ship was ready to fly, no one questioned his statement."

Though Radel's salary of $2,000 didn't match that of a pilot, it was still good enough to meet his simple pleasures—good food and a French horn or saxophone to play. At night, the sound of repair work gave way to music reverberating in the hangar.

Radel had personally seen to it that both mail planes were prepped and ready to go for the Pathfinder flight on September 5.

CHAPTER 9

PATHFINDERS

With the leather headgear pulled down tight over their heads to protect their ears and neck against the incoming storm on the morning of September 5, Miller and Gardner were anxious to get off before the skies grew angrier. Their mail planes had been ready to go for some time now, but the usual celebratory proceedings were slowing things down. Max was particularly impatient as he'd been ready to go at 6 A.M. and still, an hour later, he wasn't yet away. The longer they delayed, the nearer this storm moved. If it was bad here, who knew what flying conditions awaited the two fliers aloft. The National Climatic Data Center had made weather reports available, but data had been confined to cloud type, wind direction, and velocity all observed at ground level. What awaited Gardner and Miller aloft was anybody's guess.

At last, departure was at hand. Fortified against the elements by a heavy head-to-toe leather flying suit, Miller climbed into the cockpit and slid down behind the stick.

"Look me up when you get to Chicago, Max!" came a yell from the side. It was Gardner wishing his friend well.

Miller flashed him an easy grin and readied his hand on the throttle.

Gardner hadn't wanted to give his buddy a head start, but he'd have Radel riding shotgun. The mechanic would be there with his wrench if either he or Miller developed problems along the way. He would also be flying the more powerful aircraft. Farthest, fastest, highest, boldest—Gardner was in love with winning and superlatives had become his watermark. He fully intended on winning this contest. It was just a matter of getting up there.

But just as Miller's plane took off across the infield, the storm fell upon them, unleashing torrents of rain onto the field. Gardner and Radel stood watching the Norwegian fly off.

"Just our luck," Radel snorted. "I'll bet Miller missed it."

"Forget it," Gardner said, shrugging it off. "A bad beginning is a good ending."

With that, the two sprang into action. Stepping onto the wing, Radel climbed into the cargo hold and buckled himself in while Gardner settled in behind him. A drenched field man cranked the propeller and Curtiss ship number 39367 took off, bouncing across the grass, throttle wide open. But their ride was short-lived. Gardner, notorious for his wobbly takeoffs and landings, now found himself hobbling along the grass like a wounded gobbler, his tail skid broken. The race not yet begun and already, it seemed, Miller had landed on the better side of luck. Immediately, Turk throttled back and returned to the flight line.

Max was circling overhead, waiting for Gardner to join him, but having seen Gardner's ship limping back to the hangar, he had no alternative but to press on. He was all for fair play, but the mail in his cargo hold had a destination and it was his job to get it there. He put his Standard into a westerly heading and took off across the clouds, the very wet spectators on the ground waving him good-bye.

Down at the field, an undaunted Gardner spied an idle R4 parked nearby. He'll fly that one.

The aircraft isn't checked out, he's told.

Was it fueled and ready to go? That's all he wanted to know.

Mechanics swarm over the aircraft to prep it as quickly as possible. Gardner and Radel complete a quick preflight checkout, and then take off at 8:50 A.M., about an hour and forty-five minutes behind Miller. Gardner is wholly unfazed by the delay. Close to 750 miles of flying lay ahead. Plenty of time to make up lost minutes.

Glad to hear it, Radel responds, because he's left the fire extinguisher and their lunch in the other plane.

Up ahead, airmail's "number one" pilot was experiencing his own set of problems. The saturated air had trapped his plane inside two layers of clouds. Fortunately, a narrow path of clear sky stretched out between the layers, and Miller was able to drop his Standard into the chute. For the next two hours he maintained what he thought was the proper westerly heading, but who could be certain, given the complete lack of visibility and the notoriously faulty compasses?

Had Miller been a drinking man instead of an inveterate chain smoker he might have turned to whiskey for sweet guidance. A flat-sided glass bottle taped to an instrument panel allowed a pilot to gauge his ascent or descent just by eyeballing the liquid's motion inside. All one had to do was refrain from downing the contents, which, given the straits he now found himself, would have been thoroughly understandable.

Pushing the stick forward, Max began his descent to check his position. For all he knew he could be flying way off course. Besides, at this point, he was running low on fuel and even lower on options. He knew the chance he was taking. The ground he couldn't see might well rise up to bite him, turning him into a permanent fixture of the Allegheny landscape. The seconds ticked by as he slipped his way through the whipped gray silence. Finally, he broke through the cloud deck and found his mark. An open plot of cultivated farmland stretched out below, not the deadly woodland ridges he had expected. Straightaway, he set down, rolling to a stop just shy of the kitchen door of one Mrs. Bennett, standing there stunned at the sight before her.

Did the kind lady know where in blue blazes he was?

Mrs. Bennett took one look at Max standing before the contraption occupying the better part of her front yard, the roar of its motor scaring her egg-laying chickens off their daily jobs, and kindly informed him of his whereabouts—Danville, Pennsylvania.

Eager to gain his bearings, Max reached for one of the maps he was carrying. Printed by Henry Woodhouse and the Aero Club of America, the map detailed geographic elevations, emergency landing fields, and pertinent landmarks that aviators might encounter along what had been designated the Woodrow Wilson Airway, an 80-mile-wide skyway extending from New York to San Francisco. The president had been honored in that way due to the considerable support he had shown for aviation, having created the National Advisory Committee for Aeronautics in 1915. The country's first aviation think tank, it was created with an eye toward establishing a nationwide clearinghouse for aviation technology, and, more important, helping America catch up with the Europeans on aeronautics. The U.S. Air Mail was part of that effort.

According to the map, Danville, Pennsylvania, was about 155 miles west of Long Island. That put Miller just two miles off course. Still on track, he folded up his map and hopped back into the cockpit, anxious to stay one step ahead of his competition. Mrs. Bennett queried after him.

Didn't the gentleman want something to eat? Surely, he was hungry. Was he all right?

All was well with Max. Despite the weather, he was still out in front. All he needed now was some clear skies and for his engine to quit misfiring. Pushing the stick forward, he climbed back up the stairway.

Just forty-five short minutes later and right on schedule, Max parked his plane at Lock Haven. He immediately put in a call to Lipsner, who was standing anxiously by in Chicago, stationed inside a makeshift command center located in the downtown post office. He had instructed Miller and Gardner to contact him via telegram or telephone whenever they set down.

"Say, Cap," Miller asked. "Where's Eddie?"

"Never mind, Eddie. Where are you?"

Max gave him his coordinates and told him about the balky engine that had plagued him on the way out. Lipsner ordered him to get it fixed and be on his way.

Still on target to make Chicago before nightfall, Max enjoyed a leisurely lunch at Lock Haven's country club while mechanics changed spark plugs and saw that the Standard was properly fueled and oiled. At last, everything in place, the aviator hit the skies again confident he would soon be arriving in Cleveland.

Turk was still lagging behind, and not only was he trailing, he was fast losing ground. Stiff winds had driven him fully 30 miles off course. He landed to check his location and placed a call to Lipsner.

"Hello! This is Gardner. Where's Max?"

"You look out for Gardner and never mind Miller," Lipsner shot back. "Where are you?"

"I landed at Wilkes-Barre at 11:05. I'll get away for Lock Haven in a jiffy. Be a good fellow, Cap. Tell me where Max is."

"He just landed at Lock Haven. You might catch him if you get on the right course."

Determined to catch up, Gardner and Radel climbed into their plane and hit the skies again. But the weather had worsened. Wind-driven rain was blowing the ship across the sky. His feet on the rudder pedals, Gardner kept an ear to the staccato of feeble sputterings from his engine. It was inexplicably losing power. He had to go down—try for better weather below. Boring through the shroud, Gardner focused on the task at hand, relying on his flying skill and the sinew of youth to propel him past the fears that kept others alive. He and Radel set down safely at Jersey Shore, Pennsylvania, at 1:05 P.M. Despite the setback, Gardner remained optimistic that Radel's talent with a wrench would have them airborne again shortly.

It turned out that dirt and water were clogging the fuel line. It took some time but Gardner and Radel succeeded in at last getting their ship off the ground, only to boomerang down a short time later—this time hopelessly lost. Thanks to some local miners who had helped line up the Curtiss into the wind and crank the heavy prop, they eventually found their way to Lock Haven shortly after 2 P.M.

Gardner wasn't happy with his performance so far. Miller had left Lock Haven two and a half hours earlier. He and the sax player were falling even farther behind.

By now, Gardner could only guess where Miller was. For all he knew, his buddy was home free.

But like Turk, Miller was also struggling. He'd been plowing through gruel thick enough to bite into for the past 100 miles. Every instinct, every cultivated skill was employed to keep himself aloft.

Unsure of his location, Miller decided to descend and try to pick up a landmark. Just then, he felt a hard clunk against his fuselage. Peering over the side of his ship, he looked down to see the tip of a tree vanishing into the mist.

"That sure gave me a good scare," he said. "I hustled back up again into the fog, determined to get plenty of altitude and keep on going as long as my gas held out."

Max pressed on for another 50 miles, but now his radiator began leaking badly. He was forced to go down once again. This time his instincts led him to a break in the clouds, but the sight before his eyes was of a county fair with hundreds of people in attendance.

"There was such a mob of people that I did not land there, but went on about twenty miles to a town named Cambridge. I inquired where I was and told, 'Jefferson.'"

Miller checked his map and found his coordinates—Jefferson, Ohio. He wasn't off course by much. From here, Cleveland would be a snap. Back into the air he was sure he would arrive soon, but as the miles passed Miller realized something was horribly wrong. Setting down, he inquired about his whereabouts, then dejectedly put in a call to Lipsner. As usual, the first words out of his mouth were:

"Where's Eddie?"

"Where the dickens have you been?" Lipsner barked.

"This is Cambridge, Ohio," Max replied flatly.

"Cambridge, Ohio! What the deuce are you doing there? You're way off your course, Max, and you're still more than a hundred miles from Cleveland. What's the idea. What happened?"

Lipsner could only listen helplessly when he heard the story about how a farmer had assured Miller that he'd landed in "Jefferson," which was sufficient description from the farmer's point of view, being that everybody in those parts already knew that "Jefferson" was shorthand for "Jefferson County," the suffix amounting to an altogether unnecessary waste of time, conversationally speaking. Unfortunately for Max, the difference between Jefferson, Ohio, and Jefferson County, Pennsylvania, amounted to a detour south in excess of well over a 100 miles.

Lipsner informed Miller that his rival was still at Lock Haven trying to sort out his engine troubles.

No federal agency in the administration of President Woodrow Wilson (*right*) was more dedicated to introducing new technologies than the Post Office Department, which developed the first civil uses for both trucks and airplanes. The architects of that work were Postmaster General Albert Sidney Burleson (*second from right*) and Second Assistant Postmaster General Otto Praeger (*left*), who headed all transportation activities for the post office. Washington, D.C., Postmaster Merritt Chance (*second from left*) joins them for the inauguration of airmail on May 15, 1918. NASM, Smithsonian Institution

Multimillionaire airplane designer and racer Glenn Curtiss modified the JN-4D Jenny biplane he was building for the U.S. Army with a bigger engine and larger fuel tanks so it could fly mail for Uncle Sam. NASM, SMITHSONIAN INSTITUTION

Decades after his landmark work inventing the telephone, Alexander Graham Bell was busy helping to develop the principles of flight. Here he's flying one of his tetrahedral kites, which could lift a man into the air. Bell was present in Washington, D.C., on May 15, 1918, for the post office's first airmail flight. NASM, SMITHSONIAN INSTITUTION

Maj. Rueben Fleet was in charge of pilot training for the U.S. Army when he was given nine days to establish flying operations for the Post Office Department. He is shown here after having just flown into Potomac Park on the morning of the inaugural flight. Note the road map tied to his leg. Also note the proximity of the trees to the landing field. NATIONAL POSTAL MUSEUM, SMITHSONIAN INSTITUTION

Located on the banks of the Potomac River, the Polo Grounds in Washington, D.C., was the southern terminus of airmail service. Note the Lincoln Memorial in the upper right. JESSE DAVIDSON AVIATION ARCHIVES

Maj. Fleet confers with President Wilson at Potomac Park. The major was horrified to learn that the post office planned to extend airmail to Boston, but thought better of telling the president at this particular moment. NASM, SMITHSONIAN INSTITUTION

Lt. Torrey Webb pilots a Jenny out of Belmont Park Race Track on the southbound run to Philadelphia. August Belmont II, a major in the Quartermaster Corps, let the airmail use his raceway for free. NATIONAL POSTAL MUSEUM, SMITHSONIAN INSTITUTION

Lt. James Edgerton and his sister celebrate his successful, first airmail flight into Washington, D.C., on May 15, 1918. Edgerton, who was named to the team because his father was purchasing agent for the post office, eventually flew more miles than any other Army airmail pilot. In 1919, he became the youngest federal executive in the U.S. government when he was named chief of flying operations for the Post Office Department. NASM, SMITHSONIAN INSTITUTION

Lifelong Democrats and sons of Texas, Postmaster General Burleson (*right*) and his second assistant, Otto Praeger, work in lockstep to bring progressive reform and technological advancement to the Post Office Department.

Otto Praeger spent two decades as a
newspaper reporter, rising to Washington
correspondent for the southwest's most
influential newspaper, the *Dallas News*,
before being named postmaster of the
nation's capital, followed by appointment
as second assistant postmaster general
for the nation. NATIONAL POSTAL MUSEUM,
SMITHSONIAN INSTITUTION

Postmaster General Burleson fought to bring parcel post to the nation, which
fueled the economy by letting people use the post office to ship goods across state
lines. In this photograph, produce is carried by autotruck service introduced by
Second Assistant Praeger. NATIONAL POSTAL MUSEUM, SMITHSONIAN INSTITUTION

Maj. Charles Willoughby followed Rueben Fleet as airmail's chief of flying. The War Department was suspicious of his German ancestry, however, and removed him from the high-profile job just a few weeks after he started.

NATIONAL POSTAL MUSEUM, SMITHSONIAN INSTITUTION

A specialist in automotive engineering and aeronautic and mechanical maintenance, the spit-shined Capt. Benjamin Lipsner was the first superintendent of civilian airmail.

NASM, SMITHSONIAN INSTITUTION

The men of the Post Office Department's civilian airmail service. *Left to right:* unidentified, Otto Praeger, unidentified, pilot Edward Langley, pilot Edward Gardner, Benjamin Lipsner, pilot Maurice Newton, pilot Max Miller, and pilot Robert Shank. NASM, SMITHSONIAN INSTITUTION

At twenty-five years of age, the tall, blond blue-eyed Norwegian-born Max Miller earned $3,600 a year as one of the original civilian airmail pilots hired by the Post Office Department. NATIONAL POSTAL MUSEUM, SMITHSONIAN INSTITUTION

Straw skimmers make a strong showing on August 6, 1918, at the Standard
Aircraft Corporation factory in Elizabeth, New Jersey, when postal officials
took delivery of their first new-production aircraft. Second Assistant Postmaster
General Otto Praeger is at center, flanked on his right by Standard president
Harry Mingle and on his left by Benjamin Lipsner. Other notables include arctic
explorer Capt. Robert Bartlett (*far left*); WWI fighter ace Capt. Frederick Libby
(*second from left*); and Henry Woodhouse (*fifth from left*), editor and publisher of
Aerial Age magazine. NATIONAL POSTAL MUSEUM, SMITHSONIAN INSTITUTION

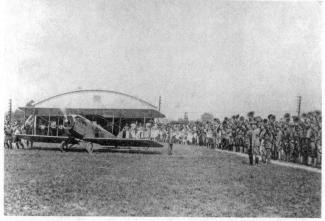

Hats off to Max Miller as he pilots his Standard JR-1B mail plane on the
first airmail flight from College Park, Maryland, to Bustleton field outside
Philadelphia. The U.S. Army ended its airmail operations the week prior, and this
was America's first-ever civilian airmail flight. NATIONAL POSTAL MUSEUM, SMITHSONIAN
INSTITUTION

Former race car driver Eddie "Turk Bird" Gardner, named so because his plane wobbled like a turkey on takeoffs and landings, was one of the old men of airmail at the age of thirty. NATIONAL POSTAL MUSEUM, SMITHSONIAN INSTITUTION

The parties lasted for three days when the airmail came to Chicago for the first time. Here, Benjamin Lipsner centers the men who made it possible—Max Miller (*left*) and Eddie Gardner (*right*). Also on hand were Augustus Post, secretary of the Aero Club of America (*far left*) and Charles "Pop" Dickinson, president of the Aero Club of Illinois. NASM, SMITHSONIAN INSTITUTION

It wasn't a man who first flew the mail between Chicago and New York. It was Katherine Stinson, who piloted the route for the Post Office Department three months before the Pathfinder flights of Max Miller and Eddie Gardner. Stinson was the fourth woman in the United States to earn a pilot's license, and in 1917 became the first woman to fly in the Orient. NASM, SMITHSONIAN INSTITUTION

Albert Burleson and Otto Praeger worked here in the grand edifice that was Post Office Department headquarters in Washington, D.C., located on Pennsylvania Avenue between Eleventh and Twelfth Streets. NATIONAL POSTAL MUSEUM, SMITHSONIAN INSTITUTION

Hollywood actor Douglas Fairbanks airmailed himself from Washington to New York to raise money for Liberty bonds during the war. Here he is on the wing, posing with pilot Robert Shank. NATIONAL POSTAL MUSEUM, SMITHSONIAN INSTITUTION

The rolling hills of the Allegheny Mountains in central Pennsylvania earned their reputation as "Hell's Stretch" because of the ever-present fog and the tree-covered terrain that afforded few safe landing sites. More airmail pilots died here than on any other part of the transcontinental route. JESSE DAVIDSON AVIATION ARCHIVES

Max Miller stops to get his bearings and top off his radiator with water in Lock Haven, Pennsylvania, on his pathfinding trip from New York to Chicago. Lock Haven postmaster Paul Brosius beams with delight. JESSE DAVIDSON AVIATION ARCHIVES

A circle marks the landing field at Beaver farm in Bellefonte, Pennsylvania, the airmail refueling stop between New York and Cleveland. JESSE DAVIDSON AVIATION ARCHIVES

The airmail hangar and repair shop in Bellefonte. The site was selected by pilot Max Miller because the land drained well and remained dry throughout the year. JESSE DAVIDSON AVIATION ARCHIVES

In mid-1919, pilot Charles Lamborn was the first to die flying across the Alleghenies from Bellefonte to Cleveland when he became disoriented in the fog and crashed. JESSE DAVIDSON AVIATION ARCHIVES

While flying the mail into Bellefonte, fog obscuring his view, pilot Frederick Robinson dipped below the cloud deck and began following the waters of the Juniata River into Bellefonte. He was killed when his plane struck a telephone wire strung across the river. JESSE DAVIDSON AVIATION ARCHIVES

The airmail service lived and died by its operational performance, which Otto Praeger used to convince the public and members of Congress of the viability of airmail. Here, members of the Belmont team pose beneath a banner proclaiming their performance record for the 1918–1919 period. Jesse Davidson Aviation Archives

Nicknamed "Sky" by his parents, the skinny Jack Knight from Buchanan, Michigan, was born to fly. He spent thousands of hours flying the mail from the cockpit of a de Havilland DH-4. NASM, Smithsonian Institution

It was E. Hamilton Lee who, as an Army instructor at Ellington Field in Texas, taught Jack Knight to fly. With an ever-present cigar in his mouth, the dapper Lee flew out of almost every major airfield operated by the Post Office Department. United Airlines Archives

Mechanics, who held a love of flying as great as any pilot, were the unsung heroes of the airmail service. They were constantly pressured from all sides, particularly from the field managers who wanted them to turn around planes faster, and from pilots, who blamed them for mechanical failures that caused forced landings. NATIONAL POSTAL MUSEUM, SMITHSONIAN INSTITUTION

The post office began flying between Chicago and Minneapolis in late 1920 with twin-engine de Havilland biplanes. Here, seven pilots on the route—including Ham Lee perched on the nose—pose with a DH at the Minneapolis Speedway. JESSE DAVIDSON AVIATION ARCHIVES

With their all-metal construction, enclosed cockpit, and single wing, the Junkers JL-6 was thought by postal officials to be the answer to many of their operational problems. However, a faulty fuel system led to in-flight fires and the death of several pilots. JESSE DAVIDSON AVIATION ARCHIVES

The year 1920 was a deadly one for airmail. Here, pilot Harry Sherlock was killed after flying his de Havilland into the Tiffany factory tower near Heller Field in Newark, New Jersey. JESSE DAVIDSON AVIATION ARCHIVES

Otto Praeger's transcontinental push westward required pilots to cross several mountain ranges, including the ten-thousand-foot peaks of the Rocky Mountains. JESSE DAVIDSON AVIATION ARCHIVES

Bundled up for winter weather, Jack Knight stands by in his cockpit to fly another stage in the February 1921 transcontinental run that would include the airmail's first-ever night flight. UNITED AIRLINES ARCHIVES

Cheered by the news, Miller was motivated to make it to Cleveland before Gardner. He took off around 6 P.M. but was repeatedly forced to land and find water to quench his leaky radiator. By the time he reached the city the stillness of night had settled over the landscape, making it impossible for him to find the Glenn Martin airfield, with its cushy "prepared surface," one of the few in the country. Instead, he settled for a dusty open field along the outskirts of the city.

Despite the hour, the Cleveland Police found their way to the Standard and took Miller's mail sacks for safekeeping. Everything stowed away, the chief of police personally escorted the tired aviator to the Statler Hotel where, despite his exhaustion, he conducted a late-night interview with a local reporter, recounting his frustration in vivid detail.

"At one farmhouse where I stopped for water, the people actually couldn't tell me where they lived and they didn't know which was the closest town or how far it was to any town. They were the dumbest lot I have ever met in my life."

For the tall, slender Scandinavian lad who had crossed an ocean to find his future, these encounters with small-town America had been nothing shy of maddening. Miller fell into bed that night convinced of his buddy's good fortune. Surely, Turk was having a better time of it.

But Gardner had hardly been able to take advantage of Miller's misfortune. The big Liberty was still giving them sizable troubles. Adding to that, the drizzle had developed into a heavy downpour before they were able to leave Lock Haven. Lipsner had instructed both men to stay there overnight. Tomorrow was another day and another leg of the race. Anything could still happen.

Come morning, Max flew his ship over to the Glenn L. Martin Aircraft Company in Cleveland, where mechanics spent the next several hours working on his radiator. It wasn't until 1:30 P.M. that he set off for Bryan, Ohio. On the plus side, the weather was improved, even though it didn't take him long to find out the radiator leak hadn't been fixed. Once again he was forced to land in search of water. By the time he reached Bryan, a sizable crowd had turned out to welcome the frustrated aviator onto Mrs. Alice Willett's field, anointed Uncle Sam's temporary refueling stop.

The crowd was abuzz. The sight of a pilot striding across the grass dressed in a leather flight suit, a pair of leather goggles on his head, was enough to get everyone chattering and pointing. Miller was even more memorable this day, as he wore his trademark white scarf about his neck. He knew it looked good streaming over his shoulder, and it came in handy wiping away the black oil that always came spewing forth from the engine. All suited up, a mail pilot drew the same stares as a U.S. Marshal swaggering through a frontier town, spurs jangling.

Max was in a hurry, though, with no time to preen about. Just thirty minutes on the ground was all he could spare while his pesky radiator was checked out by the owner of a local auto garage.

But festivities at Bryan were far from over, as Gardner and Radel had made up most of their lost time. Just six minutes later, a second flying postman came winging into Willett's field. Folks in Bryan were having a regular holiday witnessing this fraternity of aviators. Gardner, no slouch in the fashion department, understood the image his flying attire conveyed, and he took pains tending to it. On the ground, Eddie Gardner might be just a stoop-shouldered, slightly balding midwesterner from a small town, but suited up in that leather uniform he became "Turk"—a man cool under pressure, someone his peers considered to be the "very ace of mail fliers." He wore only the thickest leather headgear and the richest, most expensive leather jacket, which usually topped traditional boots and breeches reserved for cavalry officers.

Though the cavalry was fast becoming an anachronism, Gardner was riding the vanguard of a new, different type of charge, one whose traditions would not be defined by the brave and steady heart of a horse but by the *clack clack clack* of pistons.

Both pilots back in the air, Lipsner had only to sit back and see which of them arrived first. Thousands of people awaited them at Grant Park, where an evening's celebration was planned. Miller was still in the lead, but Turk wanted his stake in the roses. Though coming from behind, he had been in back of the field before, coaxing, pushing, or just plain bullying his aeroplane through every type of weather imaginable in order to cross the tape first.

"For the first time since the flight began, the weather was beautiful, except for a strong head-wind," Lipsner relayed. "At my telephone in Chicago, I was now able to appreciate and grin at the questions: 'Where's Eddie?' and 'Where's Max?'"

The afternoon wore on, slowly yawning into evening. Finally, around seven o'clock, a single plane appeared over the shores of Lake Michigan, the fumes of its exhaust creating a bluish vapor trail behind it. It was the number one Standard. Cheers went up from the crowd attending the nearby War Exposition, their voices ringing in Max, who set her down into the shadows of the unfamiliar Grant Park. Rolling to a stop, he cut the switches and climbed out.

"Where's Eddie?" he inquired without missing a beat.

Lipsner assured him that he, Max, had arrived first, in effortless style, as always. The news of his success had the aviator breaking into a smile. Miller had retained his number one heavyweight status in every way. Pilot and superintendent posed for the cameramen, the flier clad all in leather flashing his pearly whites, standing beside the ever-smartly dressed Lipsner attired in a hat and a pressed wool four-button suit. Like his boys, Lipsner was a man wholly aware of his image. He was routinely turned out as if each occasion were Derby Day and he, the proud owner of the odds-on favorite. But then, putting one's best foot forward was important both to Lipsner and to his wife, in particular, who felt that a tie was only proper if it had red in it.

The field was packed with well-wishers: members of the Aero Club of America and its local affiliate booster clubs, along with an assortment of postmasters, politicians, and national government officials. The flamboyant Augustus Post, famed balloonist, pioneer airplane pilot, and secretary of the Aero Club of America was on hand. Henry Woodhouse, clever promoter that he was, ensured that his name cropped up amid the festivities, even though he was back in New York. He had personally addressed one of the letters stowed inside Miller's mail sacks to the editor of the *Chicago Tribune*, proclaiming the New York–Chicago run as an "epoch making first trip."

*   *   *

Chicago police officers stood by as sacks of mail were removed from the gray Standard, then transferred into a waiting truck, which sped away to the city's main post office. Miller was exhausted but joyous, warmed as he'd been by the pomp and the rich chorus of cheers. But still, there was no sign of Gardner and he was beginning to worry.

"Something's got to be done about Eddie," he said, turning to the captain. "I'll bet he took the short cut over the lake to try to get here first. I know Eddie! Let me have my plane again."

Lipsner would hear none of it. What purpose would it serve having both his pilots flying around in the dark. Instead, he had another plan. Several bonfires were lit about the field, their torches serving as beacons by which Gardner could guide himself on in. But long after their embers had smoldered, there was still no sign of the Curtiss biplane in the sky.

Suddenly, Max got an idea. Fireworks! The War Exposition had already staged a rousing display earlier that evening. If promoters could be convinced to repeat the performance, maybe Gardner would be able to find his way in. Max pleaded with officials.

"I'll pay for another battle, if necessary. My buddies are lost somewhere out there over the lake."

Much to the delight of spectators, yet another colorful display soon lit the skies over Lake Michigan. But like before, darkness closed in without any sign of Gardner and Radel. Just then, Lipsner received word that a telephone call awaited him at the nearby yacht club. He and Max hurried over to find Gardner on the other end of the phone. Repairs had prevented him and Radel from leaving Bryon until nearly six o'clock that night. By the time they'd reached a little town in Indiana called Westville, darkness was fully upon them. They wisely decided to set down there for the night. He'd bring her on in tomorrow first thing.

Grabbing the phone, Max couldn't help but get in a little dig.

"Hey, Turk, I thought you were going to look me up when you got to Chicago."

It was an ebullient Lipsner who returned to the crowd to inform everyone that pilot, mechanic, and machine were safely grounded. With that, the party could continue.

The next day, September 7, Gardner would come soaring into town just after 8 A.M., completing his half of the Pathfinder flight.

Total time for Miller to reach Chicago from New York—thirty-six hours. Total time for Gardner and Radel—roughly forty-eight hours. Total time for the Twentieth Century Limited to cover the 1,000 miles of rail between the two cities—twenty hours.

From inside his wood-paneled office, Praeger stared at newspaper headlines nobody cared to read. Throughout the entire journey, the press had been having a field day. "Two Mail Planes Halted in First Trip to Chicago," wrote the *Chicago Daily Tribune*.

And the subhead, where editors like to include more of the gory details, was even worse. "Airgonaut is blown 150 miles off route over Alleghenies," it read.

Lipsner had assured reporters that the Pathfinder flight was just that, a scouting trip, adding that time was not a factor. In reality, he knew the opposite to be true. His boss had promised a ten-hour delivery time, not two days. All Miller and Gardner had done was laze their way across 750 miles of skyway with all the speed of the Lewis and Clark expedition. Praeger wanted a fleet of planes in the air, flying thousands of miles daily, each carrying 300 pounds of mail. From where he stood, the feat was not impressive. It had taken too long! The pilots must understand that failure to complete the entire trip in a single daylight period could mean the death of the entire airmail service. Both pilots would have to do it again, but faster on the return flight.

While Praeger fumed in D.C., Miller, Gardner, and Radel were living high on the hog in Chicago. Lipsner had hoped his boys would use this opportunity to recharge after their strenuous trip west. But the flight had turned Miller and Turk into overnight celebrities. There were parties to attend and special dinners held in their honor.

"Finally, I had to step in," said Lipsner. "I hated to spoil their fun, but on the other hand, I had to think of their welfare, too."

That meant making sure they were in physical condition to make the long flight back to New York. To lessen the potential of bad weather affecting both pilots, their departures would be staggered a day apart. Having won the outbound race, Miller would leave first on September 10. Gardner would follow the next morning.

Before they could depart, however, Lipsner had to repay a debt to Chicago postmaster William Carlile, who had generously allowed the captain to set up camp in his postal building. Lipsner offered him an airplane ride courtesy of Uncle Sam, and though Carlile hadn't seemed entirely keen on the offer, eventually the gentle-faced walrus of a man gamely donned a flight suit and leather helmet. As both mail planes were still in the shop, a military bomber had been lent for the occasion. Fortunately for him, the affable curly-topped Miller had won a coin toss with Gardner to fly the postmaster, guaranteeing his passenger a subdued flight rather than the white-knuckle affair that Gardner would likely have flown.

Sensing the postmaster's nervousness, Lipsner warned Miller to come down the moment he felt a tap on the back. However, a mischievous reporter overheard the conversation and, intent on having some fun, sauntered over to the parked bomber and casually informed the pilot of some new instructions.

"The signals were to be reversed, and whenever the Postmaster patted him on the back he was to go higher."

The takeoff was certainly exhilarating for Postmaster Carlile, but the excitement quickly evaporated at the dizzying height of 2,000 feet, with Chicago *soooo* far beneath him. He tapped Miller on the back, having seen enough and expecting to descend, but instead his aerial tour of the Windy City became even more of a nightmare as the ship continued to climb. People on the ground could only watch in wonder at Carlile's nerve.

"I thought they were trying to establish a new altitude record," remarked Lipsner.

He turned to Gardner standing beside him, his neck craned upward.

"For a guy who was reluctant to go up, Carlile certainly seems to like it well enough now."

At last, just when it seemed the plane would vanish into the clouds, the high-flying Miller descended and parked her back on the field. It was a wreck of a passenger who climbed out of the cockpit. Having pounded on Miller's back until his hand was sore, the hapless Carlile had succeeded only in winging himself ever higher.

For his part, Max was thoroughly confused.

"I thought the guy would never quit asking me to go higher."

All horrors exacted, the day finally arrived for Miller and Gardner to turn their ships homeward. Both would be starting with good news— heading east, there'd be tailwinds to help them along their way.

"So long, Eddie," Max shouted, climbing into his Standard. "I'll think of you when I'm walking down Broadway tonight."

Gardner laughed. "Sure, provided that radiator doesn't wrap itself around your neck."

Miller had every chance of making good on his boast. The weather was great, skies blue. He departed at 6:26 A.M. with about 3,000 pieces of mail. He soon reached Bryan 160 miles to the east, and, to save time, he flew right on past instead of coming in for a ceremonial landing. Buzzing low over town he tossed a small mail pouch over the side of his ship. He was gone before it even had time to hit the ground.

He was making great time now and had arrived at Cleveland three hours after departure when his radiator once again began acting up. A broken water connection forced the supremely frustrated Miller to set down for repairs, and he wasn't aloft again until 4:30 in the afternoon. Three hours later, with good weather all the way, he had safely traversed the Allegheny Mountains and covered the 210 miles to Lock Haven. Darkness was beginning to fall upon central Pennsylvania; still, Max was confident he could make it all the way to Belmont.

Filled with high spirits over his imminent success, he made his way to the nearest phone, eager to relay the news to the captain.

"Say Chief, I'm in Lock Haven and everything's all fixed now. My radiator had only a small leak, but I think it'll hold all right until I reach New York."

"What?" exclaimed Lipsner, thoroughly taken aback.

"I'm going to New York. I'll call you from Belmont Park before you go to bed."

"You'll do nothing of the kind."

This time, it was Max who was surprised.

"You wanted me to make it in a day, didn't you?"

Yes, of course, said Lipsner, but given the late hour the risk was far too great. Better to stay put and live to fly another day.

"But listen, boss, I've got an important appointment in New York. Besides, all my clothes are there."

Lipsner was adamant.

"I don't care anything about your appointments or clothes. You're flying the mail for Uncle Sam and you'd better obey orders. Do you think I want you flying over those mountains and New York skyscrapers at this time of the night? Besides, that radiator is very unreliable and should be thoroughly inspected. You better stay right there tonight."

Lipsner knew his decision wouldn't sit well with Max.

"Miller had not the slightest doubt that he could have made the trip safely in one day," said Lipsner. "Perhaps he never fully forgave me for forcing him to spend the night in Lock Haven, but under the circumstances I could not conscientiously have ordered him to do otherwise."

It was a somewhat deflated Miller who arrived at Belmont the following morning just before noon. To date, neither he nor Gardner had managed to make the crossing in one day.

Turk was next out of the chute, the success or failure of the Pathfinder experiment resting squarely on his shoulders.

The weather was anything but accommodating, however. Miller might had landed to sunny skies in Long Island, but in Chicago, Gardner and Radel were facing pretty grim prospects. The two Eddies were out on the field, rain pouring down around them, when Lipsner arrived at dawn. They were in favor of postponing the trip until tomorrow, but Lipsner would have none of it. The newspapers had already informed their metropolitan readers to expect a swift ten-hour return Pathfinder flight.

He took Gardner aside.

"I'd like to have you try to land that mail in New York tonight if it is humanly possible. Miller had a bad break because of the radiator. He didn't get there yesterday and it's up to you."

By now, Lipsner knew exactly what buttons to push with Gardner. He continued pressing.

"Here's your chance to hang up a record. Do you go or not?"

Turk was incredulous. Lipsner was usually so cautious. He wouldn't even let Miller attempt to finish the run at dusk despite his pleas. Gardner was his favorite, the man he purported to be the best, and yet he was willing to throw him into the storm overhead and see what happened?

Lipsner baited Gardner.

"What's the matter with you? Are you getting cold feet? I though you were my flying ace. You know our slogan as well as I do—the airmail goes out on time, rain, hail or shine. You knew that when you joined the service."

The strategy worked. The protective tarp was pulled back from the plane, and Gardner and Radel climbed into their respective hellholes, each silently dreading what lay ahead.

"Rain and cloud were so thick that I would lose sight of the ground at 400 feet of altitude," Gardner's log read. "Headed across lower Lake Michigan directly for Gary, Indiana, with a head wind of 22 miles an hour. From there I flew a compass course of 104 degrees, which landed me at Bryan, Ohio, at 8:45. Took on 38 gallons of gas and nine quarts oil. Left Bryan at 9:20. Still raining, heavy haze and fog. Climbed to an altitude of 7,800 feet and flew a direct compass course of 92. After flying for an hour and 30 minutes in sunshine above the storm, I came down to get my bearings and was on the shore of Lake Erie, directly on my course. Landed at Cleveland at 11:16. Had lunch, took on gas and oil. Was delayed one hour and 54 minutes getting filled up with gas. Left Cleveland at 1:12, clouds breaking and clear weather ahead."

The delay had been the result of a careless mechanic who had left the field with the keys to the fuel tanks stashed inside his pocket. They had lost nearly two hours by the time he was found. But Gardner was nothing if not a thoroughbred. Despite the setbacks, the lousy weather, he appeared at the top of his game, flying on course, engine humming. His biggest challenge now—time. By all estimates, it was a three-hour air trip to Lock Haven, then another three hours to New York. Any further delay would force them over the Alleghenies in darkness. If that happened, the flight would likely be canceled and another failure recorded.

Gardner arrived in Lock Haven around 5 P.M. Eastern time. Mailbags were exchanged, the plane fueled and loaded and just one hour later, he and Radel were back on a heading of 104 degrees, nothing but a sun-drenched laurel wreath crowning their glorious heads.

For the next two hours, a resolute Gardner drove his plane through the gathering darkness. But night slipped its cover fully upon them by the time they reached Jersey City.

"I crossed from New Jersey, high above the Statue of Liberty," said Gardner. "The metropolis was wonderful. Lights everywhere. Manhattan, the Bronx, Brooklyn, and to the back of us, Staten Island, Queens and far out on Long Island—lights, lights, lights."

Turk continued pushing his way through the diamond-studded darkness. Just twenty more minutes and they were home free. But it would turn out to be the most harrowing twenty minutes of their lives. The fuel nearly exhausted, Gardner crossed over Manhattan searching for the landing flares to guide him into Belmont's racetrack.

But, set against the glittering backdrop, "It was like trying to pick a couple stars out of the Milky Way. I was baffled by the lights. They all looked alike.

"I tried to find the flying field at Mineola, but that was just as difficult as finding Belmont Park. I realized that I had to set her down some place and do it soon. The streaming flash of the exhaust was blinding. And try as he might, it was impossible for Radel to communicate any helpful information to me. We were really in a predicament."

With the engine about to quit from fuel starvation, there was nothing for the pilot to do but land. Pushing the stick forward, Gardner headed down.

"My ears were numb from the noise," he said. "My eyes were burned out from the flashing exhaust."

At the last moment, Gardner spotted a dark patch in the midst of the glittering panorama of lights and headed toward it. Just because the spot was free of lights, which meant there were no buildings, didn't mean it told the whole story. It could just as easily be a rock quarry or a lake or an orchard of trees.

"I was certain this was the finish," Gardner said. "On the way down I had sort of expected to get it, but I didn't care so much for myself as I did for Radel. He was strapped in there helpless, depending on me and I had failed him."

Gardner misjudged his elevation in the dark, and instead of gliding gently to the ground, the Curtiss R4 smacked flat, snapping off the landing gear and going into a tumble. The sound of metal grinding and wood splintering filled the air. Then, seconds later, only silence. Gardner came to in a daze, convinced he was dead.

And yet a voice was calling vaguely in the distance. It sounded oddly familiar. Gardner briefly lost consciousness, only to be awakened moments later by . . .

"Take that engine off me!"

It was Radel, pinned under the airplane. Gardner, with blood streaming down his forehead and face, crawled over to where his mechanic Radel lay trapped beneath the wreckage. By now, a crowd had formed around them, drawn by all the commotion. Quickly, Gardner and Radel were rushed to Nassau Hospital near Mineola to tend to their injuries. Radel's back had been burned from spilled gasoline and Gardner had suffered another broken nose, the second one in just weeks. They were just minor injuries compared to what could have been.

In keeping with policy, the manager of the Belmont airfield was duly alerted to the accident and ordered to retrieve the mail. For their part, Gardner and Radel may not have reached Belmont, Long Island, but the letters in their cargo hold had gone down just ten miles shy of destination. For Praeger, that was good enough.

Not long after, Turk found a telegram awaiting him from the chief.

"You made a great flight. Hope you and Radel will have speedy recovery from your injuries. PRAEGER, Second Assistant."

CHAPTER 10

BELLEFONTE

With the Pathfinder flights proving that the 700 air miles between New York and Chicago could be breached in a single daylight period, all that remained was to gear up for regular operations on the new route. Stringing a series of air routes halfway across the country was as challenging in many respects, however, as any large-scale military assault.

While the intermediary stops at Cleveland and Bryan worked well because they were situated on perfectly flat land, Miller wasn't so sure about Lock Haven because of its location within the Allegheny Mountain range. He wanted to check out a nearby town called Bellefonte before making his recommendation.

Lock Haven was still the odds-on favorite to be picked, though—or so proclaimed its postmaster, Paul Brosius, who put his reputation on the line guaranteeing to everyone who traipsed through his building that Uncle Sam would be plucking their little town from obscurity and dropping it smack dab into the twentieth century. Given Lock Haven's thousand-plus population, its thriving lumber industry, and its enviable location between the west branch of the Susquehanna River and Bald Eagle Creek, he might well be right in his assumption.

But Bellefonte wasn't out of the running just yet. Two thousand people lived there, twice as many as ever called Lock Haven home. Peacefully overlooking the banks of Spring Creek, Bellefonte was known as the state's "home of governors." Five Pennsylvania governors, a California governor, and a Kansas governor lived in the community between 1850 and 1890, all drawn by its undulating hilltop streets, graceful Victorian architecture, and friendly storefronts all framing a rural picture-postcard setting.

A couple decades earlier in 1895, Bellefonte had shown its mettle by beating the nearby town of Milesburg in an economic battle for the designation of "county seat," and all that went along with it: construction of government buildings, more businesses, and new residents bringing growth and prosperity. Milesburg seemed the obvious choice at first glance. Strategically located on the headwaters of Bald Eagle Creek, it was a key transportation hub for small vessels working their way in and out of the rolling mountains. But Bellefonte had its own waterway—Spring Creek, a 20-yard-wide waterway on which the town depended. Its rushing waters drove the mills that turned out tens of thousands of wooden "single dip, strike anywhere" and "parlor" matches, plus wooden skewers for the Swift meatpacking plant in Chicago. Bellefonte would prove that Spring Creek reached even deeper into the mountains than Milesburg's Bald Eagle Creek.

Townspeople piled a flatboat with furniture to simulate a small, fully loaded cargo vessel. Then, harnessing a team of mules, they pulled it way upriver, far beyond Bald Eagle's farthest reach. A courier then dashed off to Lancaster with the news that Bellefonte sat on the true headwaters of the region, sealing its victory as the capital of the newly named Centre County, assuring Bellefonte's place in local history as a little town with big ambition.

Bellefonte's collective tenacity would once more be called into play. Aviation had changed the equation. No longer could local boosters parlay their waterway into a trump card. The plane needed no such waterways, it stopped for no mountain. New strategies would be required if Bellefonte was to become one of the links in the Woodrow Wilson Airway.

It would be the battle of Nittany Mountain to determine which town would rise above its central Pennsylvania roots, its Grange

Fair, and its dairy farmers to assume its place on the national stage. Bellefonte knew it already had one edge. Unlike so many other towns nestled in the mountains, where locals struggled under a constant barrage of winds swirling down from the hills, Bellefonte's coordinates were such that breezes were often slight and predictable.

Still, Lock Haven had something Bellefonte lacked—the inside track. The town had already shined during the Pathfinder mission in early September when Miller first visited.

Virtually every person in the county got up early one morning to watch the plane land at the local golf course. Cheers swept through the crowd as it was spotted far off in the distance. Miller was tracing the path of the Susquehanna River, threading his way upriver. It took five minutes from the time the plane was first spotted until it landed on the hills west of the Clinton Country Club.

But what an exciting five minutes it was. Postmaster Brosius could barely contain his excitement. Miller was carrying the first bag of aero mail ever destined for the small town. In return, the postmaster had stuffed a mailbag himself, and it was maybe the most memorable moment in the history of Lock Haven when the pilot and the postmaster shook hands and exchanged sacks.

Miller was piloting his Standard, and it had flown okay except that the engine was running rough, forcing him to stop once along the way to check it out. Fuel and oil for the plane had been shipped to Lock Haven a few days earlier, and it was used to quench the plane's thirst.

Just one hour after landing Miller was again airborne, gingerly nudging the throttle open, listening for signs of engine trouble. He flew a big circle around the country club, then, apparently satisfied with the timbre of his engine, drove the Standard across the sky, disappearing beyond the mountains.

"He took a long glide and flew almost due west, passing over Snow Shoe twenty minutes later," reported the local paper. "He was in plain sight of the people of that town. In crossing the Alleghenies it sailed low over the Charles Reese farm above Gum Stump and was reported from there as traveling very little above the line of tree tops."

*   *   *

Now, a couple weeks after pathfinding his way to Chicago with Gardner, the friendly aviator was back in Centre County. This time he would be making his first stop at Bellefonte. Or at least that was the rumor. Party lines were abuzz over a postal department request to set aside reserves of fuel and oil. That could only mean one thing—an airplane was coming to town.

Half the town trekked to Tom Beaver's farm on September 19 expecting to catch sight of an approaching mail ship, but the Standard was a no-show that day and the next. Still, the industrious townsfolk remained hopeful and went about their business, one eye on the sky.

Their patience was rewarded a week later, on the twenty-sixth, when word was telephoned over from a nearby town: A plane is coming your way!

Everyone dropped what they were doing and raced for the Beaver farm to see the gray JR-1B circling overhead like a hawk riding the thermals. Now and then, Miller's head would pop over the side of his ship, searching for a safe place to land. The people at the farm were jumping up and down and waving their arms.

Land here! Land here!

Miller pointed his craft at the beckoning people, and moments later he and his "mechanician" Henry Wacker were safely on the ground shaking hands and answering questions.

The people had a hundred queries for the "birdmen," as the local press called them, though Miller wasn't in a position to offer many answers.

No, I can't say exactly why I'm here, Miller said cryptically. Orders from Washington, you know.

What do you think Bellefonte's chances are of being picked as an airmail stop?

Can't say just yet, Miller responded, but Beaver Farm shows a lot of promise as a landing field.

It didn't take an experienced aviator long to figure out why. Mother Nature had clearly been kind to Bellefonte over the years, blessing it with the fast-running Spring Creek and good terrain. Situated a few hundred feet higher in the mountains than its competitor, Beaver Farm and the surrounding land drained well, keeping it high and dry through all four seasons. And it didn't hurt that Tom Beaver was the son of Civil War general and former Pennsylvania governor James Addams Beaver.

That was enough to sink any chance Lock Haven had of being chosen. Less than three weeks after Miller's visit, Ben Lipsner took the flier's advice and named Bellefonte the main refueling and transfer station east of the Alleghenies.

Not long after, Bellefonte was paid a visit by Praeger's main assistant and special representative, George Conner. He was carrying a message everyone yearned to hear.

Yes, the Beaver farm would make a perfect spot for an airfield, Conner said. And yes, the people of Bellefonte certainly were enthusiastic. All in all, the town had earned the honor and privilege of hosting Uncle Sam's Air Mail.

Except for one little thing.

Just like an army runs on its stomach, Praeger's Air Mail Service ran on money. Appropriations, hard fought for in the congressional trenches, were never enough. As a result, every dollar mattered. It was well and good that Bellefonte wanted to be part of the future, but a simple heartfelt desire wasn't enough. Bellefonte would need to pony up.

Conner sharpened his pencil. Would the town fathers mind "contributing" $1,600 toward the construction of a hangar large enough to hold three Jennies, one of which would be kept there at all times for emergencies, plus a secure shed to store oil and gasoline?

Conner didn't have to ask twice. Owners of the Bush House and the Brockerhoff Hotel would soon be home away from home for the mail pilots flying in and out every day. There would be hearty meals of freshly killed game to be dined upon, bread and wine to be served in the large first-floor restaurants of the hotels, followed by an evening smoke and a walk along Spring Creek.

Documents were signed and preparations begun in order that Tom Beaver's farm might receive its first mail flight—scheduled for mid-December.

*   *   *

While Conner was making arrangements in Bellefonte, another Praeger emissary, Col. John Jordan, was working the airfield logistics in the towns west of Bellefonte. There was hardly enough money available for everything that needed to be built, so Jordan, like Conner, was instructed to coax funds from the towns and cities where aerodromes were slated to be built.

Jordan was spending many an evening dining with city fathers, wealthy businessmen, and executives from the local chambers of commerce trying to convince them to put up the necessary money.

"Bear hard on the great advertising the city will get from its selection as one of the first aero mail routes, and on the tremendous demand for faster mail service by bankers and business men," Lipsner counseled.

He also urged him to befriend "enthusiastic women of wealth; they are everywhere and have in many cities the very fields we want and as a rule are more quickly dealt with, if of the right caliber, than men."

The advice was good. In Cleveland, city fathers donated enough land for an airfield and collected $10,000 for its construction. The City of Chicago came up with even more, $14,000, for development of airmail facilities there.

CHAPTER 11

STINSON

A young woman breezed into Lipsner's office while he had been preparing for the Pathfinder flights.

"I would like to fly the mail," she said, her small voice softening the masculine directness of her approach.

Lipsner was stupefied.

"From where I sat behind my desk, she appeared to be little more than a schoolgirl with long black curls. It took me several moments to gather enough of my wits about me to inquire who she was."

The young slip of a girl sitting before him was the female aviatrix Katherine Stinson, better known to the press as America's Sweetheart of the Air and The Flying Schoolgirl. Famous as much for her pretty face and Mary Pickford curls as for her bold aerial stunts, Stinson had carved out a reputation for herself as a brave, daring, and altogether darling aviator. She certainly had the credentials for the job.

She'd been the first woman to loop the loop, the first female to fly in the Orient, and the first *civilian* to fly the mail in Canada, hauling letters a distance of 196 miles from Calgary to Edmonton.

In 1917, she established an endurance record of nine hours and ten minutes on a 500-mile nonstop flight from San Diego to San

Francisco. She was cheered by thousands of soldiers as her plane landed at the Presidio. Surrounded by the virile men of the U.S. Army, a reporter wanted to know what thoughts occupied her mind during those long stretches alone in the cockpit. The elfin brown-eyed creature, ever aware of her femininity, flashed an impish grin, then replied in her soft voice: "Of course, the record I was trying to break. But once in a while, spring fashions."

Stinson had even flown the mail for Otto Praeger, just a couple of months earlier. Always looking for publicity, the second assistant agreed to let her fly a handful of letters from Chicago to New York. Stinson, looking for a new endurance record, said she would fly the run *nonstop*.

She arrived at Chicago's Grant Field in the silence of the morning on May 23, 1918. Just a little sprig of a thing dressed in woolens and leather for the arduous journey, she didn't require much sustenance to keep her going. Her rations for this trip were just three handfuls of malted milk balls dropped into her pockets.

"One handful is my breakfast, one is my luncheon and the third is my dinner," she said, smiling for photographers.

The postal department was up to its neck in chaos, having barely managed to survive its inaugural week experience, so Stinson would have to make the passage between cities with little encouragement from anyone in Washington.

Several Army captains were on hand, as was Chicago postmaster William Carlile, who swore her in as an official "Aeroplane Mail Carrier," then watched as she taxied to the end of the field and headed east for New York.

She had chosen a more northerly course to New York, wisely bypassing the Alleghenies. It wasn't the fastest air route between the two cities, but she wouldn't have to come down in a tree-covered mountain in case of an emergency. With a confidence far beyond her years, Stinson wove her way across the sky. If all went well, she'd see the Atlantic Ocean in less than twelve hours. The time passed slowly as she took in the scenery, but the weather was good as the rains of late had finally abated.

Stinson's mind wasn't trouble free, however. Strong headwinds were costing her precious fuel. At this rate, she'd run out of gas before reaching her destination.

Sure enough, over Binghamton, New York, just two hours shy of Long Island, the sputtering sounds of a gas-starved engine forced her down from the sky. Pushing the stick forward, she aimed toward a wide hilltop, secure in the belief that it was drier than the surrounding land because of its elevation. The week of rain had soaked everything through, however, and her landing gear dug deeply into the muddy soil, flipping the plane over onto its nose and damaging the propeller. Dozens of people raced to the landing site to help and found Stinson unhurt.

Though she hadn't reached Long Island, she'd managed to fly 601 nonstop miles from Chicago to this damnable muddy cow pasture. She had earned a distance record, as well as an endurance record of ten hours and ten minutes.

"You may tell the mothers of any young man in the flying service for me that there is no necessity for them to worry about their boys," she told the local reporters. "My flight today proves that long distances may be covered with little danger."

But Stinson was not satisfied with just the records. She had promised to bring her handful of letters into Long Island and fly them there she would. By the next day the prop was fixed and she was ready to go. But, like before, her wheels wouldn't roll on the muddy terrain and the craft once again nosed over into the dirt. Everyone rushed over to see Stinson dangling upside down from her harness.

Undaunted, the diminutive aviatrix waited several days for the ground to dry, then tried again. This time she took off, and, finally, two hours later, she landed in Long Island, having added another feather in her cap.

Even with her accomplishments, Lipsner still wasn't interested in hiring her on as a full-time mail pilot. Stinson might be a master of the loop the loop, but flying Uncle Sam's mail was grinding slug-it-out work, serious business for serious people. The pilots routinely flew in bad weather, sometimes at altitudes so high that their hands froze to the stick. Other times they'd go ducking below the cloud deck at ground-hugging altitudes, the wings of their planes whistling through the treetops. In bad headwinds, fliers struggled to hold themselves erect in their open cockpits. This little hiccup of a girl sitting before him must have hardly seemed qualified for such arduous work. What about that time of the month? How could she possibly fly then?

Lipsner could hardly be faulted for his lack of regard. At the time, a car was considered far too sophisticated a piece of machinery for the gentler sex to master—much less a technological advancement as powerful as the aeroplane. Orville Wright refused to teach women to fly, considering them far too emotional to get themselves out of a jam. Matters of science confounded ladies. Business and politics made their pretty heads a muddle. But, then, men were reasoning creatures, women were not.

With gentlemanly politeness, the superintendent took Stinson's application, assuring the young lady her name would be kept on file.

But Katherine needed work desperately. Ever since President Wilson had banned all civilian flying there was no way to earn a living. She had appealed to the joint Army/Navy board in charge of aviation several times, seeking an exception. Senator Morris Sheppard had even written the secretary of war on her behalf. But Newton Baker was unequivocal in his reply.

"The Army and Navy authorities consider that these activities are harmful rather than beneficial and have accordingly adopted the policy of confining flying in privately owned aircraft to the requirements of the Army and Navy."

The nation's entire private airplane business had been effectively shut down. Even the Stinson flying school in San Antonio had been forced to close its doors. As far as the government was considered, civilian flying was nonessential—save Burleson's airmail service.

Hoping to find some way to keep herself aloft, Stinson had tried serving her country by volunteering to fly for the Army. Baker had rejected her offer flat. Until the war ended, the only way Stinson could stay airborne was to either raise money for the American Red Cross, which she had already done, or fly the mail for the U.S. Post Office Department, which had just turned her down.

But the U.S. Post Office Department would not easily be rid of Katherine Stinson. She had come knocking on Lipsner's door full of high ambition, and she was not about to subordinate her goals because of the small matter of her sex. Diminutive though she might appear, beneath that gamine version of femininity lay a steely resolve. Exhibiting the same pluck and determination that had earned her so many aerial accomplishments, she did an end run on Lipsner and marched upstairs, personally appealing to the postmaster general.

Burleson was only too glad to see her. He remembered her recent Chicago–New York flight, as well as an earlier airmail flight in 1913 at the State Fair in Helena, Montana. The department had authorized many such exhibitions back then, few lasting any more than a dozen miles. Aviators across the country had been eager to become U.S. letter carriers, if only temporarily. For them, the ordainment was legitimizing; for Uncle Sam, it represented pure publicity for a service that had yet to find funding in Congress.

The stern, white-haired politician sat listening as Stinson argued her case. It must have been clear to Burleson that seated before him was a self-motivated individual who was no mere romantic. She possessed enough business savvy to generate a solid income from her work and put it to use helping finance her family's flying school. Like the postmaster general, she was a person who made things happen, a woman who forged opportunities out of cracks too narrow for most people to even see.

He was prepared to give Stinson a chance, despite the fact that he was no suffragist. But then neither was his president. When it came to giving women the right to vote in 1918, the Wilson administration remained as silent as the movies coming out of Hollywood. The president put it best when envisioning a future America, its tapestry of regions, culture, and ideologies one day weaving themselves into a single nation-state.

One day, Wilson predicted, America would "be of one mind, our ideals fixed, our purposes harmonized, our nationality complete and consentaneous; then will come our great literature and our greatest men."

No mention was made of women. Though women had been

fighting since 1848 to obtain the same rights as men, equality remained an altruistic ideal not yet shared by members of the male sex who assumed that granting women the right to vote would be an act tantamount to opening Pandora's box. When it came to suffrage, the progressive Wilson hesitated, claiming the states were better suited to dealing with the issue than the federal government.

The war was changing things, though, putting more women into the swell of jobs left vacant by men going overseas. Armed with a new sense of independence, American women were taking a hesitant step out of the home and climbing into the skies. Stinson wasn't the only female flier. In 1911, the gorgeous and flamboyant New York journalist Harriet Quimby became the country's first woman to earn her pilot's license, having decided that exhibition flying was loads more fun than writing for the popular women's magazine *Leslie's Illustrated Weekly*. Quimby had caught the flying bug in 1910 during an aviation exposition at August Belmont's racetrack. Just two years later, on April 16, 1912, she made history by being the first American—and the first woman—to fly the English Channel. She had the misfortune, though, of making the historic crossing the day after the world received word that the RMS *Titanic* had sunk. Her story disappeared from the newspapers almost as quickly as the ship settled to the bottom.

Still, Burleson was able to gaze beyond the mirror of the times and see something in the elfin dark-haired creature sitting before him. It wasn't just the marked intelligence, the genuine sweetness, or the drive and perseverance. Stinson had something else going for her. Though born in Mississippi, she had lived in the Lone Star State long enough to call it home, and, to the silver-haired Texan, that was good enough.

Word came down from the postmaster general's office.

Hire Stinson.

Lipsner was steamed. From the start, the captain had chafed at the way patronage undermined operations. It was his responsibility to keep things running efficiently and here he was saddled with someone not of his own choosing. And a female, no less.

"The Katherine Stinson incident had been the first time I had felt any serious outside interference in the running of the airmail service," he said.

Despite his objections, Stinson became the newest member of Uncle Sam's Suicide Club, her appointment becoming official on September 26, 1918. At a time when a woman's name was meant to appear in print only three times—upon her birth, upon her marriage, and upon her death—a front-page newspaper photograph showing Stinson standing by her biplane dressed in knickerbockers, curls tucked up inside a familiar blue-checkered cap, preparing to blast off into the skies as a bona fide aerial postman, was cause for horror in some circles. Stinson couldn't care less. The new job would have her back on the high plains.

Okay, said Lipsner, but if she was to be a member of the team, she would play by its rules. There would be no special exceptions for her.

When Stinson began to complain about the Jennies and Standards flown by the Air Mail, as opposed to the Wright airplanes she was used to flying, Lipsner hit the roof. Barely 5 feet tall and not weighing 100 pounds dripping wet, she explained how her petite size forced her to fly the double-stick Wright controls, which didn't have to be manhandled like the single stick and rudder pedal system employed by most of the planes of the day.

Lipsner didn't care. The stick and rudder were standard on all the Uncle's ships. There would be no special dispensation made just for her.

Once again, Stinson marched upstairs to plead her case before Burleson.

Who could begrudge the request of such a darling aviatrix who was forever assuring reporters that flying was as easy as applying lipstick? But she wasn't just a pretty face; she had earned her credentials feat by feat, her many flying records attesting to her skill, stamina, and determination.

By day's end a new directive had crossed Lipsner's desk. Stinson was to be accorded any type of equipment she wanted, regardless of the cost.

The incident rubbed Lipsner like a burr under his skin. He was the superintendent of aero mail. He felt he should be given a free hand to run things as he saw fit, not have his authority undermined by edicts from above. Not one, but two of his directives had been overruled. Left with no recourse but to follow the order, he ordered his mechanics to modify one of the mail planes with double-stick controls.

Her first airmail flight was scheduled for late September. She would fly the Washington–Philadelphia run. Her modified machine prepped, and with veteran pilot Maurice Newton leading the way, Stinson headed off to work.

It was common for first-timers to follow behind a more experienced mail pilot. An aviator had to learn every nuance of the land when flying point to point. In time, the small towns dotting the fields below would become as familiar as the pilot's own skin. She would come to recognize every church steeple, every schoolyard, and every cow barn along the way. She would know by name the friendliest farmers, learn which of their wives offered up the tastiest jam and homemade pies. These would be the points of her compass.

As Stinson slipped across the expanse of air, all was in balance. At last, the pint-size aviator was back where she most wanted to be, looking down on the world. She flew a textbook run, parking her ship on the airfield at Bustleton. She climbed out of her plane a full-fledged aero mail courier, adding yet another first to her already long list of flying accomplishments. Tomorrow, she and Newton would retrace their steps, making the passage in the opposite direction. This time Katherine would be flying lead, as was customary practice: the new hire following on the way out and leading on the way back.

Reporters had gotten wind of Stinson's new gig, however, and wrongly assumed her maiden flights were another competition. The recent Pathfinder race between Miller and Gardner had already shown that rivalry was a part of flying's espirit de corps. Friendly contests were accepted, promoted even. It helped the men keep climbing into their machines when common sense told them to walk away. It was only natural for the press to assume that this latest mail run was yet another contest—a battle of the sexes.

The next day, on the return run to College Park, with Stinson landing ahead of Newton as prescribed, a battle had been staged and won—in the opinion of the press. Banner headlines proclaimed the aviatrix victorious. Stinson must have been horrified. She, too, was a person of great personal pride. As much as she enjoyed accolades, she'd been given an honor she neither deserved nor wanted. Knowing as she did how Newton and the others would be insulted over the incident, knowing that those headlines would quash any hopes of meeting the men on equal footing, she began to rethink the whole equation. After all, pilots were nothing if not men of honor.

Newton, for example, the man whom she had supposedly trounced, was tangible proof of that fact. Just the day before his flight with Stinson, while hauling the mail between New York and Philadelphia, his engine had taken its final breath, then choked into silence. Stranded several hundred feet above Long Island, he was forced to search for somewhere to land. Seeing a wide open space below he glided her on in. But the wheels barely touched down before his ship went slamming into the lip of an underground cellar protruding slightly above the ground. The force of the impact sent his plane boring into the soil, hurling the bifocaled aviator straight into the instrument panel. Climbing out of the plane, his glasses shattered, nose broken, Newton had his wounds tended by a local doctor. Then dutifully filling out his accident report, he climbed into the cockpit the next day, business as usual.

Stinson's next day would not find her nearly so brave. Thoroughly humiliated by the press coverage, she turned in her badge and walked away from the job, never looking back.

Instead, she would go overseas, to France. Red Cross volunteers were badly needed. If she couldn't fly, then at least she could drive an ambulance for the sick and wounded.

Between mechanized warfare and a new strain of influenza spreading around the world, causalities were reaching epidemic proportions both on and off the front. The flu attack had come at a time when modern medicine was just beginning to triumph over diseases that had long been a scourge of humanity. But this epidemic was baffling even the brightest medical minds. By fall, nearly two hundred thousand Americans had lost their lives to the virus. Congress had pushed through $1 million to help underwrite a quick solution, but things were going from bad to worse. Suspicions flared across the country. It was those Germans again. One of their submarines had sneaked along the East Coast and released a plague of germs in the dark of night.

The nation's top doctors were at a loss. People were being urged to take precautions, wash their hands, avoid contact with anyone coughing or sneezing. But the virus was pandemic, particularly on military bases where soldiers fought, slept, ate, and drank shoulder to shoulder with one another.

"This epidemic started about four weeks ago, and has developed so rapidly that the camp is demoralized," remarked one Army doctor. "These men start with what appears to be an attack of la grippe or influenza, and when brought to the hospital they very rapidly develop the most viscous type of pneumonia that has ever been seen. Two hours after admission they have the mahogany spots over the cheek bones, and a few hours later you can begin to see the cyanosis extending from their ears and spreading all over the face, until it is hard to distinguish the colored men from the white. It is only a matter of a few hours then until death comes, and it is simply a struggle for air until they suffocate. It is horrible. One can stand it to see one, two or twenty men die, but to see these poor devils dropping like flies sort of gets on your nerves. We have been averaging about 100 deaths per day, and still keeping it up."

By the time the epidemic petered out in 1919, it had killed six hundred thousand people in America alone and twenty-five million around the globe, creating the greatest loss of life since the Black Death in the fourteenth century.

CHAPTER 12

THE STAR

Pilot Dana Chase DeHart had been flying the New York–Washington route the way Praeger and Lipsner liked it—clean. So far, for the months of September and October, he'd earned himself the best performance stats of anybody in the service.

Tall, with a long face that took on a horsey look when framed by a leather flight helmet, the thirty-two-year-old pilot nicknamed "Daddy" hadn't a clue when he showed up for work at College Park one morning what his stellar flying record had earned him.

A swarm of photographers and reporters were popping around the place like kernels in hot oil. Making his way through the crowd, he walked into the hangar to find a telegram waiting there, his name on it. It was from the chief.

"Aviator Dana C. DeHart: you are authorized to carry Mr. Douglas Fairbanks on your regular mail flight, Washington to New York."

The dashing Fairbanks was one of Hollywood's most promising movie stars and had already performed in more than twenty flicks, earning him a top salary $10,000 a week. He was also one of Tinseltown's most active supporters of our soldiers in Europe, actively giving his time to three prior Liberty Bond drives.

The war had everybody pitching in. Katherine Stinson had recently done her part, flying 670 miles through the foulest weather imaginable in order to solicit donations for the American Red Cross. Money was badly needed. The boys on the front needed food and clothes in order to continue the fight. A powerful new campaign had hit the streets, one that personified the federal government into the living visage of "Uncle Sam." The stern, white-bearded taskmaster, dressed in top hat and a Victorian waistcoat cut from the cloth of the American flag, was pointing a stern finger into the conscience of every citizen, informing them that Uncle Sam wanted them—now!

Whether it was enlisting, donating funds, or just plain conserving food and fuel, everyone was expected to join in the fight. Staples like sugar, meat, and butter were at a premium, and every scrap of wheat flour had to be saved to help fill empty stomachs overseas. Housewives were taught how to plant victory gardens. Sacrifice was the price every American was being asked to pay for what really mattered, beating the Germans.

It was patriotism that now had Douglas Fairbanks standing in Lipsner's office. He wanted to so something audacious for the latest bond drive, something that would really attract the press. He had an idea, but to pull off this action-packed feature attraction he would first need a special supporting cast.

Fairbanks was about to fly himself "airmail." He felt confident he could raise a cool million in bond sales if the postal department would be willing to supply a plane and a pilot capable of transporting him from Washington to New York in one piece. The studio publicity machine would do the rest. The result would be a certified media frenzy, as the actor was on the cusp of stardom with three new movies about to take the country by storm: *The Mark of Zorro*, *The Three Musketeers*, and *Robin Hood*.

The superintendent had by now fully grasped the value of publicity and, assured that Fairbanks's little skit wouldn't cost the Air Mail Service a dime, agreed that the postal department would participate in the stunt.

With that cue, a Liberty Bond salesman escorting Fairbanks picked up Lipsner's phone and called Pliny Fisk of the venerable brokerage house of Harvey Fisk & Sons of New York City. Fisk agreed to "purchase" Fairbanks, provided he could be delivered to his doorstep within five hours. Convinced the actor would never make it within the allotted time, the Wall Street banker and philanthropist even discussed the possibility of purchasing a million dollars' worth of Liberty Bonds, in keeping with the spirit of the performance.

Unbeknownst to Fisk, this particular script had subtext.

"At the other end of the line, of course, they didn't realize that we were planning on transporting the movie actor by airmail," said Lipsner.

Hanging up the phone, Fairbanks and his fellow cast members dashed off to begin rolling on a scene that played straight out of Hollywood.

Waiting dutifully at the airfield was Dana DeHart. Born in Los Angeles, he was one of California's first registered pilots, holding Aero Club of California license number nine. As a civilian instructor for the Army in 1917, his flight log recorded no breakages and no time lost, a reputation he maintained after joining the civilian Air Mail service. Given his safety record, it was no wonder that the stalwart aviator had been selected to play Fairbanks's aerial chauffeur. This was not a scouting mission requiring Max Miller's homing instincts. And certainly, the last thing HQ wanted was Eddie Gardner pretending he was a Hollywood stunt man. Sure and steady was what the director called for today.

Fairbanks arrived just before DeHart's scheduled departure time at noon, with the actor's car speeding across the field and pulling up to the hangar. Out sprang Fairbanks, dressed fully in character. The leading man whose dash, verve, and sheer hipness would help define the Jazz Age sprang from the car wearing a handsome leather aviator's coat. The image was tailor-made for Fairbanks.

The press immediately closed in, spurring the inveterate performer into action. Flashing a pirate's smile, he mugged for the cameras, joked with reporters, and answered their questions with a well-turned phrase and a retinue of physical gags. Then, with a devil-may-care athleticism, he scrambled onto the plane's engine housing. Standing astride the wooden propeller, he stood as if he were a pirate on the prow of a great fighting ship, sword held high.

The reporters ate it up. Still, not content, Fairbanks hoisted his leg fully waist high, and then, and with arms outstretched, proceeded to balance himself on one foot, proving to one and all the only unbalanced thing about him was his behavior.

Publicity like this Fairbanks couldn't buy. For all intents and purposes he was an aviator, and the scene playing in his head could have been written like this:

```
FADE IN


SCENE 1
INT. AIRFIELD HANGAR, DAWN

A curtain of hurting winds is stretching
over Belmont, its fury hammering against the
corrugated metal sides of the airplane hangar.
Inside, mail pilot Douglas Fairbanks sits
waiting for his turn to haul the mail. His
experience and judgment tell him not to do it.
This wasn't some localized weather pattern he
could climb through in a few minutes. To an
unlucky flier, this kind of storm could spell
the kiss of death.
     Shrugging off the thought, Fairbanks
reaches for his flight suit. Made of thick
cowhide, the suit is critical to a mail
pilot's ensemble. It must appear worn,
with just the right number of creases to
distinguish the veteran airman from the new
rookie on the block. By now, his leather
flying suit had become a second skin to
him, its soft, supple leather draping over
his limbs in thick, rich folds, making him
feel protected somehow--invincible. Dropping
himself down onto the bench, he pulls off
his street shoes and proceeds to slip on his
socks, pair by pair, until his feet have grown
three times their normal size. Not for him the
torture of having his frozen limbs pried loose
from the cockpit upon arrival.
     Fairbanks stands up, gives his feet a
stomp, then proceeds the laborious process of
fastening the double row of buttons extending
down the length of his flight suit. One by
one, his fingers work past the silver badge
marked "U.S. Aerial Mail Service" pinned to
```

```
his lapel. Then, pulling his fleece-lined
flight cap down over his head, Fairbanks grabs
his goggles off the shelf and turns to go. It's
his name on the flight board. Those mail sacks
are his responsibility to fly on through. His
hand reaches for the door when he notices
the watch on his wrist has stopped ticking.
Instinctively, he gives his arm a shake. The
first line of defense of any mail pilot is
always to shake, rattle, or roll whatever
machinery has conked out on you, be it a
cockpit instrument, engine, or watch. If that
didn't work you switched to Plan B and prayed.

FADE to BLACK.
```

Naturally, Fairbanks would have scripted his way through the storm with daring and aplomb, getting the girl at the end. After all, if a guy like Gardner, with his slouched shoulders and receding hairline, could become the object of attention all suited up, it was safe to assume that a handsome Hollywood actor poised for stardom could snag a beautiful leading lady dressed in his leathers.

Amid Fairbanks's performance, DeHart was quietly walking around the plane, inspecting its undercarriage, giving it the preflight once-over, as per Uncle Sam's flying rules for aviators. Besides, inspecting one's ship made sense. Every good pilot knew maintenance was a good way to ward off trouble en route.

At last, everything seemed a go. Springing onto the wing, Fairbanks hopped into the cargo hold atop the sacks of mail, an airmail stamp duly licked and affixed to his forehead. In a whir of black exhaust, the pair took off, leaving behind a trail of inky plumes and a group of amused reporters with stories to write up for a readership that couldn't get enough of the exploits of the mail pilots—these were the sideshows of life.

The flight was textbook. Right on schedule, DeHart set down at Bustleton. As quickly as possible, mail sacks were exchanged. Then, as the ground crew refueled the plane, Fairbanks emerged from his cramped cargo hold and ambled about the field, stretching his legs. The respite would be short as there were schedules to be maintained. Besides, the actor had a bet to claim. Preparations finished, on went the goggles, then up into the sky they both climbed, the plane's wooden prop spinning them closer to New York.

Below the flow of wash, a final burst of fall color was punctuating the decline of yet another season. Occasionally, patches of snow dotted the landscape. A sudden, cold snap had given a kick to the air, turning the ride into a purely glacial experience. DeHart knew the actor in front of him had to be lethally frozen despite the heavy leather overcoat he was wearing. But the man never uttered a complaint throughout the entire three-hour flight. To do so would have been uncharacteristic of an aviator, and Fairbanks was nothing if not a man in tune with his character. A pirate did not complain about his life aboard the high seas any more than an aviator griped about the very air that gave him breath.

At long last, DeHart spotted the familiar oval of Belmont. Down below, a reception committee of newspapermen and well-wishers stood waiting, their ferment enough to warm the ice off anyone's bones. Fairbanks and DeHart were not only cold, but starving. The moment they landed, they dove into a stack of ham sandwiches prepared for them with all the gusto of two seamen new to port. There was no need to rush. Fairbanks still had plenty of time to get into Manhattan and claim his bet with Fisk.

His hunger satisfied at last, Fairbanks allowed himself to be hustled off to the city to deliver the final scene of his performance. A reporter from The *New York Times* went along to record the scene for posterity.

```
Setting
New York City
The office of Pliny Fisk
```

```
"Action, Mr. Fisk!" cried Mr. Fairbanks.
   "I could have gone to the office of
Rockefeller, Morgan, Carnegie or any of those
guys, but just because I like you and always
did, I give you an option of matching Barney
Baruch's million-buck subscription. Dig!"
   "But," said Mr. Fisk, "our firm and I
personally have subscribed for bonds 'til it
pinched and so I don't think . . ."
   "Pinch yourself again," cried Fairbanks.
```

> "I've taken my life in my hands all afternoon
> by flying here with a nut aviator named
> DeHart, whose chief diversion on the way
> over was to pick out cemeteries all through
> Maryland, Delaware, and Jersey and then make
> a beezer dive at the tallest and sharpest
> marble shaft in the graveyard.
>
> "And why did I do it? Because I knew you
> would subscribe for a million to match Barney
> Baruch."

It was a performance worthy of an Oscar, one that earned the actor the hefty donation he was seeking. Fairbanks would turn in other, similar performances that week, his whirlwind Liberty Bond tour raising more than $5 million for the war effort. But while Hollywood's romantic actor may have put airmail behind him, he hadn't forgotten the fine efforts of his supporting cast members.

For his stellar flying performance, "Daddy" DeHart earned big Daddy O's appreciation via a telegram forwarded from Praeger. On it, Fairbanks had written: "Handled with care—arrived right side up. Great trip."

For his part in things, Lipsner received the actor's handsome leather aviator coat, which was destined to sprout legs, as often as not finding its way into Eddie Gardner's locker.

CHAPTER 13

IT'S OVER

The superintendent was burdened with preparations for the launch of the New York–Chicago route in December, so a young woman named Daisy Marie Thomas was assigned to him to help with the work. Knowing little or nothing about aviation, but a good deal about stenographic work, she'd been transferred to Lipsner's office at College Park to handle all the typing and filing. Pert and pretty, Praeger had hired her some time ago to work in his department, her father being an old Texas school chum. Efficient and pleasant, and qualified with a ladies' "business school" degree, Daisy Marie had already proven her ability to withstand the pressure cooker of the inaugural day preparations having successfully cranked out Praeger's flurry of memos, letters, and press releases. She had been with the second assistant's office ever since, helping out Praeger and chief clerk Conner.

Daisy knew all about mail pilots, at least on paper. She could tell by the ink on their applications they were all adventurers, fun-loving, hard-drinking, and breezy like the winds that had driven them to the door of the postal department. From headquarters, she'd filed their reports and typed memorandums and correspondence directed to them. Now that she was out of the city and working here on the airfield, she was a constant object of attention for the testosterone-fueled pilots.

The 6-foot-2-inch silver-tongued Max Miller went deaf and dumb when he walked into the office and saw her sitting pretty behind that desk. Nothing in his adventurous life prepared him for the sight of Daisy. Reduced to a schoolboy dunce, he found himself unable to string two words together, light up a smoke, or do anything shy of sit there in that leather sofa in front of her desk, gazing at her like a puppydog.

The petite woman from North Carolina couldn't resist such melting blue eyes frozen upon her, particularly when they came packaged with such an amiable personality.

"Max was just very nice," recalled Daisy.

The Nordic prince and the southern-born belle began dating. His upper-middle-class upbringing seemed altogether a good match for her childhood growing up in Washington, D.C. Though Norwegian born, his command of English was remarkable, his correspondence beautifully penned, each word apt and thoughtfully chosen. But then, he'd grown up in Britain, the son of a successful sea captain, or so he claimed.

In truth, Max Ulf Mueller had changed more than his name upon coming to America. The affable aviator had rewritten the affairs of his earlier life to convey an idealized image of himself, both to Daisy and to the world. Beyond the smooth talk, the breezy good looks, and the genuine likability lay a different history, one he never revealed to anyone.

Plainly obvious, though, was the affection Max and Daisy felt for each other. Joining him aloft, she would pull on a leather jacket and goggles and go flying with him, their mutual good looks making them the picture-perfect couple.

Lipsner was eager to lay his hands on some new planes for the Chicago run and had taken Miller, Gardner, and a couple new pilots to Texas to check out six Curtiss R4s being handed over by the military. To Lipsner's mind, this was a gift from heaven.

Praeger wasn't so convinced. He knew from past experiences that when it came to Big Brother you looked every gift horse in the mouth. Praeger might not be a mechanical engineer, but he talked to enough experts to know that a truck or an airplane was only as good as its engine. The R4s being offered by the Army were not equipped with the powerful 400-horsepower Liberty engine, but rather with the weaker Curtiss V2-3, a power plant known to be too heavy for the horsepower it generated. Praeger needed airplanes capable of powering heavy payloads across long distances, against stiff headwinds. The military designed planes for its own particular applications, and they rarely matched his.

Lipsner, however, was convinced that these new ships could be pressed into service for the new run. All they need do was pick them up and fly them back to New York. The timing was perfect. The team would travel to Texas by train, test the planes, and fly them back, generating publicity for the service and raising money for Liberty Bonds by performing flying demonstrations along the way.

On September 23, Lipsner arrived in Texas with his team, everyone eager to check out their new mail planes; Gardner stepped up to the plate first.

Contact!

Lipsner watched as Army personnel yanked on the R4's prop. It sputtered, then stopped. They tried again and again, but the engine failed to catch. Army personnel scrambled over the plane, trying to find the problem. As they worked, Miller climbed into another ship and took off down the grass, determined to succeed where Turk had failed. Lipsner watched as he made it halfway down the field, only to throttle back, unable to lift off. Instead he was forced to throw the plane into a ground loop to stop, damaging it in the process.

Jumping into a motorcycle sidecar, Lipsner was driven to the end of the field where Miller was standing in the R4 cockpit, his usual grin replaced by a wholesale look of frustration.

"This thing acted like it was tied down to the ground," he groused.

Seeing an opportunity to fly where Miller had failed, Gardner climbed into yet another plane and gave her the gun. But like Max, he went skimming down the field only to roll to a halt. Once again, Lipsner hopped into the sidecar and went bouncing across the grass, pulling up alongside Gardner's plane.

"I thought I could fly anything—but not this!"

Undaunted, one of the new pilots, Louis Gertson, slid into the cockpit and took his turn at the controls, ready to find the one pony buried beneath all this dung. He revved her up, then took off, his engine tamely puttering him down the field. To everyone's surprise, the Curtiss was climbing. Yes! They'd found their pony. The plane was actually nosing skyward, rising above the . . . no, it's falling now, vanishing beyond the trees.

For a third time, Lipsner leaped into the sidecar and went charging across the grass, uncertain of what he might find beyond the horizon. To his relief, he arrived to find Gertson's plane nestled safely in the boughs of a tree, an elderly woman standing at its base, gazing quizzically up at the pilot. It took the Army fire brigade to retrieve him.

Lipsner had seen quite enough. Having arrived in Texas expecting to claim his prize, Lipsner now found himself saddled with unflyable mules. Saying thanks but no thanks to the military, he promptly rejected their planes and returned to the hotel. At the front desk, he found a telegram waiting. It was from Praeger. Bad news apparently traveled fast.

"Congratulations on the junk your Army buddies handed you."

The last thing Lipsner wanted was an "I told you so" from his boss. He promptly fired back a telegram of his own.

"Congratulations not in order. Have not accepted the junk you referred to."

As fall passed into winter and the United States began to hit its stride in producing its own fighting air machines, the underpowered Curtiss R4 notwithstanding, Germany surrendered. On November 11, 1918, the day the armistice was signed, men tossed up their straw skimmers in celebration. Women cried. At last, their boys were coming home.

But trench warfare had cost mothers everywhere dearly. This war had known no class distinction. Privates fell against captains, farmers against aristocrats, their bodies punctured by the same, cutting fire. Soldiers drowned in one another's blood as poison gas filled the trenches. Sounds of a new kind of mechanical death had perverted the air everywhere—in the metal grinding of tank gears, in the staccato clanking of machine guns, and in the vacant whistle of an air bomb plummeting downward to the smoky battlefield. The United States alone had given up some 126,000 of its own soldiers, though that figure paled against the millions of deaths suffered by Europeans, where the war had obliterated an entire generation of healthy, young men.

But as of November 11 all that was over. Despite the worldwide influenza outbreak, people took to the streets, waving flags, hugging one another. In San Francisco, thirty thousand partygoers openly celebrated. Strangers hugged one another, everyone wrapped up in the euphoria, their smiles concealed by protective face masks.

In Bellefonte, the fire department roused the town by sounding the siren. Though it was only 4:20 A.M., the armistice signed just ten minutes ago by their clock, the dawn of peace had emerged over the charred battlefields an ocean away. It was time to celebrate. Before long, a bonfire would be crackling downtown and there would be a big parade at State College later in the day. The Bellefonte Central Railroad Company was offering free train rides to get there. With the event looming larger than any Grange Fair, Bellefontonians packed themselves into train cars like sardines until they filled fully six of them.

Main Streets the world over were crowded with folks celebrating the peace. In Washington, D.C., city fathers were putting together a parade worthy of the nation's capital. In honor of the victory of the brave doughboys overseas, waves of troops were slated to go marching up Pennsylvania Avenue. Someone on the organizing committee suggested an aeroplane be included in the festivities, lending testimony to the vital role it had played in the war. From reconnaissance to ground attack and aerial combat, the aircraft had shown its potential as a game-changing technology. With World War I, aviation suddenly mattered. From now on, military strategies would be expanded to include airpower.

The request for an aerial performance worked its way down the chain of command, eventually finding its way to the desk of Col. Rutherford Hartz, commanding officer of Bolling Field, the headquarter base for Army aviation, located in Washington, D.C. To Hartz would fall the task of choosing a pilot for the big parade.

Lt. James Edgerton had been stationed at Bolling Field ever

since leaving Praeger's service. His experience flying the mail had made him a valuable asset to the military brass and it showed in his work assignments. Detailed as officer in charge of cross-country flying, as well as night flying and technical development, he also chauffeured VIPs around when he wasn't busy tinkering with the latest photographic technologies to be used for aerial military reconnaissance.

He wasn't sure what to make of Col. Hartz's command to appear in his office, and he made his way across the base with some trepidation. One never knew for certain until one showed up and saluted whether news from above would be good or bad.

Straightaway, Hartz dispelled any fears.

"Would you like to fly for the big Armistice celebration?" he asked.

Edgerton listened while the commander told him what he wanted, an impressive flyover, something to give the crowd a real thrill, something spectacular.

Any ideas?

Edgerton thought it over for a moment. How about a power dive right down Pennsylvania Avenue that would blow those skimmers right off everyone's heads?

Hartz had reservations.

"What about power failure?"

Not to worry, Edgerton assured him. He would start the dive at 6,000 feet, plenty of time to pull up over the crowd before heading out over the Potomac.

The colonel liked it. Immediately, the wheels were set in motion and arrangements made for Edgerton to fly over the usually off-limits airspace around the White House and the Treasury buildings. Edgerton recalled:

"The parade was staged to catch the lunchtime crowd, so I arranged for a phone call when the parade neared the Treasury. I warmed the engine and stood by.

"The call came . . . I crossed Pennsylvania Avenue at 7th Street as the serpentine length of the parade stretched up the street. My timing was just right as I climbed in a turn over Union Station to get my altitude over the Capitol."

Edgerton was flying his favorite de Havilland DH-4, a plane he had piloted for dozens of hours testing one thing or another. He liked the DH-4. He knew her like the back of his hand. Taking her up over the Capitol he flew the plane into position.

"Now was the precise moment. With a prayer for the wings to stay put I dumped the nose over and with power screamed down upon the Avenue.

"With a last second decision for a real thriller, I swept over 11th Street between the Post Office and the Raleigh Hotel at second story level.

"As I flashed by, startled faces stared in stunned surprise from the windows."

But Edgerton wasn't finished. He had a "spectacular" to perform and perform it he would. Still hugging the ground, the pilot continued his buzz up to Fourteenth Street, the roar of his engine reverberating against the white marble of the buildings. Finally, with a turn of the stick, he finished his performance by lapping the White House. Then, veering off, his ship disappeared over the Potomac.

The crowds went wild. It had been a spectacular spectacular.

Later Edgerton heard that the District of Columbia vowed never to approve any such flyover again.

With the signing of the armistice, the military finally stopped complaining about flying the mail with the country still at war. But the peace treaty would deliver Praeger a good deal more than sweet silence. The Army was offering him a veritable air force worth of aircraft: one hundred de Havilland DH-4s with the 150-horsepower Hispano-Suiza engine, six Curtiss R4s equipped with Liberty engines, and ten twin-engine Handley-Page bombers. It was an armada that Praeger could use to expand his air service to all points west.

The armistice brought not just airplanes to Praeger's doorstep but also hundreds of decommissioned Army officers applying for jobs as airmail pilots. War veterans were signing on in droves. Flush with a ready pool of talent, Praeger began taking on fliers quicker than a child scooping up spilled jellybeans. Ten new pilots were quickly hired despite the fact that Lipsner had already rejected some of those very same applicants, feeling them unqualified or lacking in experience.

Praeger's superintendent was growing increasingly frustrated. To his mind, a pool of mediocre talents was infiltrating what had started out only a few months ago as a small tight-knit cadre of dedicated and talented men. The second assistant was inserting himself into every detail of operations. He paid as much attention to a 40-cent overage on a pilot's expense report as he did to a briefing for a congressional oversight committee. Praeger was increasingly working outside Lipsner, around him, but rarely with him. The gap between them was widening, becoming more contentious as the summer turned into fall and the harshness of winter turned the skies even more brutal.

A major disagreement was brewing on the subject of expansion. With December approaching, Praeger was pushing for Chicago like it were a green morning in May. Lipsner was adamant that they wait until spring of the next year to launch Chicago service. They weren't ready to coax a fleet of cloth-covered airplanes over the Alleghenies in wintertime. He was proud of the performance record established during his tenure. The first half of November was just as good as the prior month, and they were flying more miles. Lipsner wanted to keep it that way.

But Praeger hadn't slowed for the U.S. Army, and he was not about to do so now for Lipsner. The second assistant felt that the proper place to work out the challenges of a winter service was under a daily schedule of flying. Each problem would be identified as it arose, with information gathered over time, eventually yielding a workable solution.

At this juncture, neither man was communicating. Each was stubbornly convinced that the other lacked understanding about what it took to take the U.S. Air Mail Service to the next level. A confrontation seemed inevitable; it was just a question of where and when.

November 18 broke with dense fog pressing down on Belmont, skewering perspective, erasing all trace of depth, height, or distance. Despite the obvious danger, Eddie Gardner wasn't about to be overflown. It was his name on the board this morning, and no self-respecting pilot still standing on his feet would let someone else fly in his place.

The wheel chocks were removed and the engine began its deafening crescendo down the field, the *thump thump thump* of the propeller echoing off the heavy, saturated air.

Seconds after taking off Gardner knew he was in trouble. Just 25 feet off the ground and he'd already lost all sight of it. For the next half hour, he gripped his way down blind alleys, hoping he was heading south. Inside the whiteout, even a seasoned pilot like Turk could find himself flying straight for the ground without ever knowing it. Despite his efforts, the man defined by his instincts landed just five miles outside Belmont, where he'd begun. He had obviously been flying in circles and hadn't even known it.

Pulling off his goggles, Gardner climbed out of the cockpit, relieved to be calling it a day. No way could anyone fly through this stuff. The mail would have to be pushed through by rail.

To his astonishment, Praeger ordered him back up. The plane had a compass. Gardner should use it! At the very least, a pilot could hang a pocket watch hanging from the instrument panel. If it swung below the instruments, the pilot was right side up. If the dials somehow got below it, he was upside down.

Not one to be bullied, Gardner dug in. He knew as well as anybody that weather was part of flying. There'd been times when pilots had to start their planes inside the hangars because storms were raging so fiercely outside. And yet these same airmen had climbed into their cockpits and flown their routes to completion. Praeger regularly bragged to reporters about this. Gardner didn't expect sunny skies and tulips every day, but he had earned the right to take off and land without killing himself. He was exercising his prerogative to preserve his life and fly another day.

Praeger ignited. Nothing galled him more then an "uncompleted" on the board due to a pilot's prerogative. Publicly he might be lauding the accomplishments of his pilots—Gardner was, after all, one of the Pathfinders—but behind the scenes he was letting it be known that the U.S. Air Mail was not the U.S. Army. Gardner had taken an oath, and his refusal to fly amounted to high treason.

Another pilot was ordered to complete the run. Now it is Robert Shank in the crosshairs.

Not me, he says. If the weather was too nasty for Turk Bird to fly, then he wasn't going up, either.

Word reached Praeger that both pilots refused to fly. Without hesitating, he pulled the trigger and fired them both. The second assistant saw the writing on the wall. If pilots were standing down then, in mid-November, what would happen come December, January, February, when there was snow in New York, ice in Philadelphia, fog in Bellefonte, and wind in Chicago? The wealth of precipitation coming in winter would stop the U.S. Air Mail Service dead in its tracks. He was not about to have that.

Stunned with their dismissal, Gardner and Shank appealed to Lipsner. Gardner was particularly upset.

"I looked Eddie up and talked with him," remarked Lipsner. "His heart was broken by his dismissal, and he begged me to get him back on."

But the chief was adamant. A regularly scheduled airmail service must, by definition, be flown every day. That was the service he and Burleson had sold to Congress and to the public. That was the banner under which every pilot had already agreed to fly and fly it they would, or else.

"I was furious at the whole thing, and thoroughly disgusted at this interference," fumed Lipsner.

What Lipsner thought of as interference Praeger considered his rightful domain. He was the second assistant in charge of postal transportation for the entire country. Lipsner worked for him.

Gardner and Shank would remain fired.

Turk Bird's firing was particularly hard to take for Lipsner, who considered him his favored son. If some considered the superintendent pushy, there was no disputing that he routinely pushed in support of his fliers. He respected them. They might be freewheeling and rough-hewn, but they were bold pioneers while he remained tethered to daily routines. By nature he was temperate and refined, a man who mitered corners.

In contrast, Praeger must have seemed a chilly, calculating individual, a man for whom the end justified the means. He, too, grasped the fundamental nature of these men, understood their competitive instincts and driving ambitions. Before them he had placed goals so lofty, standards so impossibly high that the sheer pursuit of them would advance the front of aviation.

By now, the gap between Praeger and his superintendent had widened into a chasm. Feeling his power being diluted, the superintendent began to take issue over everything—the patronage, the interference, the inexperience of some of the new hires. He sharply criticized the department's plans to extend the route to Chicago in winter, though he'd been quick to toe the party line as late as December, going so far as to order the field manager of Belmont to keep pilots flying "regardless of weather conditions."

He faulted Praeger's collaboration with industry executives to spend taxpayer money modifying and improving aircraft designs when the Army was virtually giving away airplanes, including the Handley-Page bomber with its twin Liberty engines. From the day he saw them at Standard Aero, the superintendent believed they could be ideal mail carriers given their power and the enormity of their cargo hold.

Praeger, on the other hand, remained unconvinced. The aircraft was a poor performer, even with the Liberty engines.

"The planes are of a slow type, with an average speed loaded from 70 to 90 miles," wrote the well-respected magazine *Flying*. "It requires the two engines to keep it in the air with a load, the result being that with one engine getting out of order, the twin-motored Handley-Pages of that type will come to the ground, although the other engine is intact and operating under full power."

From experience, Praeger knew only too well the problems attendant upon using military hand-me-downs for commercial applications. The mechanical breakdowns the airmail was experiencing with the Jennies and other military castoffs were just like the problems he had back in 1915 when he started acquiring Army trucks to replace horse-drawn wagons.

To convert fighting ships into cargo carriers, extensive modifications would be required. Rather than throwing good money after bad, Praeger was more interested in developing newer and better ships capable of flying faster and more reliably, with greater payload capacity.

Lipsner remained convinced of his position. On Thanksgiving Day 1918, the superintendent openly challenging his boss's authority as he presented his case for the Handley-Page bomber to the court of public opinion. September's Pathfinder trip to Chicago had shown him the value of good press.

With the stage set for his "Thanksgiving Dinner in the Air," reporters arrived at the Standard Aircraft Company in Elizabeth, New Jersey, pencils sharpened, ready to give testimony to Lipsner's airborne turkey dinner aboard a Handley-Page bomber. The superintendent posed for the cameras beneath the plane's enormous wings. Then, raising a toast, he and others boarded for a grand holiday feast to be partaken of inside the craft's spacious cabin at 2,500 feet.

The newspapers ate it up.

Praeger understandably did not. A man like that would never sit back passively while his subordinate openly confronted him, using his own weapon against him. Lipsner could go to the press if he chose. At day's end, it was still this particular Texan running operations, the power of the office squarely behind him. He had the tactical advantage, and with the stroke of a pen, Praeger abolished the office of the superintendent, splitting its responsibilities into two direct reports—chief of flying operations and chief of maintenance—and Lipsner was to hold neither position.

Whether Lipsner quit first, prompting Praeger to reorganize, or whether Praeger reorganized first and Lipsner responded by quitting, the upshot was clear—Lipsner was out.

The now former superintendent sent his resignation letter to the *New York Times*, which printed it on page one.

"Capt. Lipsner Says His Action Is in Protest Against Interference with His Work," read the first subhead. "Fears Waste of Money" was next, followed in typical *Times* three-subhead style: "Special Airplanes Not Needed, He Says, While Army Ones Will Do."

Lipsner was resigning in a shroud of high-mindedness.

"I wish to resign to keep my records as first superintendent of the aerial mail service spotless," the letter read. "I read with dismay and amazement in the evening papers a statement by Second Assistant Postmaster General Otto Praeger that the air mail service was to have special airplanes constructed for carrying mail, and, at the same time, an order which he issued placing novices in charge of important branches of the air mail service."

He had even turned the knife, giving himself credit for being the guiding force behind airmail.

Praeger's fellow journalists ran Lipsner's letter without giving him a chance to comment. But that journalistic oversight gave him the opportunity to craft a rebuttal letter. Signed by Postmaster General Burleson, it ran in the *Times* two days later, albeit on the inside of the paper.

"Your letter from beginning to end is a tissue of misstatements about matters of which you should have been fully conversant," said Burleson.

As to whether the postal department planned to purchase a new airplane: "No such machine is in contemplation or in course of construction. No alterations of any character to the planes turned over by the War Department are in contemplation or execution, save the experimental modification which you requested to decrease its landing speed and the minor modification to facilitate better loading of mail in the Handley-Page."

As to the issue of novices running the airmail: "The official in charge of flying operations and the other in charge of maintenance and equipment are aviators, which you are not, and have had experience in field management and supervision, which you had not when you entered the service."

One of the "inexperienced" people that Lipsner accused Praeger of hiring was J. B. Corridon, the superintendent of railway adjustments, who Praeger had brought to Standard Aircraft for the rollout of the JR-1Bs and was now being promoted to a similarly important role with the airmail. The new head of maintenance was going to be Dr. L. T. Bussler, a former flight instructor in France who had also served on General Pershing's staff in Mexico. And Lt. James Edgerton, a young man who had repeatedly proved himself the most valiant Army officer ever to carry the mail, would now be head of operations. The three were hardly inexperienced men.

As to Lipsner's spotless record as "first" superintendent, Burleson refused to give him that honor. He wrote: "The first superintendent of the aerial mail service was Major Reuben H. Fleet of the United States Army, who launched it under great difficulties and maintained it with an enviable and distinguished record."

And as to Lipsner taking credit for establishing airmail: "The achievements of the aerial mail service were accomplished not by you, but by Second Assistant Postmaster General Otto Praeger, who has directed its movements from its inception to the present time in all its details."

This very public bloodletting was demoralizing to the pilots. It was bad enough having to haul mail across wind-driven skies for an uncaring Uncle Sam, but to watch their only champion fall on his sword was too much for some.

In protest, Max Miller resigned. "Being in full sympathy with Captain B. B. Lipsner, Superintendent of the Aerial Mail Service, in his opinion as to the contemplated reorganization plan for the Aerial Mail Service, I am frank to state that I do not feel confident in the outcome of a plan different from the one which is now being successfully operated. Therefore, it is obvious that I use my best judgment and take the stand of handing herewith my resignation."

Miller may have reengineered some of the facts of his background, but when it came to upholding its finer principles, the aviator remained steadfastly loyal. Airmail's number one pilot was turning in his flying suit and walking away with the captain. Turk Bird, Max, Shank, and Lipsner were effectively out.

CHAPTER 14

COMPLICATIONS

Twenty-three-year-old Lt. James Edgerton had been the unques-
tioned star of airmail in the days of the Army's involvement. Between
inaugural day and the time the military had pulled out of operations,
the young, confident flier had flown more legs (52), logged more flight
time (106 hours), and covered more miles (7,155) than any of the other
original five pilots operating under Fleet. Edgerton had been forced
down only once, and that was due to mechanical trouble.

He was still stationed at Bolling Field when he received a call
from postal headquarters. Edgerton listened for a while, then hung
up the phone, uncertain of what to do. It wasn't every day that a
man was asked to be chief of flying operations for the entire U.S.
Post Office Department.

Still, he had it good at Bolling. Like the postal department, the
military was working the technical aspects of aviation, and Edgerton
was playing an important role in the development of ground-to-air
communications by testing airborne transmitters and receivers.

On the negative side, advancement through the ranks wouldn't
be nearly so quick with the war over. A first lieutenant at the time,
he didn't know how long he'd have to wait for a promotion to captain. His wife, Mary Robinette, was pregnant, and Uncle Sam was
dangling more money than he had ever earned, $3,600 a year.

He spent the night tossing and turning, tying to decode whether to stay at his very satisfying job at Bolling or resign his commission to rejoin the airmail.

Next morning, he put in a call to the postmaster general.

"Good," Burleson replied, hearing Edgerton's consent. "I personally will see the Secretary of War to secure your release."

Edgerton accepted the position on December 10, becoming the youngest federal executive in the U.S. government.

Edgerton's first order of business was to hire back Gardner and Shank. Miller, however, would not be returning anytime soon. He remained loyal to Lipsner and was sticking to his decision. He stayed around, though, as Daisy was still working for Praeger.

These days, morale was pretty low. It hit rock bottom when Navy pilot Carl Smith, one of Edgerton's new hires, was killed less than two weeks after starting the job. He was at Standard Aero in Elizabeth test flying a newly modified de Havilland DH-4 when the airplane stalled and plunged 400 feet to the ground. It was the Air Mail's first fatality. Though Edgerton determined the cause of the crash to be pilot error, it cast a pallor over the entire service, made worse by terrible weather the first two weeks of December.

Gale-force winds of 50 miles per hour were recorded at College Park, and aircraft were buffeted about the sky like tin cans blown down an alley. To plow through the weather, pilots would fling themselves over the countryside, hopping chimneys at a mere 500 feet. One pilot fought the winds for nearly three hours to cover only 113 miles.

Praeger, aware of the discouragement that was circulating among his men, openly commended pilots such as former Army instructor Ira O. Biffle, one of Lipsner's hires, for his efforts in climbing into that cockpit day after day "regardless of weather conditions."

Everyone grew to loathe the month of December, but none more than E. Hamilton Lee, one of Edgerton's first hires. "Ham," as he was called, despised sitting inside an open cockpit when temperatures plummeted. It was akin to sitting inside an ice bucket. Newspapers stuffed into a flying suit helped, as did laying down a strip of fur taped across the nose. Still, given that hauling the mail was a straight fifty-two-week proposition, a guy couldn't afford the luxury of sitting frigid days out.

"You crazy?" friends had exclaimed upon hearing Ham had just signed on to fly the mail. "You'll get killed."

Lee had few options open to him at the time. He'd already been a barnstormer, and with the war over and the Army shutting down its flying operations, it was hauling the mail or nothing. Devilishly good-looking, with a pencil-thin mustache and dark deep-set eyes, the twenty-six-year-old from Paris, Illinois, traded in his job as military flight instructor and added his name to airmail's swelling ranks in December, the most teeth-chattering and miserably cold month anybody had seen in years.

Powering over the landscape, Ham tried to shield himself as best he could from the bitter wind-driven cold. This being his first mail flight for the Uncle, he was trailing pilot Lawton Smith to acquaint himself with the route between New York and Washington. Near Bustleton, he began to smell trouble—the engine was burning oil. The machine was given a quick once-over on the ground, then Lee, eager to make a good impression, was back behind the controls and once again following Smith to College Park.

All hell broke loose over Baltimore at 7,000 feet. The oil pressure gauge dropped to zero, and black plumes of smoke began pouring from Lee's engine. The power plant suddenly began clanking loudly, and the pilot immediately recognized that familiar clatter. It was sound of a broken connecting rod. Time to go down.

Fortunately, a farmer's field came into view, its rolling surface promising safe harbor. But the ground that appeared solid from a few hundred feet was actually thickened with mud. Touching down, Ham's wheels sank in, sticking his plane to the ground like rubber cement. So much for impressing management with a stellar first run. Grabbing the mail, Ham hoofed it over to the farmer's house and telephoned in the problem. A new motor was driven over from College Park and after a few hours' work, Lee was able to climb back into the cockpit and fly the final miles to deliver his cargo just before dark.

On December 18—almost fifteen years to the day since Wilbur and Orville Wright had given wings to the impossible on the dunes at

Kitty Hawk, and only a brief decade since Frenchman Louis Bleriot had flown across the English Channel, proving the possibility of long-distance flying—the U. S. Post Office Department was finally ready to push the promise even further.

A dusting of snow covered the oval at Belmont, and a crowd of onlookers shuffled about trying to keep themselves warm. Praeger was there, warmly dressed in an overcoat and brown felt hat, as were airmail boosters Hawley and Woodhouse. Edgerton was directing the operation, with help from Maurice Newton, who had become an object of sympathy and concern since his bad accident in September.

Following the crash, Newton had simply dusted himself off, and with his head bandaged, his face black and blue and horribly swollen, looking like a guy who'd just gone ten rounds with a prizefighter, climbed into his wooden crate the next morning and soldiered on. He had been quick to brush off the crack-up, preferring to take such incidents in good stride like the younger bucks. Perhaps he worried the post office might wash him out as a pilot. Keenly aware of his age, he hadn't wanted anyone to know he wore eyeglasses lest they think he was too old for the job.

But that accident had gotten to him, really gotten to him. These days, people were noticing a profound difference in his demeanor. He'd been floating around the service like a loose bolt hopelessly out of place. It was plain to Edgerton that he had lost his nerve for flying. Rather than let the poor man kill himself, Edgerton had taken him off the duty roster. Newton was a good man, though, and Praeger gave him a desk job being superintendent of the new Cleveland–Chicago Division, giving him full authority for flying in this new, important region. To help Newton get the work out, he even pulled one of the men out of the Bryan station to work as his assistant superintendent. Despite the desk job, Newton just wasn't the same.

All standing together, their moist breath condensing in the air, they watched as pilot Leon Smith prepared to depart for Bellefonte on the first leg of the trip. "Windy," as he was called, was a solid professional who had earned himself a good record. Born in the Hudson

Valley near Saratoga Springs, New York, he was a military pilot like all the others, gathering plenty of hours on the stick as a training instructor. Edgerton had hired him along with several others expressly to staff the rapidly expanding service.

Streaks of daylight were ripening the early-morning sky as the prop on the de Havilland DH-4 was spun and Windy took off for Chicago. The send-off crowd had barely finished congratulating themselves, however, when the airplane came boomeranging back around to land on the frozen ground—steam erupting from the Liberty. Ground personnel gathered around and quickly transferred the mail sacks to a new ship. Then, once more, this time for sure, the plane was away. Time lost: one hour.

Following the tracks of the Long Island Railroad, Windy went soaring westward across Manhattan's glittering landscape, passing over the hiccup of green that was Central Park before sailing over the Hudson and Passaic Rivers to Newark, New Jersey, and then onward to Bellefonte, letters stowed inside his hold. Each was stamped with one of the new designs Burleson had ordered from the government printing office. Initially costing 24 cents, the going rate for stamps had been dropping steadily until it was now only 6 cents. Despite the bargain, the public was indifferent and Windy flew relatively unencumbered.

As the plane glided into the Allegheny range, he peered over the side of his open cockpit, searching the picturesque hills and valleys for fresh impressions to guide him on a line to Bellefonte. To the astute observer, a wealth of clues lay tucked inside the rolling composite of green. One single farm could yield a dozen signs— the laundry dancing on a backyard line indicated wind strength, a herd of agitated cattle foretold the ferociousness of an approaching storm, and then, of course, everybody knew that an outhouse always faced downwind.

Windy kept inching westward toward the Beaver farm, looking for the Bald Eagle mountain range. At that point, all he needed was to find the valley upon which a white bull's-eye had been drawn in the center of an open field. The welcoming committee could handle the rest.

The residents of this solid American community had a tradition of making folks feel right at home. People in Bellefonte might be tucked away from any mainstream populace, but they enjoyed nothing more than setting down the plow long enough to renew old acquaintances and partake in some neighborly socializing as evidenced by the annual Grange Fair held since the 1870s. Best arts and crafts, best homemade jam, best apple pie—such contests, born of the land, never lack for entries, many recipes passed down through the generations, distilled to perfection. Then as now, youngsters wait for the opening day of the Grange Fair with the anticipation of a kid peering through a banister on Christmas Eve. Eager to snag themselves a blue ribbon, young 4-H members worked the barn stalls cleaning rabbits and primping goats, heifers, hogs, and sheep until their hooves shone.

The impending arrival of the airmail this morning was as widely anticipated as opening day of the Grange Fair, and virtually the entire town had turned out to Beaver's farm for the pilot's arrival. Standing in the field, they searched the skies, waiting.

But Smith had gotten lost in the verdant monotony of the Allegheny hills. Wholly disoriented, he had no idea where Bellefonte was, but the sprawling campus below that was Pennsylvania State University was invitingly free of trees. An original land-grant school from the 1860s that was now one of the leading agricultural and engineering schools in America, the university was an isolated sanctuary of learning and life for five thousand undergraduates in the heart of the forested mountains. Its voluminous, neoclassical library stood high on a hill in the center of the university and served as a natural homing beacon for any pilot overhead. It drew Windy Smith from out of the sky like iron shavings to a magnet. He landed in a field about a mile from the university. He was on his way again soon enough, with directions to Bellefonte in hand, arriving there ten minutes later.

This being a maiden voyage, the postal department shouldn't have expected everything to go smoothly, and, in keeping with the day, nothing did. Pilot Edward Johnson, who had been hired just the week prior, had ignored orders to wait first for the arrival of the New York plane and instead left the Beaver farm at 9 A.M. without any mail at all, heading for Cleveland.

Poor Windy. Whatever warmth and relaxation he might have enjoyed at the Brockerhoff Hotel would have to be forgone. His mail sacks had to be delivered to Cleveland as promised. Never having flown to Bellefonte before, let alone to Cleveland, he nonetheless rustled up a new map and then took off, heading west.

His homing instincts wholly intact, Windy finally arrived at his destination, though the same couldn't be said of Johnson. Concerned for his welfare, everyone at Cleveland stood vigil well into the night, spotlights locked onto the landing field, hoping the lost pilot might yet find his way there. They waited and waited.

But unbeknownst to them, mechanical problems had already forced Johnson down ten miles shy of their field. Without bothering to notify anyone, he had decided to call it a day. Finally, around midnight, everyone waiting at the airfield followed suit and went home.

If the westbound run fared poorly, the inaugural eastbound run never even made it off the ground since no aircraft was available for the morning flight out of Chicago. A ship had been flown in ahead of time, but an accident west of Cleveland had grounded it there. Lacking a replacement, postal officials in Chicago had been left standing at Grant Field literally holding the bag.

Clearly, the postal department had a few bugs to work out, which was made evidently clear over the next three days when not a single run was successfully completed in either direction.

Edgerton knew better than to challenge his boss directly. The Lipsner boondoggle had already shown the U.S. Air Mail Service to be a one-man operation—two if one counted Burleson. But less than a week into Chicago operations it was becoming obvious that the post office lacked the resources necessary to launch this route. Nothing was in place as it should have been. Hangars still weren't ready, and equipment was in short supply. All Praeger had were pilots and plenty of bad planes. Miller and Gardner's Pathfinder race in September had been just that—a race, not proof of the viability of a regularly scheduled service.

The new chief of flying had seen enough.

"It was high time to shut down and take stock, my first important recommendation," said Edgerton.

Four days after it had begun, the chief admitted defeat. The U.S. Air Mail would cease all attempts at flying the mail between New York and Chicago, at least for the winter. It was a retrenchment, a backtrack, and another failure for regularly scheduled service.

Praeger sat down at his typewriter and hammered out a detailed letter of explanation to Burleson. The postmaster general was fully prepared to give his second assistant a free hand, both men sharing a joint conviction to bring U.S. postal transportation up to speed. By now, the two fishing buddies had been casting a line into the Potomac long enough to develop a kind of shorthand. But even so, with the disaster of the past week, Praeger felt the need to assure his boss that airmail's reach hadn't exceeded its grasp.

Spelling out the situation in his usual no-nonsense manner, Praeger explained that the de Havilland DH-4s from the Army were dogs, poorly built, riddled with structural weakness, even those powered by the Liberty. About the only good thing he could say about the de Havilland was that they had plenty of them. On that score, he assured his boss not to worry.

"We have an ample supply of these machines at the fields to make liberal allowance for the wrecking of planes," he wrote.

No mention was made of the pilots.

In Praeger's defense, he was on war footing. Lipsner may have fought for his men, but the chief was fighting for the survival of the entire service. From the beginning, he and Burleson had battled a hostile Congress, a disinterested public, and a military that wanted total control of the airmail. In December, Army officials had nearly convinced Congress to wrest the service away from the Post Office Department and hand it over to them on a silver platter. The driving force behind much of that whirlwind was Gen. Billy Mitchell, who was continually pushing for military controlled skies, be they peaceable or warring.

Praeger respected the dashing and dynamic general, one of aviation's true visionaries. He had turned to him many times for advice. Under his guidance, the fledgling service might have some chance. But Mitchell wouldn't be in command forever, and Praeger was convinced that the airmail would languish once it lost its champion in the military. Then too, he had already seen the Army and Navy engage in petty turf battles over the airplane, each afraid that accelerating aviation development would undermine their influence in the command structure.

He took his fight to the papers. Commercial flying was an entirely different proposition from flying in the military service, he wrote, his aim perfectly poised. The Army's first consideration would always be flight training, and it would only incidentally carry the mail.

The postal department succeeded in staving off the attack, at least temporarily. But if the two Democrats from Texas were going to expand their airmail service as planned, changes would be needed, starting with the planes.

The DH-4s gifted from the military had proven that nothing comes free. The ships had been hastily slapped together to keep up with war demands, their only requirement being that they lift off, drop their payloads, fire off their rounds, and make it back to the airfield. As such, they were plagued by engine troubles, and their fuselages were unable to take the strain of landing in farmers' fields with their divots, holes, and furrows. Lightweight construction was causing them to flip over too easily, injuring pilots.

Pilot Dean Lamb, hired in early December, had barely escaped harm when he crashed on landing near Jamaica, Long Island, while testing a new landing gear. The assembly gave way, wrecking the ship.

In late December, another DH-4 suffered a broken axle while taxiing down Bustleton Field at 40 miles an hour. The airplane turned onto its nose, then dropped slowly backward onto the ground, the impact cracking the fuselage in two. It happened again two days later: same right axle, same nose over, same broken back.

"A careful inspection of the debris revealed not only poor material but faulty design," read Praeger's investigation report. "The longerons, which are the vital portions of the aeroplane, are made of a frail pine instead of ash or other strong wood and the landing gears, which sustain the shock of a plane touching the ground at between 60 and 65 miles an hour, are of thin tubing and white pine and crumple up under the strain of a normal landing."

Edgerton wasted no time in searching for answers to questions bedeviling the service. Enlisting the aid of pilots, aviation experts, mechanics, and riggers on the front lines, he and the chief began piecing together a picture of airplanes based on engine performance, tires and landing gear, instrumentation, fuel consumption, and a dozen other variables. What did the pilots think about airframe design and load-carrying capabilities? Such ideas and others were debated and together, with data compiled and verified, assembled into specs aimed at enhancing the design of air carriers.

The team identified the most important dozen or so major modifications, and the L-W-F Manufacturing Co. of Queens, New York, was contracted to make the modifications. Having just developed a new, laminated wood fuselage, the company's expertise would now be employed to strengthen the DH-4s.

Employees set to work retrofitting each ship with larger wheels and heavier axles. Longerons needed to be reinforced, landing gear fortified, the fuselage stiffened, elevators and rudders equipped with bracing wires, and rudder bars redesigned to give pilots more legroom. Engineers stabilized the de Havilland's center of gravity by repositioning its landing gear assembly one foot forward, making the plane less front heavy, less prone to burying its nose into the ground like a lawn dart. Praeger also wanted the pilot's cockpit relocated to the rear. Its present configuration sat the pilot "between 540 pounds of gasoline and an 800-pound engine." During a crash the fuel tank tended to rip loose, crushing the pilot, a tendency revealed by the investigation into the accident that had resulted in Carl Smith's death.

"The Post Office Department cannot take responsibility for risking the lives of men in planes of this character," said the chief.

The tank was hardened and more securely fastened.

Edgerton and Praeger were working round the clock trying to prop the new Chicago route back on its feet. Despite his appealing boyishness, the new hire was no wet-behind-the-ears Boy Scout who needed to be led by the hand. Still smarting over Lipsner's attack on his lack of credentials, the son of the postal purchasing agent was pushing himself hard.

But he wasn't the only one burning the midnight oil. Edgerton swore his boss "lived, ate and slept air mail," weekends and holidays included.

"There we would sit in his private office, coats and ties off and feet propped on his huge desk, at least huge in comparison to his own short, rotund proportions, as we threshed out air mail improvements," said Edgerton.

Fortunately, Praeger's office was a veritable throne room. Paneled wholly in walnut, each window was framed in solid bronze and supported by columns of thick granite. Everything about the room was oversized and opulent. Even its private bath was lavishly appointed to include a marble shower equipped with the latest, modern fixtures. Why, the coat closet alone was "large enough to hold more clothes than I ever expected to possess at one time," exclaimed Praeger.

A backdrop such as this might have turned other men's heads, but the second assistant was too clear-eyed, his powers of observation too astute, too finely honed to allow him to be fooled by the mere appearance of authority, however exquisite its trappings. Praeger understood power—in its reach and nuance, be it the power of privilege, Congress, labor unions, Wall Street financiers, or the strength of the American people when united as a whole. For all his autocratic ways, he was in every fiber of his being a humble man. Having swapped personal ambition for public service, he sought to serve the greater good by employing the full weight of the U.S. government to the task ahead. Only heaven help the bastard who got in Uncle Sam's way.

CHAPTER 15

LETTERS, WHAT LETTERS?

The failed service to Chicago might have Praeger back at the drawing board but in print Uncle Sam's Air Mail Service appeared right on track.

"Very few persons realize what an undertaking this is," he wrote. "Never has a trip by air been undertaken whereby a ship leaves for an 800-mile voyage, one each way a day, flying over mountains with very few landing places—an undertaking that six months ago would have been regarded absolutely impossible.

"When you consider that this is being done with a single-motored plane, the task is stupendous. This has never been attempted, either in America or in any other country of the world, and great credit is due to the organization undertaking it."

Praeger's statement was released widely to the media, with his staunch supporter, Henry Woodhouse, playing the story up big in his industry magazine, *Aerial Age Weekly*. Throughout the course of their relationship, the two men had enjoyed a symbiosis of sorts. In return for promoting Praeger's cause, Woodhouse had a high government official endorsing the cause of civil aviation, something he staunchly supported. A talented writer, Woodhouse had authored several books on aeronautics and regularly penned well-thought-out arguments supporting commercial aviation. Behind his deep, soulful eyes and slicked-back hair was a smart and clever man who could turn any situation into an opportunity.

Born Mario Terenzio Enrico Casalegno, a short Italian-born immigrant with a prominent Romanesque nose, he had transformed himself into Henry Woodhouse, aviation authority to whom farsighted men like Woodrow Wilson, Otto Praeger, and Admiral Robert Peary regularly turned for advice. Not bad for a kid who'd come to America from Turin in 1905 and worked his way up through the restaurant kitchens of New York. As an American, Henry Woodhouse was no more Mario Casalegno from Italy than August Belmont was a Schonberg from Prussia. Both had shed their original skins long ago. Here in the new country, a man could be unshackled from a life not of his choosing, free to define himself by the opportunities he seized, the fortunes he amassed. In America, green was no mere halftone. The color of money dominated everything right up to the Green Lady welcoming them ashore.

Despite the recent setbacks to airmail, Woodhouse was lathering support on Praeger's push westward. He boasted of flying times and proclaimed the reliability of the new mail service. Its fleet of aero mail ships had shuttled more than 90,000 pounds of first-class mail between Washington and New York in the first six months alone, a distance of nearly 70,000 miles, with much of it being flown in the face of bad weather. In print it appeared as though performance percentages were sky high.

Statistics can, however, with skill and finesse, be made to suit one's purposes, having the capacity to evade or exaggerate their topic. Such sleight of hand was not lost upon the journalist Praeger. Thus was born his system of accounting, the likes of which went as follows: Any mail successfully delivered to its destination was scored 100 percent, despite the length of time it took to arrive. If a plane's wheels never left the ground because of weather conditions, a fat zero was given and the pilot reprimanded accordingly. To record a 50 percent, however, all a plane had to do was briefly lift its wheels from terra firma, even if it never arrived at its destination. Given the hazards of flying in 1918, Praeger's unique method of computing no doubt made sense. After all, sometimes one had to grade on a curve.

Whatever the front, behind the scenes, Praeger was sleuthing through each and every forced landing report, trying to understand the problems inherent to cross-country flying. Reports and manuals covered his desk, his eye always turned to some new study promising a solution, be it to a clogged distributor or a simple radiator leak. Those problems that couldn't be solved were forwarded on to the Bureau of Standards for its advice.

Out of necessity, the chief's life had become one of calculations, cost/benefit analysis, on-time percentages, number of miles flown, and weight of letters hauled. Money was stretched thin and paychecks were sometimes late, especially toward the end of the fiscal year, causing the chief to go looking under the mattress for spare cash. Praeger the visionary had already subordinated himself to the role of accountant. Operating costs had to be examined down to the last cent. How much did a mail ship cost to fly in terms of fuel, oil, and the maintenance? Airfields weren't cheap to rent and operating hangars cost plenty in water and light bills. Where could expenses be shaved? Where exactly was the money going?

Seemingly missing from that equation was the cost of flying in terms of men.

April 4, 1919, roughly four months after abandoning the New York–Chicago route, Otto Praeger flipped on the switch again. Although L-W-F had yet to deliver on its promise for modified planes, there was no reason the men couldn't start familiarizing themselves with their runs. Practice flights would be flown to Bellefonte as a dress rehearsal for flying over the misty, often disorienting hills and valleys of the Alleghenies.

Praeger had also decided that going for broke right from the start was maybe not the most prudent way to go. So rather than attempting daily flights across the Alleghenies, the new western service would initially fly only between Cleveland and Chicago, its level stretch of terrain far easier to navigate than the mountainous leg between New York and Cleveland.

It was with a fresh supply of pilots and another $100,000 appropriation from Congress that the U.S. government once again began pushing commerce west. More good news came when Praeger found out that Edgerton was able to convince Max Miller to rejoin the service. Airmail's number one pilot was back on the duty roster. The chief had always like Max. The guy was untouchable as a pilot. Fearless in the air, he could scout a route across impossible terrain as easily as he could render a learned opinion about the inner workings of most every plane.

Whatever sentiments Miller might harbor against the chief, he was a married man now and had a wife to support. This past February, Daisy Marie Thomas of Washington, D.C., had become Mrs. Max Miller, wife of the British mail pilot, or so claimed a local newspaper, which heralded the event as an "international wedding." It would appear that Max had promised to love, honor, and obey his wife, but not necessarily lay down the whole unvarnished truth of his past. As the keeper of his own image no one knew better than Max how to tell the tale and keep it going. The son of a dashing sea captain, an English subject, sounded infinitely better than that of a restless kid who had left Norway in search of a more exciting life. This was America. Given talent and industry, even someone considered to be a black sheep could transform himself into a magnificent ebony swan.

Daisy had no cause not to believe her husband. She had seen enough of Max to know that he was kind and easygoing. As a secretary in the office, she had seen his fidelity to duty, the allegiance he showed to Lipsner by resigning. She had every reason to believe that they would be embarking on an exciting life. After all, her husband hadn't crossed an ocean to confine himself to some earthbound straitjacket of a job. Max—he saw things up there on the rim of the sky. Possibilities perhaps, or just pure, undiluted freedom. For a man like that, it could never be another day at the office.

If Miller was riding the dream, Daisy knew she would be facing a plainer truth. Married or single, all fliers had but one true love. As youngsters, they had each climbed trees tall enough to set kids twice their age to quivering. The sky was in their blood.

Miller was given first shot at flying the restart westward, along with the two other pilots—Trent Fry and Lester Bishop—both new hires who Edgerton had brought onboard in December. At the advanced age of thirty, Bishop was one of the old men of the service, but he'd garnered some impressive credentials along the way, not only as a flight instructor but also as a test pilot.

So it was an experienced trio of fliers that took off under clear skies that morning, each one piloting modified DH-4s with Liberty engines. Together, they formed their own mini mail squadron flying west toward Bellefonte. Both Miller and Fry managed to land safely. Bishop, however, clipped a telephone line with his landing gear, knocking out phone service for a good portion of the town. But what did it matter. Everybody knew already that Max was back. The man was a legend in central Pennsylvania, both as a flier and a thoroughly likable fellow. In this small, rural community of fertilizer and feed, where everyone knew every birth and every death as intimately as they knew their own last name, men like Max represented an elite. Adventurous, headstrong, defiant of authority, this amalgam of ex-military fliers, barnstormers, and automobile racers who flew under the banner of Uncle Sam's Air Mail collectively flirted with disaster on a daily basis—and all their earthbound admirers knew it. To Bellefontonians, these men in breeches and leather jackets were more than just celebrities, they had become folk heroes, part of a cadre of men beginning to be known as the Suicide Club.

Whether they came from the prairie states, the heartland, from the South, or the industrialized North, Praeger's colorful parade of characters occupied a special place in the fabric of Bellefonte, their brash youthfulness and indiscretions not only forgiven, but mined under the banner of hospitality. The antics of these flying postmen were the talk of every party line in town. Did you see "Wild" Bill Hopson riding his motorcycle up the courthouse steps? Did you hear that "Slim" Lewis flew so low over town that he had set the old weathervane atop the courthouse to spinning? The townsfolk reveled in such behavior. Residents routinely vied for the chance to receive one of Uncle Sam's own as houseguests. Their stories about life in the air were riveting, their conversation laced with all the humor and mischievous charm of flyboys enamored with life. Folks in the area knew most every mail pilot personally. Plowing the fields or milking the cows, they'd listen for the familiar cough and sputter of a plane overhead. If a long silence followed, they'd drop what they were doing and rush across the field, monkey wrench in hand to see how they might help, if only to drive the pilot into town.

Uncle Sam was paying 25 cents per mile to anyone willing to transport one of its pilots to the nearest rail depot, and fully 35 cents to any kid lucky enough to spend an afternoon babysitting a downed plane, the hills humming with crickets, daydreaming about faraway places the pilot had come from, and would likely see again just as soon they flipped this ship upside right again.

On May 15, 1919, exactly one year to the day since inauguration of the world's first regularly scheduled airmail service, Praeger's western expansion officially kicked off for a second time with flights operating between Cleveland and Chicago. In Cleveland, Eddie Gardner climbed into his airplane and, amid a rousing chorus of cheers, set out for the Windy City, arriving at his destination just three hours and fifty minutes later, including a refueling stop at Bryan.

Flying eastbound out of Chicago, pilot Trent Fry, another of Edgerton's hires, hit the skies in a newly modified Liberty-powered DH-4, arriving in Cleveland in just three hours and thirteen minutes, guaranteeing, at last, 100 percent inaugural day success.

Clearly, the decision to stop and regroup had been the prudent thing to do. A momentum seemed to be building. But ten days into the run airmail suffered its second pilot fatality. Frank McCusker was piloting the de Havilland when suddenly a flash of fire exploded in front of him. Flames quickly engulfed his ship. With nowhere to go, McCusker unfastened his harness, and at 200 feet, jumped out of the airplane. The laces were burned from his shoes, and his trousers burned off up to his knees. He was killed instantly.

As always, the papers played it up big, which might help explain why, despite the media blitz, businessmen weren't exactly jumping on the airmail bandwagon with their business. Their coveted bank notes, checks, and letters had real monetary value and from what they'd read in the papers, there was the distinct possibility of their mail going down in flames.

Not long after the McCusker tragedy, Burleson received a letter from Mr. J. W. Harriman, president of the Harriman National Bank of New York, over just such a concern. It seems the bank had lost some money, $63,000 specifically, much of it in checks and money orders, which, curiously enough, had gone missing about the same time a mail plane had crashed en route from New York to Chicago.

"We asked the Post Office Department to make an inquiry and then we compared notes with other New York banks, discovering that others had lost also," he observed.

Did Burleson know, perchance, if the missing $63,000 had been aboard that downed mail plane? The banker couldn't imagine that being the case as they hadn't paid for airmail delivery. He was understandably curious.

The routing went from Burleson directly to Praeger, who knew instantly that the date Harriman was referencing coincided with the date of McCusker's fiery crash. He had to admit that a portion of the mail was destroyed.

Harriman responded vehemently. How dare the post office put that mail on an airplane. Neither he nor the other banks that had lost money had sought airmail delivery of their bank notes, money orders, and checks. He insisted that the postal department reimburse them for their losses.

"By what authority has the Post Office Department the right to hazard bank mail in experiments? I consider it a high-handed outrage," sputtered Harriman.

Harriman took the story to the newspapers. This was a "new Burleson game" he charged, claiming the incident was being covered up by the department. Using his considerable clout, Harriman got the chairman of the Senate Post Office Committee involved.

"I cannot yet understand why the Government lends itself to experiments with valuable mail, and, when accidents occur, endeavors to hide the performance and give misleading accounts of losses. We have suffered to a considerable extent, due to this experiment, which ended so disastrously and I cannot even get the assistance of those in your Department who are responsible for the loss."

Forced to weigh in with an answer, Burleson informed Congress that the U.S. Post Office Department had no knowledge of the whereabouts of Mr. Harriman's letters. An airplane had indeed crashed around Cleveland at about the same time, as Praeger had already explained, and, yes, a portion of the mail had gone up in flames. If Mr. Harriman's money had been among those sacks of mail, it had been "damaged beyond recognition."

Case closed, at least outwardly. Behind the scenes Burleson and Praeger set to work, hammering the equivalent of hurricane shutters onto airmail's windows and doors.

A few weeks later, the U.S. Post Office Department issued a new policy. By the order of the postmaster general, sending a letter by airmail would now cost the same 2 cents an ounce as it cost to send it by regular first class. With the stroke of a pen Burleson silenced Harriman and the entire congressional posse who had gotten wind of Praeger's policy of stuffing empty cargo holds with regular ground mail in order to beef up payload statistics. From now on, any first-class mail could theoretically be placed inside a mail plane in order to provide it with the proper ballast it required, or so the postal department claimed.

In a further effort to keep the department out of the fire, it was also announced that from now on cargo holds on all aircraft would be lined with flame-resistant materials and mail sacks constructed of fireproof material. Once again, Burleson and Praeger had pulled rabbits out of their hats. Without missing a beat, they kept pushing westward.

Things were growing fast; fully twenty mechanics were busy keeping the planes running as smoothly as possible at Belmont. It was tough being a grease monkey. In the hierarchy of postal flying, they were the ones on their backs, propping up the pyramid. Not that they got much thanks for their efforts. Gravity being what it is, shit regularly fell downhill. To a mechanic, no news was considered good news. But all too often, they heard it on a daily basis—from field managers pushing them to turn around planes faster, from pilots grousing about their engine overheating or some piston misfiring. Yet, even modified, so much could go wrong on those flimsy biplanes, it was difficult keeping them in flying condition. Cables had to be regularly inspected at the turnbuckle for signs of strain, the propeller had to be kept covered to prevent it from getting warped, and wheels had to be periodically removed and checked. Adding to their troubles, inventories of spare parts were horribly low. Tires, axles, tail skids, wing struts—the list of needed parts was seemingly endless. The second assistant postmaster general might be hammering out the future of civil aviation, but it fell to the mechanics to make sure it all happened.

The job was demanding, often repetitive, and they worked out in the open hangars exposed to the cruel cold of winter and summer's suffocating heat, their nostrils always inhaling the smell of castor oil and aviation fuel. Daily, the men wiped off the wings, lest any dirt rot the fabric. Each morning, they checked for rips. Even a small, unseen tear in a wing's leading edge could, under the strain of flight, widen into a gaping rip big enough to cause a plane to crash.

Riggers were an important part of the crew, too. The way some could string a wire amounted to high art, the proper tension, the lines run up exactly the right way to take the strain of flight on the wings. When a rigger was good, he could set the wind to singing in a pilot's ear.

Despite the long hours, the insults, and the lack of equipment, scores of applications came flooding in, everyone eager to push the limits of aviation. To a mechanic, it was all about performance. If something didn't work to its optimum level, one had only to disassemble its components, then put them all back together in order to coax all those parts into sweet, syncopated harmony. There was an elemental quality to machinery. An engine never groused or bemoaned its fate, and its whine was the sound of pure unadulterated power firing on all cylinders. A man could lose himself in that kind of music. Like moths drawn to the flame they came, some with flying experience, others trying to climb onboard as qualified upholsterers. Given the applications, the postal department could afford to be selective. Mechanics were required to have at least three years' experience on gasoline motors and at least eighteen months' experience on the type of motors and planes used in the service.

If a guy was lucky enough to be hired on, he could count on eventually being required to ride shotgun atop a cargo hold filled with sacks of mail. An aero ship was a mechanic's office, and when one was downed in a farmer's field, it was the wrench turner who stuck his head into the engine compartment and, tool kit by his side, made the necessary repairs to get the plane airborne as quickly as possible. None of the mechanics liked sitting in the front cockpit with the mail, though. They all knew that in a crash they'd be flattened into a pancake by the engine.

On July 1, the full New York–Chicago route was opened for yet another time. To keep interest up, Praeger dazzled spectators with a parachute demonstration. Some of the mail pilots thought such safety harnesses to be sissy stuff, but Praeger and others in the military believed such devices would substantially improve a man's chances in the air.

The dour, serious Earl White, only hired a month prior, would be pilot in command of the first westbound flight out of the airfield at Belmont. Ground crew removed the guardrails along the oval's perimeter in order to taxi the ship through. Then, at 5:15 A.M., with dawn at his back, White took off heading west, arriving safely in Bellefonte. The mail was transferred to Max Miller, who had been specially assigned the tough Bellefonte-to-Cleveland-over-the-mountains leg. As always, the skilled aviator pulled the mail on through. Landing in Cleveland, he passed his sacks on to Ira Biffle, who arrived intact in Chicago, still plenty of light remaining in the day. Total time from New York to Chicago: nine hours.

The equation had worked smoothly, not just on paper, but in the skies. As much as eleven hours had been saved compared to sending mail by train. Even the normally tight-lipped Praeger had to be smiling. The more powerful DH-4s were not only flying fast, they were carrying up to 400 pounds of mail, compared to the previous max of 250 to 300 pounds. Farther distances, extra payload capacity, strengthened ships—critics had claimed that the maximum life of the planes would be no more than 140 hours of actual flying time. A year later, several planes had 200 hours in the air. Even all six of the original Jennies had made it through the year, flying in snowstorms and wind gales, their engines intact, each one standing as testimony to the mechanics.

*   *   *

At long last, the beginning of Praeger's transcontinental air route was back on track. Edgerton seemed to be working out, and there were plenty of modified planes and newly hired pilots to get the job done. But Maurice Newton's wife had joined the ranks of aviation widows. Her husband had never been quite the same after his accident, none of the jobs Praeger assigning him having panned out. Despite Edgerton's assessment that he had lost his stomach for flying, the aviator had resumed his old job hauling the mail. But after an uncompleted flight due to mechanical troubles put him at odds with the chief, he had enough.

"I have endeavored since I have been here in this service to carry out promptly and to the best of my ability any orders I received, and having the welfare of the Air Mail foremost in my mind," he wrote in his resignation letter. "When I got to Belmont I received your telegram asking why you should not discipline me. So I telephoned my resignation, I do not care to stay under these circumstances."

Newton left the service, but by spring, he was dead, having complained of headaches for quite some time. Though his wife petitioned at length for some measure of compensation, claiming that his earlier accident had led directly to his death, the government never awarded her a dime, saying the physician attending him the day of the crash could not be located, thus no accurate assessment could be made as to the real cause of his death. As a result, the $66.66 per month Uncle Sam would normally pay out in death benefits to survivors would not be forthcoming.

Praeger's chief clerk, George Conner, disagreed with the decision. Having seen firsthand the extent of Newton's injuries following his plane crash outside Belmont, Conner remained convinced that doctor's testimony or no, the underlying cause of that pilot's death had been sustained while in the employ of Uncle Sam. Newton's death would incite several of the men to words, Conner included.

"I am convinced that the injury received in the accident on September 25, 1918, contributed to his death," he wrote.

Throughout his tenure, Praeger would receive similar letters—pleas from fathers requesting extra funds for a son's burial expenses, letters from wives requesting compensation for dead husbands, tirades from irate businessmen, accusations from politicians, and excuses from pilots, mechanics, and clerks who couldn't get their work done. He treated them all rationally, coolly, citing government codes and regulations when necessary.

This was business. Right from the start, Praeger and Burleson had sought to operate the post office like a commercial enterprise, not some bloated government agency. That's how Burleson wanted it run and the way his second was conducting affairs. It was one thing to offer a flier a plum desk job following an injury, quite another to set precedent and pay death benefits based on circumstantial evidence. Whatever his sympathies toward Newton's wife, the chief was not one to let sentiment hold sway over realities.

Praeger was a study in contrasts, and one's view of him depended upon where one was standing. Postal employees saw him as the razor-sharp steel-eyed administrator, some of his secretaries considered him warmly paternal, while politicians viewed him as Burleson's hammer. He could be cold and impatient, yet a Texas charm lay always just below the surface.

Burleson was the one man into whose company he could escape, resting for a time on the banks of the Potomac, throwing in a fishing line, all the daily struggles behind them. For such a *sanctus sanctorum*, this cigar-chewing Texan would ever be ready, his fishing pole stashed in his closet for just such moments.

CHAPTER 16

DEAR MR. PRAEGER

The chief of flying was proving himself no slouch when it came to running the airmail. He was virtually the youngest one on the field, but his analytical mind, disciplined by military training, quickly grasped the solution to most problems. Delivery performance had lagged in the heart of the winter, only scoring in the 80s for January and February, but now that it was early summer the numbers were consistently hovering in the mid-90s. Edgerton felt vindicated.

He knew, though, that his boss wanted 100 percent success. Building on Lipsner's organizational contributions, Edgerton took accident reporting to the next level—requiring pilots to painstakingly record every detail on paper. Praeger and his team were carefully reading every report, reviewing the cause of every forced landing, searching for an emerging pattern, one that would identify weak spots, help them understand what they were dealing with.

For pilots, the task of negotiating their way around the paperwork was worse than recovering from a tailspin. It was one thing to have an engine explode and blow hot oil in your face, quite another to have to sit down with a pencil and write about it.

Take pilot Gilbert Budwig's report, filed during his first week on the job in early April: "Had been in the air about twenty minutes, making in that time three landings. On the last takeoff, when about 800 feet high, the motor dropped to 700 R.P.M. and I was forced to land, so picked the best available field and landed therein. Before the machine rolled to a stop, she hit a slight rise in the ground and was tossed into the air a short distance and since the ship was under flying speed, she at once turned over on her nose and finally rolled over on her back. Why the motor quit is at the present unknown, but I would judge from its actions [that it was] ignition trouble, since all but three cylinders cut out, and air pressure, oil and heat of the motor were all normal. Signed, Gilbert G. Budwig."

Through it all, the pilots were unfailingly polite in their reports to Praeger, trying their level best to erase the indelible "pilot error" that might otherwise stain their record. Mail pilots knew better than to argue with authority. But they also knew from experience that forced landings were subject to interpretation. A collapsed landing gear was more likely to be from shoddy construction as much as the result of a pilot's hard landing. And why should a pilot be blamed for running into a fence when it was a conked-out motor that forced the emergency in the first place?

Damage to property only compounded the paperwork. In Budwig's emergency landing, he came down in a cabbage patch, with the farmer none too pleased about having it flattened by a crashing airplane. Engine oil spilled over the ground, requiring extra cultivating before he could get his potatoes in for the season. The Belmont field manager had to personally inspect the damage and report back to headquarters so the farmer could be properly compensated. It would all go into Budwig's record.

One of Eddie Gardner's flights added a whole new meaning to term "collateral damage." Flying over suburban Cleveland, Turk was forced into an emergency dead-stick landing while over a tract of wooden two-story houses. The plane struck a rooftop, causing the fuel tank to explode, spreading burning gasoline and debris over the surrounding buildings. Half the neighborhood caught fire, and several homes were completely destroyed. Turk walked away only grazed, not forgetting to rescue the mail sacks from the hold before they burned.

Who was going to pay for the damage? the Cleveland city officials wanted to know. Send the bill to Mr. Otto Praeger, responded the irrepressible Gardner, and without missing a beat, he worked his way to the Cleveland airfield and finished the flight with a backup plane.

Such mishaps were costing Praeger plenty, but casually tossed off as mere "incidents" by the pilots, to be embellished and expanded into folklore by the witnesses. Nobody knows for sure whether it is true that Miller really did set down in some open field with radiator troubles, but when he caught sight of a farmer coming toward him shotgun in hand, he decided one hole in the radiator was better than several and quickly hightailed it out of there.

Nowhere were stories swapped and enjoyed with more relish than at the pilots' main watering hole—the American Flying Club. The tastefully proportioned white stone residence on Thirty-eighth Street in Manhattan belied the sprawling boisterousness shaking the rafters inside. Founded by several ex-military aviators, the club held a virtual treasure trove of "mementos, trophies, framed squares of airplane linen salvaged from crashes by famous men, wrecked propeller hubs, photographs of the great aces, and a collection of magnificent flight paintings by Faure."

Here, mail pilots, barnstormers, ex-military pilots, and test pilots swapped stories, played cards, hoisted a tall one with their buddies, and exchanged fantasies about the future of aviation. Guys salivated over the thought of multiengine airplanes flying nonstop across continents and oceans, with passengers onboard, even. The smoke-filled rooms echoed with laughter and flying stories, like the one about the pilot who parked his plane in a tree, then had the good humor to send Praeger an accident report telling him that "he delivered his mail to a 'branch' post office."

There was the time "Wild" Bill Hopson supposedly rode the struts of a mail plane all the way from Bellefonte to New York because he had a date in Manhattan and no other way to get there, or when Ham Lee set himself ablaze inside his open cockpit while puffing away on one of the fat cigars he liked to chew, embers spewing like sparks.

There wasn't a more likable group of guys than the fliers. But it could hardly be said that Uncle Sam's pilots were polishing the image Burleson was seeking for the postal department. Nonsense, said the men. Not everybody could play cards all night, then fly the dawn run out of Belmont sporting a hangover the size of Broadway. Harold "Slim" Lewis was the champion of that. The California-born aviator always brought in the mail, regardless of engine failures, blizzards, or whether the fog was thick enough to walk on.

As an aviator and a poker player, the lanky 6-foot-4-inch mail pilot was aces. Friends swore Slim had some tricks up his sleeve that trumped the flyboys from the East. He had a natural ability to size up a person right from the start, and for those times when he was off his luck or missed his mark he kept a couple of uncashed paychecks in his wallet for ready money.

The pilots' inclinations met with little sympathy from anybody above the rank of mechanic. Praeger had already done the math. According to his calculations, mail pilots were working on average just one hour a day.

"Sometimes, they fly a route covering several hours, and after the completion of the trip they rest for several days."

Even more reason that he expected his airmail couriers to be dependable, conscientious, and able to take direction. That meant they were not to buzz the hangars, not to perform stunts with the planes, not to give rides to civilians, and not to fly drunk. And Hopson needed to start filing his expense reports on time, and stop scribbling them on the back side of used hotel stationery.

Despite the rules of conduct, Slim kept buzzing the trains, Hopson kept dropping his sacks of dirty laundry over the side of his ship for the local launderer at Bellefonte, everyone working under the assumption that what the chief didn't know couldn't hurt them. It was bad enough they couldn't wear spurs anymore, since the mechanics complained that they were digging holes in the floorboards of the planes. But if Praeger thought the men of Uncle Sam's Suicide Club were to be maintained like a fleet of postal delivery trucks, then he was wrong.

If the pilots were insistent on flouting convention, the chief remained as determined as ever to endow the cause with a high nobility. Being a wordsmith, he was always looking for catchphrases that could help capture the essence of the service. Praeger held one phrase in particular in high regard. Its message was simple but timeless, and the former journalist couldn't help but employ it in a memo to staff: "Neither snow, nor rain, nor heat, nor gloom of night stays these couriers from the swift completion of their appointed rounds."

Praeger wasn't the only one to find inspiration in those words. So, too, had William Mitchell Kendall. As the principal architect for the New York City Post Office Building, constructed a few years prior on Eighth Avenue between Thirty-first and Thirty-third Streets in Manhattan, it was his job to find some worthy phrase to go across the entire 280-foot frieze running the length of its Parthenon-like façade. Until recently, nothing had come to mind, but one evening, while reading the writings of sixth-century historian Herodotus in its original Greek, he came across a passage that intrigued him. It described the travails of the couriers of the Persian emperor Cyrus in Egypt in 500 B.C., who braved all manner of hardship to carry messages between far-flung places.

Kendall enlisted the aid of several language specialists to help him fully translate the passage. One expert's translation lacked zing: "These men will not be hindered from accomplishing at their best speed the distance which they have to go either by snow or rain or heat or by darkness of night."

Another was a real yawner: "These neither snow nor rain or heat nor darkness of night prevent from accomplishing each one the task proposed to him with the very utmost speed."

In desperation, Kendall contacted an old acquaintance at Harvard. Would the professor tackle the job of translating the passage?

"No snow nor rain days' heat nor gloom hinders their speedily going on their appointed rounds" is what he got.

Nothing seemed just right. No slouch himself in Greek studies, Kendall put pen to paper and worked the phrase over repeatedly until at last, satisfied, he came up with the words seen today across the façade of the building. William Mitchell Kendall's eloquent expression of service proved an unqualified success, both as an inscription on the New York Post Office and as an unofficial credo for the entire Air Mail Service.

*   *   *

Even with the high ideals, there is no denying that the chief was putting his men in a vice and turning the screw. If Edgerton or Praeger or a field manager or division superintendent thought that a pilot hadn't followed operational protocol, the pilot received a black mark on his record and was docked bonus pay for miles flown. Chalk up too many mechanicals or too many weather delays and the pilot was fired, Praeger telling him exactly why in a letter.

Increasingly, pilots were beginning to rethink what it meant to be an employee of Uncle Sam. With Lipsner gone and the service rapidly expanding, the flying corps was becoming a different sort of place, not as much fun for people like Gardner. Everybody felt the pressure of Praeger's all-weather flying policy—a dictum he believed could be enforced by official edict. The pilots didn't like it and were growing increasingly more vocal about their dissatisfaction with his heavy-handed management style. When it came to incompletes on the board, a pilot was guilty until proven innocent.

Morale hit an all-time low in July when pilot Charles Lamborn died flying over the Alleghenies between Bellefonte and Cleveland. Hired only five weeks prior, Lamborn had become hopelessly lost over Snowshoe Mountain. Disoriented in the soup, he emerged from the fog nose down at only 400 feet and was unable to recover before crashing.

The weather in the mountains had been lousy all month, and the fog and thunderstorms were turning out to be just as dangerous as they feared. But day after day, pilots like Miller, Gardner, Shank, and Lee continually threw themselves into what everyone was now calling "Hell's Stretch," and for good reason. It didn't make a difference if a pilot was flying to or from Bellefonte, the Allegheny Mountains had become a serious hazard to one's health.

"In bad weather, we hung on every explosion of the exhaust with a prayer," recalled one of the new hires, Jack Knight, who had been taught to fly by Ham Lee at Ellington Field during the war.

His name was on the board one day in July for a flight from Cleveland to Bellefonte when ground visibility was an abysmal 200 feet. Still inside the hangar, he stalled for as long as possible without drawing attention. But with mail sacks already stowed inside the hold of his ship, there was nothing else but to climb into his flying suit—though "as slowly as possible without invoking suspicion that I was stalling for a few more additional minutes."

More than anything, Knight wanted to back out. Even a guy nicknamed "Sky" Knight as a young kid wanted nothing to do with flying that day. But the last thing any pilot wanted to be called was chicken. Besides, the superintendent seemed pretty determined that Jack should fly—"or else."

"Pull the blocks."

Giving a feeble wave to the chief mechanic, the skinny pilot from Buchanan, Michigan, took off. But no sooner did he clear the field than he became enveloped in mist. For the next several minutes Knight "fought the old bus" upward through the bumpy air, emerging at last above the weather at 7,000 feet, a "white sea of unbroken fog underneath as far as you could see." All he had to do now was follow his compass heading east for two hours, hope it was reading right and true, and pray that at the end of that time there would be an opening in the cloud cover over Bellefonte.

Two hours later, Knight found himself still cruising above the clouds, no break anywhere in sight. Lacking enough fuel to turn around and hightail it back to Cleveland, he pushed the nose of his ship forward and began to descend, only to pull back up again with second thoughts.

There was a distinct possibility that he and number 67 would become part of a mountainside. For Knight, there was only one thing to do—write his last will and testament. Finding an old envelope, he began jotting down his last thoughts, dispersing the sum total of his worldly effects to friends and loved ones. Then, he took a final look at the sun and down he went.

"My altimeter registered 6,000, 4,500, 3,500. Air speed raced to 140 even with throttled motor—wires screamed wildly and struts vibrating badly—still no sight of ground—just wet impenetrable fog rushing through my wings.

"2,800 feet on the altimeter and still nothing but fog. God, for just one glimpse of the ground. High points of the mountains in this locality stuck up 2,400 feet—why didn't I see them.

"Altimeter shows 2,000—still no ground—what moment will a mountain side reach up at 140 mph and end all this worry?

"Altimeter registers 1,800—1,600 still fog—fog. The elevation at Bellefonte Field is 1,800 feet above sea level."

Suddenly, from out of the mist, Knight spied a sliver of roadway on the ground and went reaching for the lifeline like a drowning sailor adrift at sea.

"I began flying down this narrow valley, twisting, turning and dodging through passes, pulling up blindly into fog, counting ten, diving back out, finally by good fortune more than good flying arrived at my terminal field."

A short time later, Knight would write down his adventure on paper—half of the story on stationery from the Hotel Jefferson in South Bend, Indiana, and the other half on paper from Hotel Yancey in Grand Island, Nebraska, glad to be alive for the retelling.

CHAPTER 17

STRIKE

Gray clouds were hovering so low over Long Island on July 22, 1919, that Windy Smith could almost reach up and touch them. It had been raining all night, puddles of water flooding the infield at Belmont. Windy walked out onto the grass, took a good look around, and called it a day. No way was he going to fly in this soup, not with this visibility. Smith might be known as "Bonehead" for having stepped into a spinning prop once and surviving with only a bump on his head, but having lived to tell the tale he wasn't about to cut his life short for the privilege of flying on a day like this—particularly when the high-compression Liberty engine on the Curtiss R-4 he'd been assigned was known to overheat when flying low and slow below the deck. And make no mistake, he'd be jumping chimneys today.

The field manager wasn't exactly sympathetic. Smith's name was on the flight board. By God, he had to go up.

But Windy held firm.

Eager to keep the mail moving, the manager put in a call to Walter Stevens, one of the reserve pilots, and ordered him to fly over Smith. But Stevens took one look at the weather and also opted out, claiming himself too new to the corps, too unfamiliar with the route to go it alone.

Pushing on down the list, the field manager stopped at Clifford Webster's name. Webster had taken the almighty fly-or-be-fired oath just two weeks before. That kind of newness usually prompted a guy to scramble into a cockpit on demand. Not so Webster. He might be a fresh recruit, but he was plenty irked over this invitation to what amounted to an early death. Nor had this been the first time in his short career that trouble had come calling. He fired off a letter to Praeger.

"On three trips I have been compelled to fly close over the housetops of thickly settled cities for a considerable distance, in order to find my way through. As under these condition a motor failure would probably result in the injury or death of people upon the ground, I consider it would be little less than criminal to continue to take such chances. As far as I can judge from the work I have already done it seems to me that the Post Office Department requires their pilots to take unreasonable risks both for themselves and for those on the ground. I believe that only exceptional good fortune has kept the death rate as low as it is. Unless there is a change of policy I do not think I shall care to remain in the Aerial Mail Service very long."

The mail sacks were still waiting to depart Belmont. For the fourth time that morning, the field manager got on the horn and placed a call—this time to good, old "One Hundred Percent Ham" Lee. The former barnstormer never particularly liked the moniker. He knew from experience that trying to keep up with a rep like that got a pilot killed. But despite the fact that he wasn't due out for several more days, and even though the weather was downright vicious, he nonetheless hoofed it out to Long Island, ready to fly the mail on through.

Upon arriving, he learned the larger truth. No way would he fly over Windy, at least not with the Curtiss R-4. Like Smith, however, he offered to fly a Curtiss Jenny, claiming its 150-horsepower Hispano-Suiza engine could be flown at lower altitudes without overheating.

Washington was notified. No mail was going out of Belmont Field. Praeger ignited. The men had promised to fly whenever called upon, whatever ordered. There were no caveats in this equation. They had taken the oath, all of them. Those mail sacks had to leave Belmont today. The weather in Washington was fine. If skies there were socked in, the men could use the instruments on their panel to fly over the deck.

The second assistant's response was swift and severe. The two new hires who refused to fly would remain on the payroll, but the more experienced Windy Smith and Ham Lee were sliced off just like Gardner and Shank had been last winter.

The discontent that had been smoldering in the corps erupted. Most of the pilots were former military fliers. Five of the aviators that Praeger had hired in December to fly the Chicago route were aerial aces from the war, meaning that they had not only accepted the challenge of flying combat, but also lived long enough to shoot down five or more planes. They were prepared to risk their lives for their country, but being forced though blinding weather over some of the meanest stretch of terrain this side of hell for a couple sacks of mail was unacceptable. Praeger had gone too far. Progress should not come at the price of a man's life.

On July 23, Praeger found the following telegram on his desk.

The summary dismissal of pilots Lee and Smith without investigation or justification is considered as a direct attack on every pilot in the aerial mail service inasmuch as it was merely their misfortunes to be the ones in position to have to refuse to fly in order to protect their lives. Their reinstatement pending such investigation is requested. In order to be fair we will defer action for 24 hours. This everlasting fly regardless of weather conditions or resign must cease as we are as human as the rest.

Pitting themselves against the bullying tactics of a deskbound bureaucrat ordering them to fly, fly, fly, twenty of the pilots were refusing to do just that unless Praeger reinstated Windy and Ham.

Accusations were hurled back and forth, Washington claiming the pilots had lost their nerve, and pilots claiming Praeger had overstepped his bounds. Postal headquarters even accused the field manager at Belmont of mishandling the situation. He should have been tougher on the pilots, demanding they fly instead of requesting them like a maiden aunt to tiptoe through the raindrops. And Smith should have been booted off the field right after refusing to fly instead of being allowed to hang around, bad-mouthing operations and scaring the others off.

Windy, though, remained staunchly convinced of his decision not to fly. He was not going down without a fight, and he fired off a letter to the chief.

"It is might easy Mr. Praeger for you to sit in your swivel chair in Washington and tell the flyers when they can fly," he wrote. "You think it is impossible to fail to come through. Only yesterday I flew through terrible rain storms with the result that when I got in here that paint was knocked off my wings and my propeller badly torn. Pilots have been killed and only last week one of the best flyers in the United States lost his life when he tried to obey your orders and come through with the mail. Mr. Lamborn is the man I refer to. You do not regard a man's life with the least of respect, nor do you stop to consider the number of planes that have been smashed up with a big expense to the Government. It matters very little as long as you can run things in your own way."

Praeger sat down and did what he did best—address the situation on paper, issue by issue. In a rush to quell the sentiments weighing in against him, he issued a detailed report rebuking the pilots for their unwillingness to fly with the big Liberty. It was bunk to think the Curtiss R-4 required a minimum flying speed of 100 miles per hour to function properly. Everyone knew a pilot had to damn near whip the beast into flying at such a top speed.

"Also they know that its lowest flying speed is not in excess of 55 miles an hour, as demonstrated a recent official test by the Air Mail Service. This is possibly 5 miles an hour more than the small type JN-4H."

Praeger continued on the offensive, claiming the R-4 was actually safer than the smaller JN-4H, as it was less prone to flip over during a forced landing on wet ground and because the pilot's cockpit was positioned farther away from the engine. Studies proved him out.

For three days the mail didn't fly. The standoff had the press salivating over the story. This joust easily topped the fight with Lipsner back in December. What about all these aero ships, a reporter from the *New York Times* wanted to know—was it true that ten planes had crashed in the last two weeks alone, costing the department $20,000? Was it true that the airplanes were unsafe to fly?

No, what the pilots were saying was nonsense, Praeger told the reporter. Yes, there had been a number of forced landings lately, some serious but most causing just slight damage. He assured the newspaperman that such set-downs happened all the time and that a competent repair crew kept all flying machines in order. Both sides went back and forth. Praeger felt betrayed by the pilots. To him, this had been insubordination of the highest order. He felt sure that they had colluded to disrupt the delivery of airmail.

"The department cannot leave the question of when to fly and when not to fly in each instance to the judgment of a dozen different aviators. If this were done, it would be impossible to operate a mail schedule with any degree of dependability and the air mail would have to be abandoned."

This was the most frustrating time of his tenure with the postal department. He couldn't help notice that the United Kingdom's Royal Air Force was flying its mail through infernal British weather each day without much grumbling from its men.

"There is not much indicting in these reports of English pilots refusing to fly for lack of visibility as only 2.2 percent of their 2,450 trips failed on account of weather," he noted.

In fact, Europe was building a continentwide network of airmail routes despite the devastation wrought by the war. England was initiating two daily mail routes, one from London to Paris, the other from Folkstone, England, to Cologne, Germany. Already, Italy was flying a mail route nearly 500 miles long. France, too, was pressing its powerful multiengine planes into service and had recently posted to fly mail between Paris and Bordeaux. A passenger service had been inaugurated between Berlin and Weimar in war-torn Germany.

America might have been the first country to get a scheduled airmail service off the ground, but Europe was now pulling ahead, its air routes growing in leaps and bounds while Praeger struggled to keep his fledgling service afloat. The only first his pilots had recorded lately was laying claim to having engineered the world's first pilots strike.

The friction generated by the conflict naturally attracted the attention of Congress, and the honorable William Christian Ramseyer, a popular Republican congressman from Iowa, called Postmaster General Burleson to task. It was high time to bring attention to this matter.

Time was something Burleson could appreciate, having so little patience for anyone wasting his. The postmaster general once asked a man whom he considered a giant bore "how much he thought his time was worth."

The fellow hesitatingly allowed that 50 cents an hour was a fair valuation.

"Here then," said Burleson, proffering a silver dollar, "give me two hours exemption from your society."

Burleson would be able to handle the inquiry just fine. And his second could do the same on his front. Praeger had already proven himself a tough negotiator in his dealings with the Chicago political bosses some years back while setting up his truck routes. Over the past several years, he and Burleson had weathered far too many a skirmish and a few pitched battles to become anything less than master tacticians.

In an effort to hammer out a settlement, pilots Charles Anglin and Ham Lee went to Washington on July 26 to meet with Praeger and his management team of Edgerton, superintendent J. B. Corridon, and Charles Stanton, superintendent of the Eastern Division.

Anglin, who was called "Pop" by the other pilots, continually pressed Praeger for answers.

"Just what does that order mean—that the mail must go when it is ready to go?"

Praeger's response left little room for debate.

"The order means that the pilot must fly when he gets the order to fly or, in accordance with the understanding and agreement with pilots on their employment, tender his resignation."

Back and forth the discussion went, with Anglin doing his level best to give Praeger an inside view of airmail from the pilot's perspective. As Edgerton sat there listening, he surely had to know that

Pop was wasting his breath. Some time back, he'd already tried giving Praeger the same bird's-eye perspective of the service by strapping the second assistant into the cockpit.

"With the pretext of his examination of a new field, I got him into the air for his first flight. It was a clear day, but I finally found my objective, a small cumulus cloud a few miles northeast of Washington. En route in a straight line, I pointed out major features of the landscape. Casually I entered the cloud, then to emphasize an important point, spun out. Washington was in plain view. With throttle pulled I tapped him on the shoulder and asked, 'Where is Washington?' Dazedly, he looked all around and shook his head in bewildered fashion. After I pointed, and then aimed the ship, he finally recognized the city. He turned to me with a sheepish, little boy grin."

Like the pilots, Edgerton felt the chief sometimes made excessive demands upon pilots beyond the bounds of contemporary safety. Praeger didn't mind him thinking that, as long as Edgerton didn't publicly take the side of the pilots. He was careful to keep his distance. This was between Praeger and the pilots. Everyone else watched in the grandstand.

Anglin brought up another sore spot—salary. Starting pay was now only $2,000 a year. After thirty flying hours, $200 was tacked on up to $3,600. Max Miller, who had been hired at a starting pay of $3,600 little more than a year ago, had, following his reinstatement, found his salary cut back to $3,000 a year. The pilots wanted all starting salaries raised to $3,000 a year.

But Pop was trying to draw blood from the proverbial turnip. Postal coffers weren't exactly overflowing. The entire airmail budget for 1919 amounted to $100,000, and that paltry sum had been hard fought for in Congress. This year would find Praeger shifting another $600,000 out of his railroad and powerboat budgets in order to make up the shortfall between airmail expenditures and outlays.

The chief refused to enter into negotiations on the matter. One crisis at a time. He assured Anglin that twin-engine planes would soon be pressed into service, and salaries would be adjusted accordingly for any fliers wishing to pilot them.

For days, the men negotiated politely, their contentiousness couched in steady, civilized tones. But in the end, Praeger looked at Anglin from across his desk and summed up his position by saying:

"I have to fight Congress for appropriations. I have to fight the public that does not believe in airmail. Now, if I have to fight you pilots, too, there just won't be any air mail.

"As Second Assistant Postmaster General my job will go on, but it will be you pilots who will have no job."

The press was crying out for a resolution. Having turned the spotlight of attention on the conflict, they had succeeded in endowing it with a larger-than-life celebrity that the entire nation was now watching. A former correspondent, Praeger knew better than anyone that fueling the fires of dissension among the ranks could only damage his service in the end. The crashes, the narrow misses, the conflicts—their ferment was helping to sell newspapers, and he understood that the story wouldn't go away until he shook Anglin's hand.

Praeger relented, somewhat. A new policy on foul weather flying was instituted. From now on, it would be the field managers, not the postal officials in Washington, who decided on whether a pilot went up in bad weather or not. If a pilot believed the weather unfit for flying, the field manger would make a test flight himself. If in his judgment the visibility was good enough to fly through, the pilot would oblige and take the ship up. If not, he'd be given a bye, no black mark upon his record.

Ham was to be reinstated at full salary, as were the two lesser-experienced pilots. Praeger admitted that "an error of judgment was made on the part of the manager of the field in calling upon pilots Stevens and Webster to fly the New York–Washington route on that date. One of these pilots had never been over the route and the other had only made one trip, which was not sufficient to enable him to pick up land marks on days of poor visibility."

But Leon Smith—after that scathing letter—was off the team. The pilot whose father had once nicknamed him "Windy" because he "talked too much" had gotten his wind up and told the chief where to head off. Praeger hadn't forgotten; Smith's days as a flying letter carrier were over.

Mail resumed flying after that. All the combatants returned to their respective corners, each side convinced of its victory. Finally, the men had more of a say in the flying game. Windy, by thumbing his nose at Praeger's fly-or-be-fired dictum, had opened the door for his buddies to step through and voice their own discontent over postal policy. But the chief was confident in his triumph. Let the press and the pilots claim what they would. At the end of the day it was Praeger hiring the field managers, men who were often chosen more for their administrative skills than for their flying talents. Their allegiance would understandably be toward operations, not for placating the whim of each pilot. If he chose, he could send foxes to guard his henhouses.

CHAPTER 18

WILSON

Albert Burleson was known as the "magician" within the Post Office Department—up early with the birds each day battling the Army for control of airmail and jousting with former colleagues in the House of Representatives to keep the service funded. With President Wilson as his shield, he could remain impervious to the slings and arrows while bringing efficiency to the department, its wheels running along party lines, or so critics routinely charged.

Burleson saw no reason not to employ his considerable politicking skills in order to lay down a path furthering Wilson's ideologies and political interests. It all boiled down to fidelity—whether supporting the home state or backing one's political party, it was a quality expected of Burleson since the day he was born in 1863.

His father, Edward Burleson Jr., had fought for the Confederacy during the Civil War. He had also been a Texas Ranger as well as a delegate to the Constitutional Convention of 1875. But the Burleson pathway to battle dated back even further. Albert's grandfather, General Edward Burleson, had become one of the "Heroes of the Revolution," the Texas Revolution, that is. Just weeks after the fall of the Alamo in 1836, Gen. Burleson fought alongside Sam Houston and 750 other Texans in the Battle of San Jacinto. On that bright April morning when he and others took their revenge against Mexican general Antonio Lopez de Santa Ana and fifteen hundred of his soldiers, it's likely that he used the war cry "Remember the Alamo" to spur his men to victory. Having won the Mexican War, many of those heroes went on to make their fame and fortune in Texas, including Gen. Burleson, who served as vice president of the Republic of Texas.

Burleson had the self-confidence to handle whatever the press could dish out. He was an easy villain—his imposing posture and grave countenance made potent by a hair-trigger temper and a brusque management style that valued thrift and economy over the individual needs of his three hundred thousand postal employees. He and Wilson joked about his media thrashings regularly. Such lambasting came with the territory. Burleson was content in the knowledge that he was doing right, both by himself, by the president, and by the American people he served.

That sentiment was mutually exclusive, as evidenced by the fact that Burleson was the only member of Wilson's first cabinet to be reappointed when Wilson won a second term in 1916. The silver-haired umbrella-carrying Texan may have been born into privilege, but he shared the common values of thrift, honesty, and personal sacrifice with the president, the son of a Presbyterian minister. Add in Otto Praeger, a man of similar character and equally stern countenance, and airmail had been endowed with the power of the holy trinity.

But whatever help and political cover Burleson and Praeger may have received from the Oval Office over the past several years was slow in coming these days, the president thoroughly worn out from the stress of war. Only sixty years old, he was already a frail man, his efforts to push through his progressive reforms while negotiating the country through the conflict had taken a toll on his health. The low point came during the summer, when the basic tenets of a peace treaty he had labored to develop at the end of the war were collectively rejected by Congress.

"The Fourteen Points" were to have been his lasting legacy to peace, the means by which his domestic policies, bonded by a solid morality, could become the architecture of an American policy abroad. Notions of free trade, open agreements, democracy, and self-determination were derivations of the domestic programs that progressive reformers had been supporting for two decades. Where many countries believed that only self-interest should guide foreign policy, in the Fourteen Points Wilson argued that morality and ethics needed to become the basis for a foreign policy born of a democratic society.

The guardian of that morality would be the League of Nations, the last of his Fourteen Points. For Wilson, establishment of the League of Nations would be the only good thing to come of the horror of this war. It alone seemed capable of providing the forum by which a new world order could emerge to safeguard the peace for future generations. Without it, all the heartbreak had been for naught.

Yet for all its high ideals, the Fourteen Points failed to find favor with legislative bodies in America, England, or France. The Republicans controlled the Senate by one vote, and the party of Lincoln was not inclined to break partisan politics in order to approve the League.

Wilson knew what he had to do. He would go on the road and peddle the concept directly to the American people, hoping to build a groundswell of support that the Republicans wouldn't be able to ignore. Though already frail, he roused himself for the task ahead, embarking on a grueling 10,000-mile whistle-stop tour of the country. Determined to make his dream succeed, the president pleaded his cause day after day, his oratories intelligent and passionate, often rousing the public to thunderous applause. At last, the old articulate Wilson was back stirring people's emotions. It seemed as if the League of Nations might have a chance, after all. But after 3,500 miles on the road, the president's migraines began flaring up again. Wilson's health was failing. He long suffered from hypertension, even while president of Princeton, often surrendering to debilitating headaches. Then as now, he refused to take his doctor's advice and rest, instead driving himself through long, often eighteen-hour, days. His head throbbing, gripped in horrible pain, the president continued his tour, each stop punctuated by the same stretch out across the bed, eyes closed in the darkness of the Pullman, waiting for the next railroad stop, his next speech.

His second wife, Edith Bolt Galt, was worried. The stress of the speeches, the relentless travel—it was killing him. He needed to rest. Ignoring her pleas, Wilson pressed on to Pueblo, Colorado, to speak before a crowd of thousands. It was Wilson at his best, ascending to the heights of his ideals with an old eloquence and passion as he urged the audience to support the concept of an international league aimed at furthering world peace.

The speech, though brilliant, cost Wilson dearly. That night, his blinding headaches worsened, leaving him badly weakened and ill. His doctors had seen quite enough. The president simply had to return to Washington. If he didn't rest voluntarily, he would collapse. Thoroughly worn-out, it was a broken man who returned to the capital late September, knowing that the document into which he had poured so many hopes and dreams would die in Congress.

Only four days after arriving back, the president's wife found him sprawled out across the bathroom floor, unconscious, a severe cut to his head. Hurrying down the hall, she rang up Wilson's chief usher on a private line, lest White House operators overhear.

"Please, get Doctor Grayson, the President is very sick," she urged.

Admiral Cary Grayson, the president's physician, rushed over immediately. What he found devastated Wilson's wife. Her husband had suffered a terrible stroke, leaving his entire left side paralyzed. For days he hovered near death, unable to do anything beyond eat or drink.

Determined to hide the truth about his condition from the public, the press and even members of the president's own cabinet, Edith closely controlled access to her husband. No one came in or out without her personal approval.

As October became November and Christmas came and went, Republicans started growing suspicious. Rumors of Wilson's ill health had already been circulating through Congress, as doctors and nurses were routinely seen coming and going from the White House. There were whispers of his wife acting as regent. Everyone wanted to know what was going on.

Inside the White House, the president was growing stronger with each passing month, but clearly the stroke had stripped him of the ability to govern. As a statesman, he was virtually lifeless. In desperation, Edith and the doctor concocted a scheme. They would invite a group of Republicans to the White House where the president would be propped up in a chair, waiting, his paralyzed left arm hidden beneath a blanket.

"We're praying for you," said one of the visitors.

"Which way," quipped Wilson.

It was a stunning performance, his old wit silencing any rumor of disability. But it could not resuscitate his beloved League of Nations. Five months after his stroke the League went down in a Senate vote, his highest vision toppled. Wilson muddled through his remaining year in office, passively staring at newsreels and motion pictures sent in from Hollywood, wholly removed from the sea of events in which he could no longer participate. Communications with the president had all but ceased; only those deemed important by Edith were allowed into his sick room, earning her the moniker "the first woman President."

Wilson's stroke had paralyzed more than his body. Cabinet members found themselves lame ducks cut adrift in a Republican-controlled Congress. Burleson and Praeger became virtually sitting targets for any politician wishing to take potshots at the outgoing administration. Increasingly, airmail was being labeled "Burleson's Folly" or "Praeger's Folly" and even "Wilson's Folly."

Realizing that time could well be running out on the service, Praeger began pushing the transcontinental route even more vigorously. He would start by extending the New York–Chicago route west to Omaha, an additional distance of 440 miles, then push straight on through to San Francisco.

The buzz phrase around airmail hangars was "Frisco or bust."

From now on, everyone's sights would be set beyond the broad well-watered Mississippi Valley to the great plains. From there it was over the Rockies and beyond the great Salt Lake desert, moving across the Sierra Nevada, and into the rich fertile valley of California. Any transcontinental push, however, would require substantially better planes than what Praeger had in his fleet. Without them, crossing the 10,000-foot elevations along the way would be near impossible.

In December, Praeger got his wish when he was delivered a new de Havilland DH-4 that was modified with not one, but two power plants. He also received a twin-engine Martin bomber he felt sure would gain him the necessary power and altitude he was seeking to push the route west. Eager to test them out, the chief put them to work hauling mail along the short New York–Washington route.

On the DH-4's maiden trip, he was rewarded with a record 630-pound cargo carrying run. Less than a week later, the twin-engine Martin plane was able to bypass Philadelphia entirely, completing the trip from New York to Washington in two hours, all the while hauling an eye-popping 1,066 pounds of mail. Given the plane's long-distance capability, Praeger was able to eliminate Bustleton Field as a refueling stop, the expense of maintaining flying operations there no longer necessary. The facility was converted into a repair depot.

Flying operations at Belmont were also being moved. For too long pilots had reckoned with the unforgiving weather off the coast of Long Island, its fog and mist continually dogging their flights. Then, too, there were reports that Maj. Belmont's staff at the track had grown weary of the disruption to horse racing and training caused by the aerial activity, not to mention the buzzing of the track.

Flying operations were moved to a small field owned by Paul Heller in Newark, New Jersey. Designating it the official new northern terminus of the airmail during the winter of 1919, Praeger inducted Heller Field into the growing pantheon of lousy airmail facilities, using the occasion to denounce the military's continued attempt to control all government flying.

The continued expansion of airmail had the ground underneath Eddie Gardner seemingly falling away. Instead of a mentor like Lipsner, he now had to contend with a chief of flying, a chief of maintenance, a chief of construction, a chief clerk, division superintendents, field managers, maintenance officers, and an operator in charge of radio experiments who, together, were forming the weight of an impenetrable governmental organization bearing down on him.

Even ever-reliable One Hundred Percent Ham was catching it over an unscheduled stop near Bustleton, forcing him into pages of correspondence between him and management. It had taken a letter to Praeger from the assistant superintendent of repairs before Ham Lee was cleared of all charges.

Hopson was forever getting into hot water over his expense reports. Praeger wanted them submitted promptly by the tenth of each month, while Hopson preferred storing them up for three months, presumably opting for a larger one-lump payout. Despite Praeger's reproaches, Hopson kept right on losing his expense vouchers and handing in his expense reports late, scribbled in illegible handwriting on hotel stationery.

The post office wasn't so much evolving as much as it was mutating into something unrecognizable to the pilots who had been there in the early days, a whole year and a half ago. New aviators were being hired, old ones reassigned to different airfields along the routes like so many pawns on a chessboard. And still, the ever-present order to fly, fly, fly through all weather came bearing down upon them. For Gardner, the fun-loving former racecar driver, the heady days of flying the Uncle's mail were already over. Not for him a slumped state of servitude. He'd been married once, hadn't liked it. A committed bachelor, Gardner made it his business to go where he wanted, whenever he wanted, spending his greenbacks as he saw fit.

In October 1919, Turk Bird flew his last run for the Suicide Club. A month later Robert Shank resigned. The two pilots, who just one year ago had defied Praeger's authority by refusing to fly out of Belmont, were again calling it quits. The two would set up a little flying operation in Atlantic City, hauling tourists around in a Curtiss JN-4C.

Max Miller was the only one still standing from the original group. The handsome blue-eyed Norwegian had been transferred several times already, but like always, he took it all good-naturedly. Miller was still working to get his old salary reinstated in order to help push his life forward. Daisy knew that despite all the relocations that kept them from settling down and buying some furniture, one day they would attain the dream they were working toward.

*   *   *

In hindsight, it seems inexplicable that Praeger would have chosen such a dangerously small field as Heller unless he believed its location near Manhattan would speed up existing ground handling times. Situated in the industrial quarter of Newark, the field was stuck like a caramel between the teeth of a fireworks plant on one side, and the Tiffany jewelry factory on another, and pulled up short by a canal strategically located at the far end. So hazardous was the site that factory workers at the Tiffany plant routinely placed bets as to whether or not planes landing and taking off outside their windows would make it.

Praeger's flying postmen weren't exactly odds-on favorites.

"When a new pilot would come in for his first landing the employees of Tiffany's would line up on the ramp to observe. They were usually rewarded with a spectacular splash in the canal, a wild ground loop or a nose-up into the mound," said one of the pilots.

If the glide path was too short, the pilot would drop down onto the warehouses, too long and he'd sink into the canal beyond. The only way to land without mishap was to drop out of the sky like a wounded bird, then bank sharply before landing. It was an aerial maneuver of the highest order and often beyond the skills of most mail pilots. Realizing this, management strategically dumped a large mound of dirt at the end of the runway to keep planes from running into the canal.

Landing at Heller Field was tough enough in a regular plane, much less trying to land one of the behemoth, new twin-engine Martin bombers now part of the fleet. Adding to the test, the winter of 1919 had delivered some of the worst weather in years. Lacking any heat in the hangars, mechanics were being forced to start the engines in zero-degree temperatures.

"These engines were mounted so high that it was impossible to turn the propeller by hand, forcing them to be started with electric starters which drew their current from small storage batteries nearby," said one individual. "It was the custom to fill up with warm water and warm oil, but in spite of these precautions, the starter would slowly grind the prop around, time after time, without a single explosive response from the engine exhaust. This naturally drained the storage battery and during all this time the water in the radiator was cooling off and approaching the freezing point and the oil in the crank case was getting constantly colder. Even the injection of a little ether through the engine pit-cocks frequently failed to bring the desired response. Next, some of the boys would sense the approaching freezing point and stop to drain the radiator and fill it again with hot water. In the meantime, the little old storage battery had gone dead and a new battery had to be installed and connected up. All this was going on at about 5:00 A.M., with a crew whose spirits fitted the time and weather."

None of that was of concern to pilot Slim Lewis, though. Despite a foot of snow covering the field, he climbed into the cockpit of his Martin one morning, and without any snow skids he set out to fly the mail to Cleveland.

Someone yelled, "Go!"

The men holding the tail promptly raised it into the air while those holding the wings began running forward—propelling the ship through the snow and down the field.

Like always, Slim made it where others would have failed.

As the year 1919 drew to a close, Praeger and Burleson were hoping Congress would give them something more than coal for Christmas. Praeger estimated he needed close to $3 million to extend the route from Chicago all the way to San Francisco.

As always, reactions to their budget request were typical. Those who still wanted to see the military running operations thought that starving the service of money would hasten the process. Others, including the Railway Mail Clerks Association, were against appropriating funds to airmail strictly on principle.

If there was one common reaction, it was the belief that attempting to fly mail on a continuous 3,000-mile journey from one end of the country to another was just left of insane—particularly in light of the disastrous military experiment in October. Looking to promote the value of joint Army/Navy air operations, Gen. Billy Mitchell had dispatched sixty-three airplanes of all makes and models, fighters to bombers, on a round-trip flight from Mineola to San Francisco. By the time the dust settled three weeks later, seven pilots had been killed and many others injured. All told, twenty-five planes crashed.

The race dashed Gen. Billy Mitchell's airmail hopes and created suspicion in Congress about the Post Office Department's push westward. If the U.S. military couldn't cross the breadth of the country, what made Praeger think he could make it over the snow-capped Rocky Mountain peaks? It simply couldn't be done, not with existing airplanes.

Praeger and Burleson knew better. Years back people had said that the railroad would never replace the stagecoach, folks claiming locomotive equipment to be a hazard. Never—ever—could railroads be made safe, not as a mode of transport. Armed with long memories and an unerring vision, the two Texans faithfully donned their hip waders once more and went fishing in shark-infested waters for the money with which to expand the line westward.

CHAPTER 19

A KILLER YEAR

The U.S. Air Mail Service sputtered into 1920 wholly spent from its annual funding battle with Congress. Despite Burleson and Praeger's political wrangling, January saw just $850,000 added to airmail coffers, hardly enough to underwrite existing service much less extend it all the way to San Francisco. The new year brought more mixed news, as the favorite vice of the airmail service—from Burleson and Praeger on down to the flying corps—was about to be abolished.

January 16 was nearly upon them, and Max was downright worried. Though not a drinking man, he felt certain the streets would be chaotic at midnight, the hour Prohibition became law. Given that he was off working, he urged Daisy to stay inside and away from the pandemonium surely to come.

The straitjacket presented by having the entire nation go dry was a bizarre juxtaposition to the new dynamic emerging from the ashes of World War I. America had survived a global battle, sobered but resilient, its collective optimism still intact. Gone was the austerity and deprivation, the death and the disillusionment, the climate of mistrust whipped up by the government's quest to root out troublemakers and search under every rock and bedpost for spies. "Postmodernism," the term that had been coined in Germany in 1917, had spread across the Atlantic and was poised to kick off a wholesale social release that would find its beat in the Roaring Twenties.

Americans wanted to kick up their heels, dance cheek to cheek, drink gin, and smooch in the backseats of automobiles. In their efforts to bring moderation to the masses, legislators had inadvertently provided people with the cover they needed to do just that. Before the ban on liquor, most ladies wouldn't be caught dead inside a bar. But thanks to the efforts of the Temperance Union, women across America had only to whisper their secret password to a pair of undisclosed eyes peering out from behind a thin slot in an alley door to find themselves deliciously free—whether it be to sip a champagne cocktail, listen to the jazz punching through ragtime, or just start shaking away rigid behaviors and antiquated mores.

The underground banquet was perfectly timed to the other major change to the U.S. Constitution in 1920—the newly ratified Nineteenth Amendment, which gave women the right to vote beginning August 26. And what better upbeat to celebrate with than jazz—that new American rhythm. Prohibition might be giving rise to a subculture of shady bootleggers and mob types whose fortunes would be derived from illegal liquor sales, bars, and speakeasies, but it was also giving jazz performers a broader venue in which to perform. Before long, every back alley in Chicago and New York would be enlivened with the distinctive sounds of New Orleans. As black musicians like twenty-one-year-old Duke Ellington experimented with offbeats, painters like Georges Braque and Pablo Picasso were bringing their innovations to the canvas in Europe, trying to best one another with fresh, new perspectives. Cubed or jazzed, the world was changing the way it looked at itself.

While America kicked up its heels, Praeger and Burleson still faced the same old deprivations when it came to airmail. The chief continued what he'd been doing right from the beginning—reallocating federal dollars. Each year, to the tune of several hundred thousand dollars, he would siphon away funds from railways, powerboats, and other transportation modes and divert them into airmail coffers. So long as money was used to defray actual operating expenses and not to purchase new equipment or set down new routes, all was perfectly legal. Praeger conducted his money transfers under a watchful eye of an auditor from the Treasury Department. However, being ever astute at the numbers game, he made certain that few line items were recorded in his ledgers. A complete inventory of the airmail wouldn't even be taken until the end of the 1922 budget year.

Thus, wholly determined but positively underfunded, the chief and the magician forged ahead with their plans for the transcontinental run. Praeger's team had already cut its eyeteeth convincing officials in towns and cities east of Chicago to pony up for airmail hangars and fields, and it was prepared to do the same as it went west through Iowa City and Omaha. While they worked on the ground, pilots were flinging themselves across the flat midwestern terrain, trying to familiarize themselves with the airspace between the two cities in preparation for the inauguration of the Chicago–Omaha line.

However, disaster struck again when the postal department was just days away from launching the new route. The division's recently appointed superintendent, William McCandless, was killed while riding as a passenger in a de Havilland mail plane. Having traveled to Omaha to check out final preparations, he was heading back to Chicago to attend opening ceremonies when strong headwinds forced his plane down in Iowa. Upon landing, a gust of wind sent the ship swerving sharply and straight into a large elm tree.

"The impact of the ship against the tree sounded like the collision of two railroad cars," said an eyewitness.

As the dust settled, the full wreckage of parts came into view, with the plane's fuselage now upended beneath the tree. McCandless was seated in the front passenger seat and crushed by the fuel tank. The pilot seated behind him managed to escape without major injury. Omaha field manager William Votaw was particularly devastated. Only a last-minute change in plan had prevented him from being on that plane. At the eleventh hour, McCandless had decided to fly on ahead to Chicago.

Despite the tragedy, on May 15, 1920—as scheduled, and on the second anniversary of airmail—Praeger officially launched service between Chicago and Omaha. The dress rehearsal over, pilots would be expected to fly the routes with uncompromising success. By now, the men flying west from Chicago would know to keep the railroad tracks in their sights in order to reach Iowa City. They would come to recognize the little town of Wheaton, Illinois, by its water tower, identify Geneva by the intersecting Chicago and North Western railroads, and come to follow the Rock River, confident that it would lead straight into Dixon, Stirling, and Rock Falls. In time, they'd see that Clinton, Iowa, was the best spot to cross over the Mississippi River and that by following the waters of the Wapsipinicon River for the next 24 miles, making sure to keep the tracks of the Chicago Rock Island and the Pacific in sight, they would arrive in quick succession over Tipton, Iowa City, Monroe, Des Moines, Atlantic, Council Bluffs, and finally into Omaha.

But several more legs remained to go before the route could be officially connected coast to coast. The Alleghenies were nothing compared to the challenge of plowing across the deserts, prairies, and vast mountain ranges that comprised the great American West. Pushing the mail toward San Francisco would force pilots across dangerous stretches in Wyoming, Utah, Nevada, and California. Just west of Cheyenne, Wyoming, lay terrain known as "the Hump," where the Laramie and Medicine Bow mountains rose up, "rocky and sharp like the fangs of a wolf."

Continuing on, a pilot had to navigate the 150 miles separating Rock Springs, Wyoming, and Salt Lake City, Utah, finding some way through the Wasatch Mountains. Survive their peril and it was on to the Great Salt Lake Desert—a barren, inhospitable expanse that threatened any flier pushing to Reno, Nevada. At any time, a searing dust storm could sweep across the barren landscape, bringing a pilot low. Should a man go down there, he would wither as quickly as scrub brush before he ever reached a settlement, in some places a hundred miles distant. Fortunately, things cooled off considerably just east of Elko, Nevada, where the Ruby Mountains lay quiet but deadly, their jagged snow-clad peaks towering 10,000 feet above sea level. About the only way a flier could make it through was to fly the "secret pass" and keep a sharp weather eye out for the ridges on either side. Pilots prayed that engine trouble or blinding weather wouldn't arise in any of those places, otherwise they'd be just another statistic.

Despite the daunting challenges, pilots, mechanics, and staff kept on propelling the route westward with unbridled enthusiasm, everyone aware of the great step forward they were taking.

Said Edgerton, "It elated us to conquer time and space."

But on many occasions, the limits of their enthusiasm were stretched thin. Nineteen twenty was turning out to be a deadly time for airmail. Harry Sherlock, a baby-faced war veteran stationed in Bellefonte, had been hauling Uncle Sam's mail for a mere six weeks when he crashed into the smokestack of Tiffany's factory while trying to negotiate his way into Heller Field. Men had poured out from everywhere. Together, they had pulled Sherlock's limp body from the wreckage and rushed him to the first-aid office at Tiffany's. But he was dead before they even got inside.

On March 31, the *Newark Evening News* ran an oversized picture of the dead pilot juxtaposing his boyish face against the rubble of the plane smashed against the Tiffany smokestack. Sherlock had survived a world war only to die hauling a bunch of letters across the sky.

In grief, Sherlock's mother traveled to Heller Field. Trying to sort through the meaning of his death, she felt a bile rise in her throat. Heller Field was a disgrace, a death trap for all who were forced to fly in and out of there. The factories, the telephone wires—how could the U.S. Post Office Department call this a legitimate airfield? Fueling her anger was the lack of any official acknowledgment or condolence from Washington regarding her son's death. Inflamed, she put pen to paper and voiced her vitriolic sentiments to Praeger. Mrs. Sherlock was furious over the lack of heartbeat coming from the office of the second assistant postmaster general.

The chief responded in a succinct one-page letter, his remarks perfunctory, offering only the briefest of condolences. "Our acquaintance with him was rather brief," he wrote. "Nevertheless he endeared himself to all with whom he came in contact with by his sunny disposition and pleasant manner."

In its short term of existence, airmail had already lost fourteen men, including two mechanics who were struck in the head by spinning propellers. There was no disputing the fact that Praeger had the courage to risk it all for a cause. But as August rolled through, many were questioning whether the chief was risking the lives of his pilots for an idea whose time had yet to come.

Edgerton lay awake at night, his thoughts troubled. He had hired some of the men who had died in the past year.

"Their deaths haunted my thoughts and dreams many long nights," he said. "How do you weigh progress against the cost in human life, not impersonal life, but the lives of friends who are your personal responsibility?"

McCandless, Sherlock, and others like Clayton Stoner, who crashed in the fog between Chicago and Cleveland, Richard Wright, who either fell or jumped from a burning plane, and N. C. Montis, who crashed when his engine quit on takeoff—all good men killed while flying blind through fog, running into smokestacks at Heller Field, struck in the head by whirling propellers, burned to death, crushed by fuel tanks, and let down by faulty equipment. If some of deaths were unavoidable, others might have been prevented had some sort of communication network been available to help solve the problem of navigation. To Edgerton, radio was the answer.

He wasn't alone in his assertion. There was consensus in the aviation community that radio communications would improve long-distance flying if weather patterns could be tracked and reports dispatched regularly between ground personnel and pilots in the air. So convinced was Edgerton of its need that he'd been spending what little time he had available at College Park experimenting with various ground-to-air communications system. Armed with some findings from the Bureau of Standards, a spare Curtiss RL-4 and a couple used pieces of radio equipment from the military, he had set to work.

In August, Praeger invited Edgerton into his office. A new feeder route between Chicago and St. Louis had just been added to the line. Also, mail deliveries were being outsourced to Florida–West Indies Airways to start moving the mail across international waters—between Key West, Florida, and Havana, Cuba. However, the second assistant had been unsuccessful in negotiating a deal to lease telephone and telegraph wires to pass information along the expanded network. In order to supply the growing transcontinental service with a communications capability, it would have to be done themselves. Then, he dropped the bomb. Praeger would soon be leaving to attend the upcoming Congress of the Pan American Postal Union held in Madrid.

"When I return in a month I expect you to have a complete chain of radio stations to cover every airport upon the transcontinental route, installed and in operation."

Edgerton sat before him, wholly stupefied.

Then, the news got really ugly.

"You have just $20,000 to pay the bill," announced his boss.

Edgerton accepted Praeger's challenge, and, as part of the new assignment, Edgerton would shift from chief of flying to chief of radio while his friend Charles Stanton, a former second lieutenant in the Army Signal Corps, would take over his old duties.

"Charley sat there, mouth agape," noted Edgerton.

That night, as airmail's newly installed chief of radio headed home to his wife and family on Capitol Hill, he considered the paltry experience he brought to the job. He had no professional background in radio, just an abiding interest and some experiments he'd conducted at Bolling Field a while back. But he did pass an exam some years ago authorizing him to operate a commercial radio facility. That accounted for something. And maybe more important, Edgerton had youth, imagination, and enthusiasm for the prospects for radio communications.

"Confidence blinded me to the impossible," he remarked later.

With Praeger steaming his way toward Spain, Edgerton got down to business. Rudimentary radio stations had already been installed at College Park, Bellefonte, Bryan, Iowa City, and Hazelhurst, Long Island, now designated the northern terminus for all transcontinental runs. To reach the West Coast, Edgerton would need nine more stations. No way would he be able to purchase power lines, batteries, vacuum tubes, and tools; construct sheds and masts; and hire personnel with the amount he had been allocated. In keeping with the tradition set by Praeger and Burleson and upheld by everyone affiliated with airmail, Edgerton went scrounging. Edgerton managed to track down some unused airplane fabric with which to barter for the several motor generators he had his eye on. A thorough rummaging through Navy supply rooms yielded a dozen arc transmitters.

"We were the best beggars in Washington," said retired major Leon Lent, who was named the new superintendent of airmail, and to whom Edgerton and Stanton would report.

Edgerton then set off across the country to establish the new facilities. He stopped first at Omaha, his old birthplace, in search of funds. The city had suffered through some terrible blizzards the past few years, even some tornadoes. Because of it, the mayor was more than willing to underwrite one of its favored sons with funds for a station that could also transmit emergency information to residents. Buoyed by the response, Edgerton continued on.

"Each success induced others," he exclaimed.

By the time his month was up, radio stations had been installed in Omaha, North Platte, Cheyenne, Rock Springs, Salt Lake, and Reno. To save money, Edgerton had convinced the Navy to share its existing radio stations at Chicago and San Francisco.

When Praeger returned, Edgerton walked him up to the rooftop of the Post Office Department located at Pennsylvania and Eleventh Avenues, now designated command central for radio. With what looked like Dr. Victor Frankenstein's laboratory before him, Edgerton explained the workings of the metal antennas and transmission wires. Praeger listened as Edgerton gave him an overview of the situation, the stations he'd set in place, the cooperation he'd garnered from cities along the route. He's set up operational manuals, outlined procedures, and assigned call letters and frequencies to each station. Though each was separated by fully 200 miles, they would be able to talk with each other via radio transmissions, sharing weather observations like wind speed and direction, and notifying each other of aircraft arrivals and departures. It seemed at long last that pilots would be flying secure in the knowledge of what weather they would face up ahead.

The chief's face softened as Edgerton finished explaining his new communications network.

"I will never forget the little man as he rubbed his hands in glee," he said.

By early fall, the New York–Omaha route had been pushed farther west to North Platte, Nebraska, followed by Cheyenne, Rawlins, and Rock Springs, Wyoming; Salt Lake City, Utah; Elko and Reno, Nevada; and finally into San Francisco. In all, a total of fifteen landing fields were strung together like pearls on a necklace, the chain of terminals forming a route spanning from the Atlantic to the Pacific, the longest distance between any two stops being the 248-mile stretch between Omaha and North Platte.

With the installation of Edgerton's transcontinental radio system, some measure of dependability seemed to have been bought to the very hazardous business of flying the mail. But although pilot communications were improved, the ships they were flying were most decidedly not.

Upon first glance, the new Junkers single-wing airplane appeared perfect for the challenge of cross-country flying. Designed by the German professor Hugo Junkers, the JL-6 monoplane had a fuselage fabricated not of wood and cloth but wholly of metal. Given the construction, the Junkers could theoretically be left standing on the field all day, under the beating noonday sun or during a rainstorm, and not suffer any damage. Then, too, it was presumed that its all-metal construction would all but eliminate the prospect of fire—every pilot's nightmare.

Maj. Lent had been openly enthusiastic about the plane. He and Eddie Rickenbacker had flown across the country in a Junkers, its closed cockpit encapsulating them in comfort. The planes were built of a light-metal alloy, capable of carrying a payload of 1,000 pounds, their engines capable of cruising for six hours on low-grade fuel, as compared to the three-hour capacity of the Liberty, which required high-octane gasoline. It didn't take a mathematician to see that the Junkers could significantly reduce operating costs.

The plane looked even better when Praeger was able to buy eight of them, with four spare motors, six landing gears, ten tail skids, six props, two full sets of wings, and six radiators for only

$200,000. Gen. Mitchell, by comparison, was paying $30,000 apiece for the aircraft.

But good deal or not, the twin-engine planes weren't working out as expected. Even the more experienced pilots were having their share of troubles flying the Junkers. Wesley Smith, one of the airmail's steadiest pilots, had taken off from Chicago heading to Cleveland in one of the metal monoplanes when a leak in the fuel line ignited. Smith suffered serious burns from the fire, but lived.

The next pilot wouldn't be so fortunate.

The first day of September 1920 started out much like any other when Max Miller climbed into one of the new Junkers. He was flying his regular route from Hazelhurst to Cleveland, mechanic Gustav Reierson riding shotgun. Not long after taking off, however, the nose of the plane was engulfed in flames. Folks on the ground watched as Reierson began throwing mail sacks out of the ship. Then the Junkers went down.

No one knew what happened. Max was the best flier in the corps. The cause of the accident was a mystery. With a heavy heart, it would fall to Lent to inform "Tommy," as Daisy Miller was affectionately called, about the disaster.

"It seems as if our hopes and aspirations had tumbled about us with a sickening thud," said Lent.

The crash near Morristown, New Jersey, was front-page news across America. Airmail's number one pilot, Max Miller, was dead.

"A flaming plane, shrieks of pain, a crash and an explosion," screamed Morristown's *Daily Record*. "Flying low, evidently in trouble—and, according to some, already in flames—the plane tried to head into the trees to break the fall. It crashed to the ground just short of a clump of trees, and with a frightful noise, the gasoline tank exploded. Both pilot and companion burned to a crisp."

Even the normally terse Praeger took the extra step and sent a telegram to Miller's mother in Norway, conveying to her the sad news. Then, all too quickly, the wheels of the funeral were set in motion. The handsome blue-eyed Norwegian was buried in Washington.

As author of his own image, Max Ulf Moeller would have been

pleased to know his death affected so many. Despite the continual reassignments, the succession of cities he had been forced to work out of, he'd remained steadfast, ready to pilot any ship. If there had been chapters of his life he'd been unwilling to disclose even to Daisy, there emerged through the omissions and fabrications an inner portrait of a man who became in the end more than the sum of his youthful desires. One thing was certain, though. No one ever loved the sky more or flew it better.

Just one week later, on September 8, Praeger inaugurated Uncle Sam's first nonstop, transcontinental airmail flight. Amid great fanfare, two planes took off simultaneously—one from San Francisco, the other from New York—each stopping at flying fields in Bellefonte, Cleveland, Chicago, Omaha, Cheyenne, Salt Lake City, Elko, and Reno. Without beacons or landing lights, pilots were restricted to daylight flying. But unlike the military's disastrous pell-mell leap across the country the prior year, Praeger's men arrived at their destinations intact, their cargo delivered just three days after leaving. Newspapers across the country proclaimed the event a singular triumph. Airmail had beaten the railroad by nearly a full day.

The September feat had pilots working overtime trying to get the new transcontinental fully operational. Everybody felt they had a stake in the action: managers, pilots, ground crew, mechanics, and radio operators. If a flier failed to show up during daytime, they'd light up the field with oil drums, or lights from parked cars—anything to help their guy home.

"Radio operators and station managers were coming to work at two or three A.M. so all the weather information possible, gathered by radio and telephone, would be available for the pilot by take off time," said the confident Tex Marshall, who began flying out of Chicago and Omaha in 1920. "When a plane failed to arrive at its destination did everyone take off and go home when darkness came? They did not. They hung around, anxiously awaiting some word."

There seemed to be no letup in the anxiety. Every airfield in the system was seeing its share of trouble. Near Rock Springs, Wyoming, pilot Christopher Pickup, who had just been hired in August, ran out of fuel while airborne. He managed to clear a grazing herd of cattle below, but ended up parking his ship squarely across a set of railroad tracks. The plane was fortunately cleared before the next train came through. Dean Smith, another of the more recent hires, was flying out of Chicago when his engine quit over a field seemingly covered with cattle. His accounting reflected his ordeal.

"I made a steep turn that finished in a sideslip, then went into a skid to kill the speed; I was in a dead stall coming over the fence, angling for a lane that would miss all the cows. Too late, an amiable-looking cow walked in front of the plane. The wing tip caught her fair amidship, the impact pin-wheeling the plane end over end, wings, nose, and tail all breaking off as we went around, until there was little but me and the cockpit left when we came to rest. I stood up, quite unhurt; the cow did too. But the cow was lopsided, caved in on one side and pushed out on the other. She gave one reproachful moo, then lay down and died."

Smith filed his report to headquarters.

"Flying low. Engine quit. Only place to land on cow. Killed cow. Wrecked plane. Scared me. Smith."

Understandably, the rigors of flying the Western Division caused some of the pilots to develop quirks and superstitions. One wouldn't take his ship up unless his favorite stocking cap was affixed snug on his head. Another needed that old watch of his tucked safely inside his pocket, the same one that had faithfully kept time over in Europe, despite the relentless shelling. Walter Stevens, who was one of the reserve pilots whose refusal to fly in 1919 led to the strike, often went up with his dog Lady.

Stevens had ping-ponged from the west back to the east. As long as he didn't have to fly out of Heller Field, he'd be fine. He loathed it there and with good reason. The prior December, he'd landed the first twin-engine Martin bomber on the miserable little field. While rolling at high speed just after landing, a group of youngsters appeared from out of nowhere. He swerved, but without brakes and with children running everywhere, one of them was struck by the spinning prop and killed instantly.

On September 14, two weeks after Miller's death, Stevens was in the cockpit of another all-metal Junkers from the airmail fleet. He was with mechanic Russell Thomas flying between Cleveland and Chicago when the plane went down. Like Miller's Junkers, and the one that had crashed before that, Stevens's plane had caught fire and was last seen plummeting out of the sky like a fireball. Both pilot and mechanic were killed.

Seeking sanctuary in answers, Praeger created an engineering section aimed at hunting down the mechanical questions that were plaguing them and assigned Lent to lead it. Lent's investigations, along with others being conducted, showed that the Junkers's fuel system was built with weak copper fittings that permitted fuel to leak onto the hot engine.

"We seemed not to realize, as any sensible person would have done, that whether metal would burn or not, 80 gallons of gasoline would," said Lent. "Our previous thoughts of a fire-safe plane were at once shattered and dissipated."

Everyone was growing weary—pilots, mechanics, administrators. All the deaths, particularly Miller's, hardly seemed possible. The Junkers held such promise. But September was destined to become darker yet.

Fred Robinson was a sunny pilot of twenty-three, his lazy smile and smooth stubble-free face attesting to his easygoing demeanor. The young aviator had already faced the vertical hazards at Heller Field, but he found himself unprepared for one of the horizontal obstacles that were springing up across the country. Tall poles strung with telephone lines and electrical wires were becoming more commonplace, particularly in the big cities.

In late September, while flying the mail into Bellefonte, fog obscuring his view, Robinson dipped below the cloud deck and began following the rushing waters of the Juniata River into Bellefonte. No witnesses could attest to the final story—whether he saw the flash of telephone wire strung across the river before it snared his landing gear or whether the technological web caught him unaware. Either way, it flung his de Havilland into the water, sending him irrevocably to his death.

A thin metal wire would also be the undoing of pilot Bryan Mc-

Mullen less than a month later while flying between Chicago and Omaha. The *Washington Post* reported the accident:

> At 6:20 o'clock Mrs. George White, wife of a farmer at Bald Mound, near Batavia, saw the airplane descending and called her husband. They were watching the airplane glide towards the ground when it struck [a] wire, flopped over like a giant bird that had been shot, and landed in the field upside down.
>
> Almost immediately it burst into flames, and White and his wife rushed to the rescue of the aviator. The flames were so intense, however, they could not get near enough to aid him and his body, strapped to the seat, was almost entirely burned up. The larger part of the mail cargo was also destroyed. McMullen had been flying quite low for some miles prior to the accident, showing he either had lost his way in the fog or was having some trouble with his motor.

Not long after, Irving Murphy barely avoided the same fate. Following takeoff from Bellefonte one day, an engine fire began raging out of control. Able to put his ship down, Murphy found himself held tight by his harness, unable to escape the flames licking his shoulders and pants.

Having witnessed the accident, a nearby farmer came running over. Despite the flames engulfing the ship, he climbed aboard the wing and tried yanking Murphy from the cockpit by the back of his jacket. But the straps held fast. With flames devouring Murphy's torso, the farmer reached into his pocket, pulled out a knife, and began slicing through the webbed belts fastened about the pilot's chest. The very oxygen in the air seemed to vaporize around them. Any moment now, the fuel tank itself would explode. In a frenzy, the farmer continued sawing until at last, the pilot cut free, both men tumbled to the ground, just as the fuel tank exploded. They were taken to Centre County Hospital where doctors tended to the farmer's blackened back, hands, and face. Murphy was terribly burned, but lucky to be alive.

Given the accidents, Bellefonte was fast becoming as much a final resting place of mail pilots as it was a refueling stop. Even

"Wild" Bill Hopson nearly broke his neck after his engine quit at 150 feet. Plowing into a wheat field, his plane folded up like a jack-knife. Anyone else would have become a statistic. But the good-looking daredevil pilot who had consistently managed to escape management's guillotine that lopped off any pilot not conforming to its rules had crawled out of the wreckage, none the worse for wear.

But so many others hadn't been as fortunate—pilots, mechanics, division superintendents; the deaths were mounting. Even Burleson himself was beginning to have misgivings about the whole thing.

Nearly everyone was ready to call it off. Everyone, that is, except Praeger.

CHAPTER 20

KNIGHT

I f the past year had airmail gasping for breath, 1921 had the service all but flatlined. President Warren Harding's election had given the Republicans control of both the executive and legislative branches of government. The Democrats were on the run. Burleson's adversaries, in particular, were emboldened. The ten-time congressman and chairman of the House Committee of Post Offices and Post Roads, Rep. Halvor Steenerson, a man with a "bitter hatred" for the postmaster general, was loudly proclaiming that funds earmarked for railroad operations had been wrongly diverted to airmail.

Adding to the turmoil was a congressional investigation that promised to play out luridly in the press, a number of discrepancies having been revealed between the public proclamations of airmail success and its actual performance. Throughout much of 1920, arrivals and departures had averaged being nearly an hour late between New York and Washington. As a result, airmail was slower and more costly than the train. The New York–Cleveland air route hadn't fared better.

"During the period between April 1 and December 31, 1920, only 55 percent of the flights scheduled from Cleveland to New York were found to have been actually completed," stated a report.

"Mail on these flights arrived on the average three hours and 33 minutes late, which meant that in most cases it could as well have remained on the train from which it was taken at Cleveland. Similar results were obtained on the westbound flights."

To those serving on the Joint Commission on Postal Service that was formed to investigate matters, it was clear that the postal department had expanded too quickly: "It led to the induction of personnel into the service much more rapidly than it could be trained, with bad maintenance and forced landings as a consequence. It starved essential research in radio communication and weather service, despite expenditures on the entire service of $4,649,158, nearly double the amount Congress had intended to appropriate."

February brought even more bad news. In a single week, the service lost four men to air accidents.

Flying the Chicago–Minneapolis feeder route, which had just opened in November, pilot Kenneth Stewart died in a crash of a twin-engine de Havilland outside Minneapolis. Days later, pilots Hiram Rowe and William Carroll were with mechanic James Hill in a Junkers flying out of Chicago when the plane caught fire and went down, killing all three men. This was after Praeger's team thought they had solved the problem of the Junkers and the big transport planes.

In response, the service grounded all of its Martin bombers, its Junkers, and its twin-engine DH-4s.

But the change had come too late. The media was in feeding frenzy mode, Steenerson was attacking from all sides, and the Joint Commission was relentlessly digging into Praeger's ledgers. In a very public series of hearings, legislators considered airmail to be hardly worth the price, either financially or in the cost of lives. They planned to recommend to the larger legislative body that 1921's proposed $1.25 million expenditure for airmail be cut from the budget, effectively shutting down operations.

A fortune had already been spent, nearly two dozen had died, and with a near certainty that Congress would kill the service, it appeared that everything had been for naught. Praeger, the pilots, the grease monkeys, every secretary and clerk—all their attempts at keeping airmail afloat, at moving it forward, they'd all just been chasing the tail of some dream that lay forever outside their reach. The years of struggle, all those deaths, were seemingly for nothing. The U.S. Air Mail Service appeared to be taking its last breaths.

Out of time and out of options, Praeger made a bold move. If his math was correct, flying the mail nonstop coast to coast would take just thirty-six hours, half the time it took for trains to cover the same distance. That would be the *aha* moment that could prove once and for all the superiority of airplanes over trains. Even a Republican-controlled Congress would have to acknowledge such an accomplishment. But to make it possible, pilots would be required to do something they have never done before—fly at night through the pitch of darkness. It was the only way.

The plan was simple. Two planes would take off from San Francisco heading east while simultaneously two mail ships would depart New York heading west. The hope was that at least one of them would arrive intact on the opposite coast. The date was set for February 22, the anniversary of George Washington's birthday.

Praeger, a one-man publicity machine, was whipping up interest in the groundbreaking event, encouraging civic groups in towns along the air route to help out the pilots who would be battling the darkness overhead by whatever means available—bonfires, car lights, torches. In no time, Praeger had succeeded in getting the whole country rooting for them to make it.

As the day approached, mechanics and ground crew filled the hangars, everyone working overtime to ensure that the single-engine de Havillands were in perfect running condition.

But winter skies couldn't have been uglier come Washington's birthday. Pilots Ernest Allison and Elmer Leonhardt fought their way out of New York on that cold, winter morning. Icy conditions forced Leonhardt down in Pennsylvania, damaging his plane in the process, but Allison managed to push the mail on through to Cleveland where his mail pouches were transferred to Wesley Smith who, despite the worsening weather, made it to Chicago where Bill Hopson was waiting.

By now, gusts of thick, white flakes were blanketing Checkerboard Field. Still, if anybody could get through the snowstorm, it was Wild Bill.

"Bill was a terrific pilot, unequaled at pushing through thick weather," said Dean Smith, who had flown with him when both men were stationed at Omaha.

Bucking his way through the blinding snow, Hopson fought his way into the storm only to be forced back down minutes later, humbled by a power mightier than himself. The westbound run was run effectively finished.

The fate of the Air Mail Service now was in the hands of the two eastbound pilots. Farr Nutter and Ray Little had departed San Francisco at 4:29 A.M., both having successfully crossed the Sierra Nevada landing safely in Reno—most of the time flying in the dark—they were well ahead of breakfast at seven. There, the mail was turned over to two relief pilots, who went charging off into the clear morning air like two pony express riders. They both landed at Elko, Nevada, at 9:24 A.M., and after a change of planes were back in the air just seven minutes later heading to Salt Lake City.

Then, the unthinkable happened. Taking off in the oxygen-thin air of Elko, located nearly a mile above sea level, one of the relief pilots, William Lewis, stalled his plane at 500 feet. Unable to pull out, he crashed and died upon impact. Lewis, a pilot with the airmail for only a month, was set to be married in March. Despite the horror of the scene, his mail was retrieved and passed to a standby pilot who continued the journey eastward for Utah.

Two planes were still in the air, still forging a path across the western sky. By the clock, airmail was still ahead of the rails. But things were slowing down. The first pilot out of Elko had reached Salt Lake City at 11:30 A.M. and passed his mail sacks on to the next man in line who immediately took off toward Cheyenne. But en route, mechanical troubles forced him down and not until close to 5:00 P.M. did he reach his destination. With darkness upon them, mail sacks were handed off to another pilot, who pushed on to North Platte, arriving at 7:48 P.M.

Now it was Jack Knight's turn to do his part. With a small bandage covering the broken nose he received in a crash a week earlier, he was ready to go. But repairs to the airplane kept him on the ground for another three hours. It had already been a long day for Knight as he had previously flown from Omaha to Cheyenne and then back to North Platte.

"I would not ordinarily be selected for this leg of the journey because my afternoon flight had been a trifle wearisome," he had told field manager Votaw. "My broken nose was paining me and not improving my eyesight. But it happened that I was the only pilot available in Cheyenne."

While Knight cooled his heels, the other pilot, Harry Smith, was still pushing the mail eastward. Having departed Cheyenne he had come and gone from North Platte and was heading toward Omaha. Journeying across the midnight landscape, and guided by the Union Pacific Railroad, Smith followed the luminescence of the Platte River and the light of the bonfires set by people at Grand Island.

Back in North Platte, Jack Knight finally crawled into the cockpit of his plane and climbed into the skies at 10:44 P.M., heading for Omaha. Like Smith, he had only to peer over the side of his ship to confirm his course by the light of the bonfires blazing below.

"I felt as if I had a thousand friends on the ground—Lexington, Kearney, Grand Island, Columbus, Freemont slipped by, warm glows of well-wishers beneath the plane's wings. And then, I saw the lights of Omaha."

In a way not seen since the inaugural flight back in 1918, this transcontinental undertaking seemed to ignite the public's imagination. People were once again reinvesting themselves in the possibilities of flight. Towns along the route had joined in the adventure by lighting fires, painting the names of their hamlets on barn roofs so pilots would know where they were. The sight of a U.S. mail plane winging its way across thousands of miles of open country was stirring a nation's collective pride.

Smith arrived first in Omaha at 11:35 P.M. But he was clearly exhausted from his effort.

"We didn't even suggest he carry on because of his condition," said Omaha field manager Votaw. "We offered him a ride to his hotel, which he immediately accepted."

An hour and a half later, Knight parked his mail ship on the field at Omaha, to the delight of a crowd numbering in the thousands. As his wheels touched down everyone started applauding and shouting his name, their breath punctuating the cold night air. Votaw greeted a very tired and cold pilot with hot coffee and a couple of fresh doughnuts. Then he gave him the hard news. Knight was the only pilot still flying. His replacement—the man who was supposed to fly the next leg from Omaha to Chicago—had been snowed in. He never even made it to the airfield. There was no one to fly the next leg.

Knight looked at him, his gaze direct.

What about Wesley Smith and Bill Hopson? he asked.

Votaw told him they were done. Nothing left but for Knight to call it a night. Already the crowd was beginning to disperse, the cold driving all but the most diehard away.

"We can't let it bust up here," Knight exclaimed. "I'm going to take it through, so get out the maps and I'll be on my way after that coffee and two cigarettes."

"But Jack," argued Votaw, "you have never flown this route, from here to Chicago, even in daylight."

Votaw couldn't find a map, but Knight never even flinched, pointing to the maps tacked up on the wall of Votaw's office.

"What's the matter with giving me those maps?"

They tore the maps off the wall and examined the route the best they could. Knight was told to follow a course to Iowa City whereupon he could land and refuel. He should look for the Rock Island Railroad in Des Moines to guide him eastward. At that point, bonfires would light his way toward Chicago.

Knight climbed into his plane.

"Leave the lights on for an hour. If I'm not back then you'll know I'm on my way. If I get lost I'll sure as heck come back."

With no beacons, and no flares attached to his wings or searchlights to guide a flight path across the sky, Knight took off around 2:00 A.M., encouraged by the field manager's illuminating words to look for "burning waste" at Atlantic, Iowa, some 50 miles distant.

To those waiting word back east, things seemed pretty bleak. At postal headquarters, Praeger could only pace inside his plush office to see if the dream lived or whether daybreak would find him and Burleson shuttering up operations. At this point, it all boiled down to the men. From the start, he had pushed his pilots to their limit, some even beyond. But not once did he underestimate their endurance. He had seen too many accident reports come filing across his desk—Shank's, Miller's, Gardner's, Hopson's, Newton's, Knight's— each account stripped of its emotion until it read like an actuarial report.

Though Praeger may not have admitted it, every pilot in his employ had shared a common faith. This wasn't about legitimizing their claims or vainly trying to keep their names in front of the press. This transcontinental flight represented a personal validation for each of them, proof that flying was more than some romantic notion. Its science mattered—to defense, to commerce, and to each of them. But all of it was resting in Knight's thin hands.

"Those of us who had our fingers crossed for the success of the experiment were ready to sell out for a good box of cigars," remarked Ham Lee.

Old Hundred Percent Ham had taught Jack everything he knew about flying, having been his flying instructor back at Ellington Field in Texas. Skinny kid—wasn't about to let himself get washed out like so many of the others. Practiced and practiced until he got his landings and takeoffs right. Edgerton, too, knew that Jack was the real deal, the two having trained together back at Ellington Field in the First Squadron. Despite Jack's determination and skill as a pilot, prospects looked bleak.

Guided by his compass heading, Knight enjoyed fair skies as far as Des Moines, but from there, the weather deteriorated badly, with snow plaguing him straight into Iowa City.

"By this time I was flying over territory absolutely strange. I knew nothing of the land markings, even if they had been visible. I had to fly by compass and by feel. The throbbing rhythm of the motor didn't help matters. It was almost a lullaby. I gripped the control stick with my knees and began slapping my face to keep awake. I stuck my face over the side of the cowl and let the rushing zero air bite my cheeks almost raw."

To make matters worse, this leg of the trip offered few distinguishing landmarks.

"I got pretty lonesome," said Knight. "At times, the moon was totally obscured by a heavy black layer of clouds. It looked as if the whole blooming world was sleeping hard. There's a sense of isolation that's hard to describe. But my faithful old Liberty roared out, fighting the wind and dragging my ship along at about a hundred miles per hour."

Knight hit Des Moines in just over an hour.

"I could see the lighted dome of the capitol and Fort Des Moines showed plainly under my right wing a bit later," he said.

He pressed eastward, at times the low clouds forcing him to fly dangerously close to the ground.

"Flying was pretty bad at this altitude. The air was rough and the valleys were packed with fog. Next I began to get snow flurries and I knew with the wind shifting I was slowing to 85 miles an hour. Then I lost my horizon and got to wondering if I'd reach Iowa City."

What Jack didn't know was that the Iowa City ground crew had all gone home after being inexplicably told by Omaha that all flights had been canceled, even though Knight was very clearly in the air. All that is, except the Swedish watchman.

"All the crew except me left for home," he said. "Later, Ohio called advising the trip was continuing east, but I was unable to get ahold of the rest of the employees so I made preparations to handle the trip alone. It was 12 below zero and I would stand outside and listen for Jack's motor as long as I could stand it and then I would run back in the 5 x 5 shack, just room to get in and back out, and listen with my head out the window. Finally, I heard Jack's motor, sounded like over Coralville, about two miles northwest of the field. By the time I had placed two railroad flares in the center of the field, Jack was already shooting for them, and I had to run to get out of the way."

In contrast to the crowd at Omaha, only the Swedish watchman stood waiting to greet him in Iowa City. Cold and hungry, U.S. Air Mail's skinniest pilot wolfed down a ham sandwich while the watchman poured alcohol into the radiator to keep the motor from freezing up. Then, with the engine running the whole time he was on the ground, he quickly beat a path back up into the sky.

"I didn't dare eat any more for fear it would put me to sleep. It was 6:30 A.M., Wednesday. The rest of the way I flew by instinct. I just pointed the plane's nose for Chicago and kept going. Snow whirled around the ship for a while and the wind blew stiff from the east. It was hellishly cold. But as the day grew brighter, I saw the gray smoke of Chicago mixing with the clouds and it was the finest sight I have ever beheld."

But as he approached the city, his engine began to cough. Knight forgave it wholeheartedly. The ship had done its job. In Chicago, another relay pilot picked up the mail sacks and flew them on to Cleveland. From there, Ernest Allison finished the run into Long Island.

Total time for the transcontinental flight: thirty-three hours and twenty minutes. Total time for the railroad to make the same journey: four days. Airmail had bested the train by nearly sixty-five hours.

Exhausted though he was after landing in Chicago, Knight immediately wired his boss with news of his success.

Knight quickly received a telegram back from the chief.

"Accept my hearty congratulations for your splendid performance last night under most difficult weather conditions."

Knight responded back.

"Any one of the airmail pilots would have done the same because we were all keenly interested in seeing that aviation and air transportation was given a chance to develop."

The pilots' collective bravery turned events in their favor. Public reaction to the fabulous success of the cross-country flight, which would soon become known as Jack Knight's night flight, was overwhelming. Within days, Congress reinstated the U.S. Air Mail Service's $1.25 million budget by a two-to-one margin. Nine days later, President Harding and his Republican administration took office, leaving Second Assistant Postmaster General Otto Praeger and his boss, Postmaster General Albert Sidney Burleson, out of a job.

Praeger threw a farewell dinner for his boss at Washington's venerable University Club. Together, they had ushered in the future of mechanized mail deliveries, taking the U.S. government from horse-drawn mail wagons to auto-trucks and now to mail planes. Praeger had always maintained that in government, as in the private sector, people fit into three categories: "the effective, the merely spectacular and the failures."

The fighting Texan and his second, through their idealism, masterful political maneuverings, hard work, and pragmatism, had taken on all comers and made history. As Praeger prepared to clean out his desk, he sat down and penned a letter to his boss and long-time friend, Albert Sidney Burleson.

In cleaning up the work of the Bureau of the Second Assistant Postmaster General in anticipation of leaving a clean slate for my successor after March 4, I am struck by the vast amount of constructive work that has been accomplished not only in my Bureau but in all the other Bureaus of your Department.

The work that has been done in your various Bureaus has been due to your initiative and encouragement and to your broad business policy of setting tasks and exacting results there from, leaving the executives under your free and wide authority in working out the problems.

The scope of this work in my Bureau has covered not only the weeding out of extravagance and far reaching improvement and enlargement of the service but it has also included the amelioration of working conditions of the personnel—always with the view of giving the public the greatest amount of service for the dollar by exacting an honest return for the money spent for labor, material and contracts.

I consider that the great heritage I can leave to my children has been my connection with the Administration of President Wilson and particularly such service as I have been able to contribute towards helping you make your administration of the postal service the most aggressive and most advanced in the history of the Post Office Department. For this opportunity and for your ever fair and liberal support of my endeavors, I thank you most earnestly.

EPILOGUE

Twenty-six airmail pilots, mechanics, and personnel died in the service of the U.S. Air Mail between May 1918 and February 1921. With the service averaging one fatality per month, an airmail pilot could expect to fly less than two years before dying on the job. After the war ended, it was clearly the most dangerous job in the world.

Fueled by a common bravado, courage, and naïveté, the pilots of the U.S. Air Mail Service chartered the first unknown course to what is today a worldwide network of air transportation in which individual aircraft routinely transport tens of thousands of pounds of cargo and hundreds of people on nonstop flights in excess of 6,000 miles.

Otto Praeger, in a letter to William Hopson and the other pilots who had participated in the epic transcontinental flight, acknowledged their very personal contribution to the future of aviation.

> My Dear Mr. Hopson:
> On the eve of my separation from the Postal Service, permit me to thank you most sincerely for your excellent work in flying the mail on the record breaking trip from San Francisco to New York on February 22 and 23. It is something to be proud of but

it should be a matter of still greater pride to you and to all the pilots in the service that you are each day delivering the goods as they have never been delivered in aviation in any country in the world. I thank you for your excellent work.

Sincerely yours,

Otto Praeger

Second Assistant Postmaster General

In the years to come, more airplanes would crash and many more pilots would die. The path forward was clear, though many who were there at the beginning wouldn't witness the full triumph. This is what happened next.

THE U.S. AIR MAIL SERVICE

The epic-making transcontinental day/night flight on February 22, 1921, proved once and for all the value of airmail by connecting New York and San Francisco in only thirty-three hours—a full three days faster than the train. Overnight, airmail had been elevated to a level of national importance.

Day-to-day operations, however, were about to shift dramatically as Democrats Albert Burleson and Otto Praeger gave way to the incoming Republicans led by the new president, Warren Harding. Appointed in 1921, Postmaster General William Harrison Hays and his second assistant, retired colonel E. H. Shaughnessy, would now be placing a premium on safety over expansion. There would, in fact, be a retrenchment of service, and little, if any, night flying at all. The new philosophy was simple: fly fewer routes, but fly them more consistently and with fewer accidents.

By the summer of 1921, when the cutting was done, little was left of Praeger's network of sky routes. Gone were the two feeder routes out of Chicago, south to St. Louis and north to Minneapolis. Also cut was the crown jewel of the entire service—the New York–Washington run. The airfield at College Park, Maryland, was abandoned, as was the original field at Bustleton, Pennsylvania. Heller Field at Newark went, too. Total savings for the U.S. Treasury was $675,000.

When the smoke cleared, the nation was left with only one air-mail route, but it stretched nearly 3,000 miles between New York and San Francisco. The transcontinental run epitomized what airmail did best—deliver mail faster than trains. But night flying would be for a later day. For the time being, cross-country flights would only be during daytime and in good weather.

The post office would throw all its planes into the task. There were enough Jennies, Standards, and de Havillands by now to afford each pilot his own personal ship. It would be his to customize, to baby, or to kick if something went wrong. Pilots wasted no time in imprinting their own insignias onto the fuselages like World War II bomber pilots. Soon, though, Shaughnessy realized the inefficiency of operating disparate aircraft types and settled on the DH-4 with the Liberty 12 engine.

Like Burleson and Praeger, Shaughnessy expected that the private sector would ultimately take responsibility for flying the mail.

"The Department, true to its traditions, wants air transportation of the mail because in that direction lies rapid transit," he explained. "The Department, however, does not feel that it should operate an Air Mail Service any more than it should operate a steamboat service or a railway service except until such times as the commercial interests of this country are ready to step in and take over the burden."

With fewer routes being flown, and hundreds of fewer hours in the air each month, the U.S. Air Mail Service was able to show significant improvements in reliability and reduced operating costs. Between July of 1921 and September of 1922, not a single Air Mail employee died in a plane crash. For the accomplishment, the Air Mail Service won aviation's most important prize—the Collier Trophy.

Established in 1911 by *Collier's Weekly* publisher Robert Collier, an early president of the Aero Club of America, the trophy is unlike any other in aviation in that it honors the advancement of aeronautics as a craft, rather than recognizing a new speed record or a high-altitude flight.

The citation read: "The Air Mail Service has flown 1,700,000 miles on the transcontinental route for a year's time in all conditions of weather without a single fatal accident. This performance denotes substantial progress in the practical application of airplanes to the purposes of commerce and other peaceful pursuits."

Sadly, Shaughnessy was not able to participate in the award as he was killed with ninety-seven other people when the roof of the Knickerbocker Theatre in downtown Washington collapsed during a blizzard.

Postmaster Hays replaced Shaughnessy with Col. Paul Henderson, a serious and studious business manager who served in ordnance during the war. His father-in-law was Chicago congressman Martin Madden, who clashed with Praeger during the mail motorization of Chicago in 1915. Building on airmail's momentum in early 1923, Hays and Henderson decided it was time again to tackle night flying, and in the spring of 1923 work began on a lighted airway between Chicago and Cheyenne—the same section that Jack Knight flew for Praeger two years prior. Knight himself was put in charge of figuring it all out.

The pilots' see-in-the-dark ability would be made possible with the installation of large gas beacons manufactured by General Electric to illuminate the airway from city to city. Nearly three hundred beacons, one about every 3 miles, would be placed along the flat 980-mile route between Chicago and Cheyenne. Each would flash six times a minute, blinking out a homing signal visible from dozens of miles away. Five primary landing fields were constructed, with the key feature at each being a 500-million-candlepower searchlight revolving atop a 50-foot tower. Thirty-four lighted emergency landing fields would also be established.

The airplanes were also modified for night flying. Cockpits were retrofit with luminescent instruments so pilots could see the dials, landing lights were added, and sidelights were added to the wingtips—a red light went on the left, and a green light on the right, just like in naval vessels. Completing the safety equipment was a pair of high-intensity flares with little parachutes that could be jettisoned from the airplane and illuminate the landscape for a mile around at 1,000 feet.

President Harding died of a heart attack in August 1923, and Postmaster General Hays resigned to become president of the Motion Picture Producers and Distributors of America Association (where he would administer the Hollywood moral code for the next two decades). Airmail continued unabated under President Calvin Coolidge's postmaster general, Harry New, and by year's end aviators were routinely navigating the blackest of night.

For establishing regular night flights between Cheyenne and Chicago—an accomplishment never done before—the U.S. Air Mail won its second consecutive Collier Trophy as the most important aeronautical achievement in America during 1923.

The Collier Trophy continues to be given today by the National Aeronautic Association (the successor to the Aero Club), and the actual 525-pound bronze trophy, with its swirling visions of man reaching for the sky, is on display at the National Air and Space Museum in Washington, D.C. To date, the U.S. Air Mail is the only back-to-back winner of the trophy, and it joins the elite club of aircraft builder Glenn Curtiss and instrument designer Elmer Sperry as the only other two-time winners.

In 1924, the lighted airway was extended eastward 308 miles from Chicago to Cleveland. Then in July 1925, night mail came to New York when engineers crossed the Allegheny Mountains with a line of beacons that stretched all the way to the Atlantic Ocean. By the end of 1925, an unbroken, illuminated chain from New York to Salt Lake was operational. The Post Office Department spent $542,000 lighting the 2,000-mile distance. Flying day and night, the pilots of the U.S. Air Mail Service could complete the entire transcontinental trip in about twenty-nine hours (with eastbound tailwinds).

Praeger closely followed the progress of airmail and was unmistakably proud of its success. "Four short words, 'Get the mail through,' express the spirit of the United States Air Mail," he wrote in 1925. "They are continually on the lips of the 46 pilots, the 40 radio operators, the 70 caretakers of night-flying beacons and the 500 others engaged in this vast transcontinental enterprise."

The year 1925 was pivotal for the airmail for another reason. New was still postmaster general, but there was a fresh second assistant onboard who would continue a string of strong postal transportation czars stretching back to Praeger. Warren Irving Glover was also studious with round glasses like his predecessor Henderson, but with an eye for the flair. Often seen in the summer in a white suit and silk tie, Glover was a five-time New Jersey state legislator. He would stay in the job for seven years and work to transition government airmail to the private sector.

The first step came that year with passage of the Kelly Act, which made it possible for private companies to earn up to 80 percent of the value of the postage it carried. Named for Pennsylvania congressman Clyde Kelly, the legislation was intended to help railroad interests by getting the government out of airmail, but in the long run it did the opposite by enticing a number of powerful businessmen to get into aviation. The postal department put many of its north-south feeder routes up for bid, and by the end of 1925, four small start-up airlines began flying the mail. The investors came from all walks of life but had one thing in common—a desire to make money from the nation's first commercial aviation enterprise. They included: Cornelius Vanderbilt Whitney, heir to two separate family fortunes; future Pan Am Airlines founder Juan Trippe; Canadian financier and former *Wall Street Journal* reporter Clement Keys; chewing gum heir and future owner of the Chicago Cubs baseball team Philip K. Wrigley; and *Los Angeles Times* publisher Harry Chandler.

Some of the great airmail pilots from Praeger's day, like Jack Knight and Ham Lee, would be hired to fly for these fledgling carriers and would be joined by new aviators like Charles Lindbergh, who flew the Chicago–St. Louis feeder route in the years before his Atlantic crossing.

Each of the privatized routes would feed into the east-west transcontinental run, which, for the most part, would still be flown by Uncle Sam with government pilots. Privatization efforts continued into 1926, with the government auctioning off a variety of new routes, including Seattle to Los Angeles, Chicago to Detroit, and Detroit to Cleveland. Automaker Henry Ford was the wealthiest man in Detroit, so it was no surprise when he won the rights to the two Detroit runs. The Ford Motor Company was investing in aviation in a big way, first spending $500,000 to buy the Stout Metalplane Company and then infusing it with $2 million in capital. The fruit of that transaction would come in the form of the

4-AT Tri-Motor, a legendary monoplane powered by three Wright Whirlwind engines, which would carry mail—and passengers—on the mail routes in the coming months.

By mid-1927, the U.S. government was done flying the mail. All airmail assets—planes, hangars, fields, beacons, and personnel— were transferred to the Department of Commerce's newly created Bureau of Aeronautics.

The final airmail flight to be flown by a member of Uncle Sam's Suicide Club came on September 1, 1927. Over the coming decades, the companies that won the rights to fly the first privatized airmail routes would evolve into some of America's most important airlines, including United Airlines, Delta Air Lines, and Trans World Airlines.

TOP AIRMAIL PILOTS (1918–1927)

Pilot	Miles Flown
James Knight	417, 072
William Hopson	413,034
Harold (Slim) Lewis	365,625
E. Hamilton Lee	382,426
Dean Smith	365,719
Harry Boonstra	303,428
Harry Huking	226,850
Ira Biffle	193,515

AIRMAIL BY THE NUMBERS (1918–1927)

FUNDING: $11.6 million
REVENUES: $5.3 million
MILES FLOWN: 13.7 million
FORCED LANDINGS: 4,437 (weather); 2,095 (mechanical)
PLANES CRASHED: 200
FATALATIES: 43 total deaths (32 fatal crashes killed 32 pilots plus 9 mechanics/passengers, and 2 personnel were killed on the ground by spinning propellers)

SECOND ASSISTANT POSTMASTER GENERAL OTTO PRAEGER

Each of us has a glory, a prospect of greatness that, given the opportunity, soars upon the wind like a God-given destiny. Second Assistant Postmaster General Otto Praeger was the right man at the right time. He recognized the opportunities afforded by flight and, with the help of Postmaster General Albert Burleson, was able to give wing to the world's first scheduled airmail service.

Come February 1921, Praeger was forced out of his job. He understood perfectly. Politics is politics. Woodrow Wilson was done, mentally and physically. After eight years of Democratic control, the country wanted a change and Republican Warren Harding, the twenty-ninth president of the United States, reflected that.

Two decades as a newspaper reporter, more than a year as postmaster general of Washington, D.C., and six years as chief of transportation for one of the largest government agencies in the world gave Praeger an impressive résumé. Still, the world didn't come knocking at his door. Only fifty years old, at the top of his game, he was quickly disappearing from any prominence.

He took a job as manager of sales and promotion for a pharmaceutical company in St. Louis. He and his wife, Annie, lived there for a time, but returned to D.C. when she became ill. Annie died in mid-1924, and with his two older sons grown and out of the house, Praeger and his youngest boy, nineteen-year-old Herman, moved to New York City, where he advised large mail-order houses and industrial companies on postal regulations and requirements.

The highlight of his New York years came in 1925, in the form of an unexpected invitation from Gen. Billy Mitchell to personally watch what even today is arguably the most important aerial demonstration since Kitty Hawk. The one-star general and the second assistant postmaster general had battled for many years over control of airmail, but there was always mutual respect.

Mitchell was still pushing his concept of "Airpower" and felt that aircraft were being severely underutilized by the military. Fighter pilots got lots of press during World War I, but airplanes played a limited tactical role—unlike in World War II, where bombers were used to destroy manufacturing plants, disperse troop concentrations, disrupt communications, and demolish enemy cities. By the mid-1920s, Mitchell was one of the few who felt that the bomber was ready to play a larger role in warfare, and he boasted that an airplane could sink the battleship. In an experiment that established his legend, a pair of twin-engine Martin bombers successfully sank two decommissioned battleships, the *New Jersey* and *Virginia*. Praeger was there:

> I witnessed this performance as guest of General Mitchell on board the transport *Chaumont*, which carried General Pershing and his staff. I saw one of the bombs leave a plane. It looked like a big black cigar streaking downward in the sky, and it scored a direct hit on the deck of the *Virginia*. The gun turrets of the battleship were sheared clean off, and with it all of the superstructure of the ship. Then the battleship turned end up and sank to its grave.
>
> The report that circulated among newsmen who were aboard was that when the battleship was swept clean by the blast, General Pershing turned to a high officer at his side and remarked, "There goes the Coast Artillery."

Praeger continued his consulting work until 1928, when an offer came that shook the cobwebs from his life. He was approached by an emissary of the government of Siam (to be renamed Thailand in 1939), which wanted to establish an airmail service. Praeger was recommended for the job by President Wilson's former ambassador to the country, Francis Sayre. If interested, Praeger would join other American advisers working in Siam, including former New Hampshire congressman Raymond Stevens, the king's foreign affairs adviser, and Dr. Hugh McCormick Smith, head of the U.S. Bureau of Fisheries during the Wilson administration, who was helping the country manage its fish and turtle populations.

Praeger accepted the job and began this challenge accompanied by his new wife, an Oklahoma gal named Carrie Will Coffman, a woman twenty-seven years his junior, a year younger than his oldest son. They married just before the ship departed and honeymooned aboard the slow-moving vessel—to many raised eyebrows as the new Mrs. Praeger had registered under her maiden name as co-occupant of Otto's stateroom.

"The captain demanded to know whether she thought she was in Greenwich Village, and added that there would have to be a wedding ceremony at sea or the production of a marriage certificate if she expected to sit at the captain's table," Praeger recalled.

Many a toast was raised to the happy couple during the two-week 3,000-mile trip from the West Coast to their new home in the land of his Majesty King Prajadhipok. Educated in England and France, the diminutive king was an early proponent of democracy and viewed the development of an improved infrastructure as a way to bring the country out of its economic depression.

For five years, from 1928 to 1933, Praeger was postal adviser to the Royal Siamese Air Mail and managing director of the Aerial Transport Company of Siam, which flew tourists to the southern ocean resorts of Phuket as Siam's first commercial airline and was the predecessor of today's Thai Airways.

A glance at a map and geography of Siam makes it clear why the country desperately needed airmail. It is an amalgam of terrain, from the bamboo metropolis of Bangkok, to Chaing Mai elephant country in the teak forests north of Burma, and the idyllic South Pacific environs of the narrow southern isthmus on the Andaman Sea. Always hot and humid with two typhoon seasons, the country has 2,000 miles of coastline and hardly any miles of paved road. From north to south, Siam is 1,200 miles long, and the only way to transport mail from one end to the other was by elephant, sampan, or creaking bullock cart. All in all, it was a perfect place for the distance-shrinking capabilities of the airplane.

Praeger and his wife loved their life there, absorbing the lemon grass–flavored culture. He started a second family. Mirroring his first go-around as a father, he had three girls this time—Janet, Elinor, and Helen—all born to him and Carrie during their time in Siam.

Twelve years after leaving the employ of Uncle Sam, Praeger returned. All five members of the Praeger family said their good-byes to the South Pacific and settled in Depression-era Washington, D.C. His new job was assistant to the president of the U.S.

Merchant Fleet Corporation of the U.S. Shipping Board, where he would help to regulate American ocean commerce, supervise freight and terminal facilities, and administer government funds to construct and operate commercial ships.

Praeger stayed with the commission for three years, and in 1936, at sixty-five years of age, he semiretired and moved to San Diego with his wife and three children. He bought a 16-acre lemon grove in Escondido, but before he ever had the chance to test his green thumb he found his first year's crop ruined by a rare overnight freeze. With no crop to sell and bills piling up, Praeger lost the grove to the bank, though he was at least able to keep the house.

With virtually no income, Otto would park himself out in front of the house and shoot rabbits with his rifle. He taught the girls to handle a gun, and the family ate a lot of rabbits that year. His wife, Carrie, brought in an income by teaching music full-time. Despite their financial struggles, she ensured the house was filled with laughter and music. It must have frustrated Praeger to sit by and watch his wife manage things by herself. But by then, he had developed terrible arthritis in his hips and could barely get out of bed for a year. The children were raised mostly by Carrie, with Otto interacting with them more like a grandfather than a father. He read a good deal of Dickens and still cherished the bound set of the author's works his colleagues gave him when he was the D.C. postmaster. Eventually, he took the cure during a lengthy visit to the Salton Sea region south of San Diego and managed to get back on his feet by 1938.

Praeger kept in touch with a few friends during those years working for Uncle Sam. Regularly he wrote Burleson, who by now had retired to Austin, Texas. Both gentlemen were still fighting the good fight for the Democratic Party, and though Burleson was no longer in politics, the inner workings of government continued to be a defining aspect of his life.

"I see by this clipping from the *Evening Star* that you handed out a wallop to the enemy," he gleefully wrote to Albert Sidney a couple months before President Franklin Delano Roosevelt clobbered the Republican candidate in the November 1936 election. "I suppose you are noticing that the straw votes are coming out strong for the administration. The *Washington Post*, which carries the banner for the Liberty League and all of Roosevelt's enemies, doesn't find much consolation in the poll conducted by Dr. Gallup for the Institute of Public Opinion."

The lean years continued for the Praeger family. Otto had regained his strength, and though he was nearly seventy years old, he decided to return to work.

"The impetus, I am certain, was purely financial," said his daughter Elinor. "He did volunteer work that summer at the local Democratic headquarters to test his strength, and then flew to Washington to find a job. He was gone several months, and we were not certain that he would be able to land anything."

Praeger had hoped that his lifelong devotion to the Democratic Party would help him land a position of responsibility, but there weren't too many jobs for seventy-year-old relics of a prior generation. He was finally hired for the lowly position of liaison between the United Youth Administration and other departments of the federal government. The administration was a pet project of first lady Eleanor Roosevelt, who feared that the idle and unemployed youth of the Depression era would become a lost generation. His only consolation was that the girls and Mrs. Praeger had joined him to live in Washington.

Praeger couldn't have been any farther away from the center of politics than he was in 1941, but he ended up being pulled back into the fray in an unexpected way.

President Franklin Delano Roosevelt expected to be embroiled in the European conflict sooner or later, and he was in the process of developing a plan for wartime censorship. Praeger was keeping busy at the National Youth Administration, but it was way below his talents and he was itching for something more. Some clever fellow thought it prudent to dust off the history books to see how President Wilson handled censorship during the nation's last war, and, under the subject of squelching dissenting opinion in the media, two names topped the list: Albert Burleson, now dead, and Otto

Praeger. They tracked down Praeger and hired him to impart his knowledge to the next generation of government censors working at the Office of Defense Transportation.

"In spite of his advanced years he still has the capacity for planning, organizing and leadership," wrote the person who interviewed him for the job, who also noted that Praeger listed Texan Sam Rayburn, longtime speaker of the U.S. House of Representatives, as a personal reference.

Praeger worked dutifully throughout the nearly five years of World War II—even through a minor heart attack in 1943—until he was virtually the oldest employee of the Office of Defense Transportation. Mandatory retirement at seventy-five years of age ended his career (most likely against his will) in 1946.

He spent his last two years lazing around their big house on Thirty-fourth Street in the District of Columbia. He continued to read Dickens and the newspapers and listened to the news on the radio several times a day. He didn't care too much for sports, so it really bothered him when all the radio talked about was a black man, Jackie Robinson, joining the Brooklyn Dodgers. His wife continued to teach piano, and they took in boarders. The house had six bedrooms, and two or three rooms were always rented out. The new people coming and going provided an endless source of interest to Otto and he could easily spend the evening chatting with the people living under his roof.

At the age of seventy-seven, Praeger died of a heart attack in his home in Washington, D.C., on February 4, 1948. His wife, Carrie, died three years later at the age of fifty-two.

Though Praeger rarely talked about his days as second assistant postmaster general, he did live long enough to see his accomplishment with the Air Mail Service recognized. On the twentieth anniversary of the U.S. Air Mail, May 15, 1938, the post office honored him in a press release. It said, in part:

"To you, perhaps more than any other person, must go the credit for the vision and the perseverance which results in the creation of this new and now highly important branch of the postal service. From the 218-mile route which you, as Second Assistant Postmaster General, established between Washington and New York in

1918, our domestic and foreign air mail systems have grown until they now embrace 62,000 route miles over which the most modern transport planes last year flew more than 70,000,000 miles."

Later that week, Praeger participated in a live radio interview from San Diego with Reuben Fleet, who was at the time the city's most important citizen as the founder and president of Consolidated Aircraft, one of the nation's most important defense contractors. He deflected all credit for the achievement of airmail to Praeger.

"The success of the air mail in its early days was due almost entirely to the dynamic personality and the determination of Otto Praeger. Every possible stumbling block was placed in his way to prevent him from starting air mail service."

Otto Praeger's obituary in the *New York Times* called him the "father" of airmail in both the headline and lead. The obit was ten inches long in newspaper jargon, which is about a single half-page column. Not the longest obituary ever written, but not bad for an obscure civil servant.

POSTMASTER GENERAL ALBERT SIDNEY BURLESON

Control of the nation's mail and communications infrastructure had been considered so vital to the country's security that the man in charge of the post office has been a member of the president's cabinet since the founding of America. With the Postal Service Act of 1792, President George Washington elevated Postmaster General Samuel Osgood to the same level as Secretary of State Thomas Jefferson and Secretary of the Treasury Alexander Hamilton.

However, history has not been kind to the postmaster general position in the intervening two centuries, and the men who are remembered to have filled that slot usually come down to one, Benjamin Franklin—if, indeed, any names come to mind at all. Still, there is no denying that Albert Sidney Burleson was one of the most politically influential and effective postmaster generals in the history of the nation. When Burleson's post office recorded a surplus in 1914, it was the agency's first year in the black in more than three decades. At the end of his eight-year tenure, the agency recorded a net surplus of about $135 million. At the same time, the number of parcels delivered by the post office increased ten times, from three hundred million in 1913 to three billion in 1921.

His reforms reached down to the individual mailbox, the shape of which he standardized and which still applies today. He made postal money orders cashable at every post office in the nation, which gave people a simple but secure means of transacting business. He also struck a blow against patronage by working to ensure that all postmaster generals passed the civil service exam.

And, of course, he was in charge of the U.S. mail when it introduced scheduled delivery by motorized vehicles and airplanes.

In January of 1921, one of Texas's favorite sons finally returned home after spending nearly twenty-two years in Washington, D.C., first as Austin's legislator in the U.S. House of Representatives (1899–1913), and then as postmaster general in the cabinet of President Woodrow Wilson (1913–1921).

Those who knew him best, though, didn't think about things like budget surpluses when his name came up.

"The outstanding personal attributes of Albert Sidney Burleson were courage and fairness," said his most fervent supporter, Otto Praeger. "Many man are animated by high ideals but lack the courage in critical situations to translate those ideals into action. Albert Burleson was fortunate in a heritage of courage that enabled him to emerge from 50 years of dynamic public life, head erect and with a high reputation for fair dealing and dependability."

Burleson was fifty-eight years old when Wilson's second term ended, but unlike his friend Praeger, he had no interest in continuing the fight. He remained a vocal supporter of the Democrats and progressive issues, and he cheered when Franklin Delano Roosevelt won the first of his four terms in November 1932, but his days of public life were over. He owned thousands of acres of grazing land and retired to his home in Austin to enjoy it. Good luck followed him there.

Some three decades before, he had bought 12,000 acres of virtually worthless land in west Texas for $1 an acre. He wasn't even sure then why he bought the property, situated as it was in one of Texas's more arid regions and with little use for even grazing. So when oil prospectors wanted to drill experimental oil and gas wells on the land in 1926, Burleson leased them the rights for the same paltry $1 an acre, receiving in return a one-eighth royalty on any crude produced. Shouts of *eureka* soon followed, and Burleson's one-eighth share was soon bringing in $4,000 a week.

He eventually earned millions of dollars from the bonanza, but its wealth would be saved for his wife and three children. His life remained one of cultured modesty, and one of his great joys continued to be an annual hunting and fishing trip to Mexico with friends like fellow Texan Gregory Watt, who served with Burleson as the attorney general in Wilson's first cabinet.

He also took great satisfaction in the strong women in his life—his wife, Adele, a published playwright, as well as his daughter Laura, who became active in the Democratic Party in 1910 at the age of thirty and was a vocal supporter of women's suffrage. She had the political bug like her father and in 1928 became the first woman from her home county to be elected to the Texas legislature.

He didn't miss the political battles but was quick to slap down those people who criticized Wilson, particularly after the president died in early 1924. Burleson took special umbrage with those who falsely hinted that much of Wilson's campaign of progressive legislation over two terms originated with the postmaster general. Burleson saw the flattery for what it was, a thinly veiled attempt by Republican conservatives to discredit the reforms of the former president by implying someone else was the author. Such quarter even came from a Wilson adviser, former Navy secretary Josephus Daniels, who, as a newspaperman, couldn't resist asking Burleson for the true story. Burleson pulled no punches in his response.

"As you say, no one was in a better position than I to know that Wilson did his own thinking and that the wonderful program of reform legislation put through during the first six years of his Administration was his own and originated with him. You are right; I was the go-between for the president and the Congress. This was not of my choice, but his; and whereas it was an arduous task and at times a very disagreeable one—yet I felt I owed this service not only to the man who had so honored me, but to my party as well."

Toward the end of his life in 1936, Burleson took up the banner for campaign reform. He worked with a Senate committee to draft a plan limiting individual campaign donations to $25,000 and capping party spending at $1 million.

As to the relationship between Burleson and Praeger, it was not complex. Like an old married couple, they could almost finish each other's sentences. As such they were able to present a forceful two-man front that institutionalized both motorized ground vehicles and flying airships into the federal government in a single three-year period. The vision behind those technological leaps for the benefit of the people has yet to be matched today by any government entity.

History credits Praeger with being the true vision behind the establishment of airmail. Humbly, he looked at it differently.

"The title of 'Father of the Air Mail' often has been bestowed upon me by well meaning partisans in and out of aviation circles, but the real 'Father of the Air Mail' was a man who always stepped to the front when responsibility had to be assumed, and who invariably receded into the background when honors were passed about. That man was Postmaster General Albert Sidney Burleson. He conceived the plan of speeding up the United States Mail by introducing the airplane into the postal service as a fixture, like the railway, the steamship and the automobile. All the rest of the persons who were directly or remotely connected with this important work were, like myself, only the favored instrumentality for translating Postmaster General Burleson's vision into the far flung operation known as the United States Air Mail."

Burleson was equally complimentary of the people around him. Praeger liked to tell the story of the day that Thomas Edison called upon Burleson while the inventor was in Washington as head of the Naval Consulting Board during the war. Edison wanted to thank him for the handling of labor and censorship issues. Burleson graciously accepted the thanks but called for his four assistant postmaster generals to join him. It took a few minutes, but soon the assistant postmasters first through fourth were standing silently and respectfully before one of the world's most important inventors.

"These are the men, Mr. Edison," said Burleson, "who have done the work for which you have praised the Department."

Albert Sidney Burleson died of a heart attack in his home in Austin on November 24, 1937. He was survived by his wife, Adele Steiner Burleson, and three daughters.

In 1971, under the administration of President Richard Nixon, the postmaster general was stripped of his cabinet position.

MAJ. REUBEN HOLLIS FLEET

Maj. Reuben Fleet was a pilot for fewer than two years before being named, first, the head of Army pilot training in the United States, and, second, flying chief of the first airmail service in May 1918. Those two laurels were to be followed by a career that continued to make an impact on aviation for decades to come.

After leaving the airmail, Fleet furthered his aviation skills with an advanced flight training course at Brooks Field in San Antonio, Texas, and then was named officer in charge of flying at Mather Field in Sacramento, California. A stint overseas came next, and Fleet spent two months at the Graduate School of Advanced Flying for Flying Instructors at Gosport, England. Returning to the United States in January 1919, he was reassigned to McCook Field as the influential senior contracting officer in the Army Air Service.

He held that position until late 1922, when he resigned his commission to join the Gallaudet Aircraft Corporation as its general manager. Gallaudet was mildly successful building Curtiss floatplanes, though its only claim to fame today is that in 1908 it became the first officially registered aircraft manufacturer in America. Fleet learned the ropes of aircraft manufacturing for the next year and a half at Gallaudet, before venturing to start his own company in the very competitive, already overcrowded field of airframe manufacturing.

World War I had been a fruitful time for airplane builders, and nearly a dozen were manufacturing planes for the War Department. The Loughead brothers, Allan and Malcolm, who would change their name to the more easily pronounceable Lockheed, built their first airplane in 1918. William Boeing was building seaplanes and had already sold dozens to the Navy. The Glenn L. Martin

Company had split from the Wright Brothers, and Martin's chief engineer, Donald Douglas, would soon go off to found his own company—the famed Douglas Aircraft Company.

But with the war over and the market already saturated with hundreds of surplus airplanes, the government was about to turn off the spigot for defense contracts. It was in this environment that Fleet invested $15,000 of his own money and $10,000 of his sister's. He wouldn't start his company like the others did, in their garage. Fleet was a pilot, but his strength lay in management, in organization. He used his money to buy the assets of Gallaudet, as well as the designs for a training plane owned by General Motors's Dayton-Wright Company. No one had ever built an aircraft company like that before, and the name of his new company said it all—Consolidated Aircraft.

Fleet also had another skill that he used to great effect—salesmanship. He knew everyone in the military and private sector from his years as the Signal Corps's contracting officer. Tapping those relationships, Fleet talked his company into a number of contracts, and eventually sold some two hundred primary trainers to the Army and Navy over the next decade. He even branched off into the nascent field of civil aviation with the Fleetster, an all-metal aircraft that could carry eight people.

Then, in 1929, the good luck that seemed to follow Fleet throughout his life disappeared in one tragic moment. It was Friday, September 13, and he was on the last leg of a cross-country flight with his private secretary, Loretta Golem, also a licensed pilot, when their Wright-powered aircraft lost power and crashed about 150 miles west of Buffalo, New York. Golem succumbed to her injuries a day later, and though Fleet would survive, he would spend the next seven weeks in the hospital with multiple bone fractures.

Fleet recovered and returned to the helm of Consolidated. Flying boats were the bread and butter for most manufacturers in the 1920s and 1930s, and Consolidated's entry into the field was the large XPY-1 Commodore monoplane. It won some sales, but Fleet needed new designs to keep up with the competition, and his wintry Buffalo home and its ice-filled harbor were not suited to year-round flight testing. After nearly twelve years in Buffalo, he moved

Consolidated to San Diego in 1935. It was a massive relocation, stretching 3,000 miles coast to coast, and involved four hundred plus employees and 157 train-car loads of material. No one had seen the likes of it before.

It was in San Diego that Consolidated developed its most successful airplane, the PBY-1 Catalina flying boat. The Navy liked it so much that it placed a $22 million order for the plane in 1937—at the time the largest defense contract post–World War I. Hundreds of Consolidated Catalinas would fly reconnaissance and search/rescue missions during World War II.

An even bigger deal would come Fleet's way in 1939 when the U.S. Air Corps, successor to the Army Signal Corps, asked him to back up Boeing and coproduce the B-17 bomber. No thanks, said Fleet. His chief designer, Isaac Machlin "Mac" Laddon, who had known Fleet since their Army days and was the designer of the Catalina, had a different bomber in mind—one that they believed was better than the B-17 in almost every way. Nine months later, in December 1939, Consolidated would fly its new design. The Air Corps would designate it the B-24 Liberator, and it would rain down bombs on Germany and throughout the European theater for the duration of World War II. More than eighteen thousand were eventually built.

San Diego suited Fleet, and Fleet suited San Diego. In the years prior to Pearl Harbor, the city by the sea was best known for laid-back tourists and drunken sailors on shore leave. That changed when Consolidated arrived, and San Diego was transformed into an industrial giant. The year America entered the war, Consolidated booked nearly $5 billion worth of airplane orders and grew faster in 1941 than any company in American history had ever grown in any other one-year period. By 1943, Consolidated employed forty-one thousand people in San Diego, and the legend of "Rosie the riveter" was coined for the women working there. Fleet's huge manufacturing facility, with the phrase "Nothing Short of Right Is Right" emblazoned across the façade, dominated the cityscape. A resident had only to gaze into the sky at any moment of the day to see a Consolidated-built bomber or seaplane flying overhead.

Fleet owned 34 percent of the company, and in 1943 he sold it to the relatively small-time manufacturer Vultee Aircraft for $10 million—ending a twenty-year run at the helm of Consolidated, though he would continue as a senior consultant. The company that Fleet started in 1923, however, wasn't finished making its mark on aviation. The new Consolidated-Vultee company, more commonly known as Convair, would become one of the nation's most important defense contractors.

The year 1945 then brought Fleet some measure of notoriety when he found himself in the pages of the *Guinness Book of World Records*. The listing read: "The greatest alimony ever paid was $11,550,000 paid by Reuben Hollis Fleet, the U.S. millionaire aircraft manufacturer, to his second wife Dorothy in 1945, after their separation, following 'verbal abuse.' " It made for a good read, but some years later Dorothy Fleet corrected the record. The settlement was for $1.25 million, she said, with some millions more from ownership of property and stock shares.

Convair exited the war with another big contract, development of the Air Corps's next bomber, the B-36. It would be the first aircraft designed with intercontinental range to strike deep into the Soviet Union, and Convair would build nearly three hundred B-36s through 1954.

In mid-1946, Reuben Fleet left Convair for good. The company would change hands in 1949 and see continued success with a delta-wing fighter called the F-102 Delta Dagger. Another change of ownership would come in 1953 when Convair merged with shipbuilder Electric Boat. The new company would be renamed General Dynamics, but the moniker Convair would live on as a division within GD and play an important role in the space program of the 1960s.

As Consolidated grew, so did the city of San Diego—with continual prompting and support from Fleet, who had become one of its wealthiest residents. Fleet contributed to the building of Harbor Drive and Linda Vista, as well as Lindbergh Field and its 9,000-foot runway to handle the long-range B-36 bomber. Fleet also helped tackle one of the city's most constant problems—access to water. He served as chairman of the city's Water Reclamation Commission and grappled with water rights issues that helped bring Colorado River water to the Southland.

Fleet was inducted into the Dayton, Ohio, Aerospace Hall of Fame in 1965. His biography there reads, in part: "Above all, Reuben Fleet was an unabashed patriot. He believed in the basic virtues which made his beloved country great—self-reliance, personal integrity, respect for truth, living within one's means, devotion to duty, thrift, belief in God, love of country."

On May 15, 1968, the fiftieth anniversary of the inaugural airmail flight, Fleet was designated "Airmail Pilot No. 1" at a ceremony at the Smithsonian's National Air and Space Museum.

He died in 1975 at the age of eighty-eight.

LT. JAMES CLARK EDGERTON

The adventurous Nebraska-born Lt. James Edgerton, who owed his place on the inaugural mail flight on May 15, 1918, to his father's connections, more than proved his mettle first as pilot, then as chief of flying, then chief of radio. His experiments with radio led to the establishment of a postal-run broadcast system that spanned the United States, bringing market news and weather reports from the Department of Agriculture to pilots and anyone with a home radio.

However, this free government-run radio operation soon caught the attention of people like David Sarnoff, president of the Radio Corporation of America, who was interested in using private funds to build a similar network, which would be sustained by advertising and the sale of radio receivers. Herbert Hoover, secretary of commerce in the Harding administration, was sympathetic to what the post office was trying to develop but sided with commercial interests.

Seeing that his radio work was to be deemphasized at the postal department, Edgerton resigned from the service on December 31, 1922. Over the next decade he worked as a representative for several airmail contractors, and then in 1932 was appointed a member of the Reorganization Committee of the Department of Commerce in charge of aeronautical matters. In 1933, he was named executive assistant to Assistant Secretary of Commerce in Charge of Transportation Ewing Mitchell.

Following the outbreak of World War II in 1939, he was asked to help organize a civilian flight-training program. He was recalled to active duty in 1940 and named executive officer to the air operations officer of the War Department. He was promoted to lieutenant colonel and assigned to Eglin Field, Florida, as director of research, where he worked on pressurized cabins and high-altitude equipment.

He retired in 1945 due to heart troubles and moved to Florida, first living in Fort Lauderdale and then Miami Springs, where he served on the city commission for two terms, as well as the Dade County Water and Sewer Board.

In 1973, he died at the age of seventy-seven at his home in Boca Raton, Florida. He was survived by his wife of fifty-five years, Mary, and their two daughters.

CAPT. BENJAMIN B. LIPSNER

At fewer than four months, Capt. Benjamin Lipsner's tenure with the U.S. Air Mail Service was shorter than that for most pilots. It was a bittersweet departure for Lipsner, who harbored great aspirations for aviation. But he lived a long life and witnessed the achievements of Lindbergh and the *Spirit of St. Louis*, Col. Paul Tibbetts and the *Enola Gay*, Chuck Yeager and *Glamorous Glennis*, and Neil Armstrong and the *Eagle* lunar module.

After leaving government service, he worked as a consulting engineer for several airlines and oil companies. He also headed his local American Legion Aviation Post in Chicago.

For his part, Lipsner's role in aviation, particularly as he got older, was as a booster, regaling radio and television hosts and American Legion crowds with stories about airmail's pioneer days and—his favorite subject—his personal role as "Father of the Regular Air Mail Service."

But success has many fathers, and like many great technical achievements, the airmail story boasts several creators, plus many others who were there at the birth. Lipsner's quest for recognition began in 1921 with a letter to Will Hays, Albert Burleson's successor, who now served President Warren Harding.

"You can readily understand that the distinction of being the first Superintendent of the Aerial Mail Service is not necessarily due to exceptional ability," he wrote, "but is, nevertheless, a most fortunate appointment and one that I cannot help but cherish for the benefit of myself and posterity; and, that I may in my after years leave to my sons positive proof that circumstances made it possible for their father to enjoy."

The government response came from the U.S. Air Mail superintendent C. F. Egge, on behalf of Second Assistant Postmaster General E. H. Shaughnessy.

"The Air Mail Service was established May 15, 1918, with equipment and flying personnel furnished by the Air Service of the Army. Major Reuben H. Fleet of the Army Air Service supervised and directed the work while the Army had control. He was considered the first superintendent. Mr. Praeger decided early in July to have the Post Office take over the flying activities and on July 15, Lipsner was appointed superintendent to assist in organizing. The Post Office Department took the service over on August 12. Lipsner resigned under pressure December 6 of the same year. As a matter of fact, Mr. Praeger personally supervised the Air Mail Service and I would say that Mr. Praeger was the first superintendent of the Air Mail Service, notwithstanding Lipsner's claim."

It was obvious that Lipsner would get nowhere in 1921, when many of the postal department officials were holdovers from the Praeger years. Lipsner had no official contact with anyone from the postal department for the remainder of the 1920s, but he reopened the question in 1930 in a letter to Walter Folger Brown, postmaster general for President Herbert Hoover. His argument in short: Otto Praeger offered him the job of first civilian airmail superintendent, and he resigned his military commission to take it. End of story.

Brown asked his second assistant to look into the matter, and the verdict came back a week later. Lipsner had won his title as the first superintendent.

"I am unable to locate anything in our files indicating the designation of Maj. Reuben H. Fleet as officer in charge of the aerial mail service, but I do find communications signed by him dated May 18, 1918, with the following title, 'R.H. Fleet, Major, J.M.A., Signal Corps, Office in Charge Aerial Mail Service,' though he was not designated as Superintendent because, as I understand it, military regulations would not permit of an officer's carrying a civilian title.

"On July 13, 1918, an order was issued by the Second Assistant [Otto Praeger] appointing Capt. Benjamin B. Lipsner Superintendent of the Division of Air Mail Service effective July 15, 1918, which made him the first civilian supervisor of the air mail service, his appointment carrying with it the title of Superintendent."

In 1951, approximately three years after Praeger's death, Lipsner published one of the best-known accounts of the founding of the service. In his book, entitled *The Airmail: Jennies to Jets*, Lipsner places himself at the center of every important airmail decision from the inaugural flight on May 18, 1918, until the end of that year when he resigned from the service. The title page of the book identifies Lipsner as the "first to hold the title, Superintendent of the United States Aerial Mail Service."

In one passage from the book he writes: "I continued to keep my eyes on all worth-while developments in commercial aviation, watching and studying every aviation activity, particularly every move by the Post Office Department, since I felt that the airmail was my baby."

Lipsner died in 1971 on the day before Christmas, at the age of eighty-four. In 1982, his family donated his archives to the Smithsonian Institution's National Philatelic Collection. Included in the material was the original wooden dispatch board that Lipsner designed to track pilots and planes. The other prize in the Lipsner collection was the full-body leather flight suit worn by Douglas Fairbanks during his war bond flight with the Air Mail Service in 1918.

PILOT JACK KNIGHT

Pilot Jack Knight joined the U.S. Air Mail in 1919, first flying between New York and Chicago, and later between Omaha and

Cheyenne. Following the triumph of the February 22–23, 1921, transcontinental night flight, Knight immediately became the most famous man in America. Other aviators in the same situation might have parlayed fame into an acting career in Hollywood or started their own flying circus to tour the country. Knight went back to flying his regular 460-mile airmail run between Omaha and Cheyenne.

By 1923, though, he yearned for new challenges in the development of aviation technologies and was named chief pilot for Experimental Night Flying. When the postal department began regular night flying between Chicago and Cheyenne, Knight was the lead pilot. And when the personnel of the U.S. Air Mail won the 1923 Collier Trophy for the establishment of night flying, Knight—as the man most responsible for the accomplishment—could just as easily have been chosen as the sole recipient.

He stayed on the route for the next four years, and by late 1927, when the U.S. government ended its participation in airmail, Knight was the most senior pilot in the service, having traveled 417,000 miles over 4,300 flying hours.

Knight then went to work for Bill Boeing and Eddie Hubbard's Boeing Air Transport, which won the rights to fly mail between Chicago and San Francisco. He flew for BAT until 1934, at which time the big company was broken up by President Franklin Roosevelt. A company called United Airlines was one of the spin-offs from the breakup, and Knight went to work for United flying the Chicago–Omaha run, and later the Chicago–Denver route.

United Airlines captain Jack Knight retired from active airline flying in 1937, with his last job in the left seat of the twenty-one-passenger DC-3 Mainliner built by Douglas Aircraft. He had spent twenty years as pilot in command and logged eighteen thousand hours in the sky (the equivalent of two solid years), and he had seen 2.4 million miles of terrain pass beneath his wings since he first took the stick in 1918. He had climbed to the top of the pyramid and was recognized around the world as the man who had flown more miles than anyone, ever—the equivalent of ninety-six times around the planet.

In his own words, he was now a "kiwi, a funny kind of bird who has wings, but doesn't use 'em."

Not wanting to let him retire, though, United appointed him their unofficial ambassador with the title of director of public education. Knight was now a salesman of "aviation confidence," and he spent his time traveling the world talking about the value and safety of flying.

At the start of World War II, Knight joined the Civil Aeronautics Administration, which had oversight responsibility for pilot training and certification, as well as airway development. From there, Knight found his way to the Defense Support Corporation, kind of a go-to agency for vital war materials. It acted as a broker buying aviation fuel for the air force. It purchased and stockpiled various medicines for the armed services, including quinine for malaria and serum for typhus fever. The corporation also cornered the market on Cuban-grown sugar and molasses, which were important ingredients in efforts to develop synthetic rubber.

American researchers were going full bore trying to create rubber in the laboratory because natural sources had been in short supply since the Japanese cut off supplies from Southeast Asia. The shortage became so acute during the conflict that it was virtually impossible for a private citizen to buy a new tire.

The Defense Support Corporation thought there might be sources of natural rubber in the Amazon jungle region, and Knight was part of the team sent to explore. He contracted malaria while there and was never able to shake off the disease. It weakened him so badly that Knight was unable to recover from a serious fall. He died at the age of fifty-three in 1945.

Jack Knight's last flight came a couple days later over Lake Michigan, when his family scattered his ashes to the air.

PILOT EDWARD GARDNER

Eddie Gardner left Uncle Sam's Air Mail Service in October 1919, hoping to recapture some of the excitement he experienced the prior year in tandem with Max Miller on the New York–Chicago Pathfinder trip. Gardner's message to his friends that Christmas: "I am still going higher."

Using connections he had made at the Standard Aircraft Corporation, he was hired to demonstrate planes for the Nebraska Aircraft Corporation, which had bought up a huge stock of Standard airplanes, parts, and Hispano-Suiza engines and was reselling them to the general public. It was the perfect job for Turk Bird, as he was able to fly the company's airplanes in fairs all over the country. The very stunts that the Air Mail Service frowned upon were exactly what his new employer wanted him to do.

Gardner never tired of performing his aerial maneuvers, and eighteen months after joining Nebraska Aircraft, he was still throwing his Standard around the sky. There was nothing particularly special about one such aerobatic performance, for a show in Holdrege, Nebraska, about 190 miles from Lincoln, on May 5, 1921. It was just like the dozens he had flown in the prior months. This one, however, ended tragically.

"Gardner went into a tailspin at 1,200 feet and appeared at all times to have complete control of the ship," said former mail pilot Ira Biffle, who was at the show to watch his old friend. "It seemed to me that he tried to land from the spin, as he was just in a good position to making a landing."

The next moment, though, before anyone could realize what happened, the airplane plowed into the ground. Gardner survived the impact but his face was smashed and a doctor thought his skull had been fractured. Gardner was transported by train to a better hospital in Lincoln, but he went into a coma and died early the next morning.

He was buried in his hometown of Plainfield, about 35 miles outside Chicago.

PILOT WILLIAM "WILD" BILL HOPSON

Originally assigned to fly out of Bellefonte, William Hopson requested transfer to the west and was soon flying the Chicago–Omaha route—though not without incident. In 1925, he crashed his de Havilland into an Iowa field full of corn. In 1926, he recorded no fewer than thirteen forced landings. Any pilot other than the personable Hopson would have likely been fired, but the various field mangers and superintendents always backed up his assertion that the landings were due to weather or mechanical difficulties.

When airmail transferred to the private sector in 1927, Hopson went to work for National Air Transport, which held the rights to fly between New York and Chicago. It was while flying that route in October 1928 that his plane disappeared after passing over Clarion, Pennsylvania, about 70 miles east of Pittsburgh.

Nobody knows what sort of mechanical trouble bedeviled Hopson that night, but people on the ground reported seeing flares dropped over the side of the plane to indicate the crash site. It was not uncommon for rescuers to take hours or days to find a downed pilot, and it was every airmail aviator's nightmare to survive a crash but succumb to injuries while he waited for rescue—cold, bloody, and alone on the side of a mountain or deep in the woods.

Hopson's airplane sheared off the top of a tree and careened off another tree before it struck the ground, where it broke apart. Fire quickly spread through the wreckage. There were 1,000 pounds of mail aboard and 900 of it burned. Hopson was thrown from the plane, and his charred body was found nearby.

The story would have ended there, with Hopson being just another airmail casualty, if not for the nature of his cargo that night. Rumor had it that he carried a stash of diamonds, and if true, the diamonds would still be there, no matter how hot the fire. Sure enough, someone picking through the carcass of the airplane a couple days later found one. Word spread of the find, and soon hundreds of people were trampling the scene of Hopson's death. Several more diamonds were even found. The post office launched an investigation, and the gems were soon tracked down and returned to their rightful owners.

Hopson was survived by a wife and a fifteen-year-old son. When he died he had spent eight years flying the mail and covered more than 400,000 miles, second only to Jack Knight.

PILOT KATHERINE STINSON

An official pilot for the U.S. Air Mail for two days in September 1918, aviatrix Katherine Stinson took her considerable piloting skills and left for Europe, where she was determined to help her country in any way she could, driving an ambulance for the Red Cross.

She remained in France after Armistice Day and unsuccessfully fought for permission to fly into Germany to deliver the mail to soldiers of the victorious occupying army. At the time, the airplane was really the only way for the Allies to reach deep into the country because so many of the roads, bridges, and trains had been destroyed.

During this time, Stinson became a lightning rod for anguished parents and relatives desperate for information about missing sons and fathers. She regularly received pleas for help, such as this one.

"I hope that I have been rightly advised that you have taken up the Red Cross work in Paris and that you will be available to make flights in search of any boys who may have been left in Germany," wrote one father. "There are so many conflicting reports about some of the boys that (maybe) there is the remotest possibility that the information which the Government sent about (my son) being killed is not true and that he may have been taken prisoner, severely wounded and later transferred to some hospital in France or Switzerland or some other country. All these things I am desirous of finding out."

But Stinson was in no position to help. The stresses of the war had compromised her health, and she was forced to return to the United States after contracting tuberculosis. She went first to a New York sanatorium, then to Santa Fe, New Mexico, in 1920, where it was hoped the climate would help to restore her health. She was finally cured four years later, but rarely, if ever, did she fly again. In 1927, she married Miguel Otero Jr., a former military aviator and one of the state's prominent judges. In their vows, they pledged never to pilot a plane again. Moving from aviation to architecture, Katherine designed several houses in the Pueblo architecture style, garnering several awards for her designs. She and her husband reared four adopted children.

In her later years, when interviewed about her flying career, she claimed forgetfulness when the questions turned to her involvement in airmail.

Katherine lived a long life and died after a lengthy illness at the age of eighty-six in Santa Fe. Years after she had packed away her flying goggles, Katherine said wistfully: "I had hoped there would be a place for women in modern aviation, but there isn't."

And yet she did affect many, including the girls of The Brearley School in Manhattan in December 1919. In their eyes, Katherine Stinson had punched a hole right through the sky. They sent her a Christmas package and wrote this letter.

> Dear Miss Stinson,
>
> We are Class VII of the Brearley School. There are fifteen of us, tall and short, good looking and not so good looking, ages anywhere from 15 to 17, and all very full of admiration and excitement over flying. So when Miss Dunn, our English teacher, who had heard about you from Mrs. James, suggested that we send you a Christmas box, we jumped at the idea and began to wonder what you would like.
>
> We wondered what color your hair was, and whether you liked music and someone wanted to know if there was any rule as to an aviatrix's taste in candy. So if you find anything strange you mustn't be surprised for all we had to go on was a black and white photograph.
>
> We only hope that you have as much fun opening our box as we have had packing it. We had a Christmas party in your honor, grape juice and cake with sticky frosting two inches deep. We owe all our enjoyment to your credit, but if we feel the after effects we will blame only ourselves.
>
> Good-bye and much Christmas cheer from Class VII every member of which would give everything to be someday what you are now.

MAJ. CHARLES WILLOUGHBY (WEIDENBACH)

It may have appeared in the summer of 1918 that Maj. Charles Willoughby was destined for obscurity. The first Army airmail superintendent to follow Maj. Reuben Fleet, his career was seemingly derailed by accusations of being a German sympathizer. He was unceremoniously shipped off to Kelly Field in San Antonio, but it was there that he would begin a stunning climb to becoming one of the highest-ranking military officers in America—and also one of the nation's staunchest anti-Communists.

After Kelly, he reverted back to the infantry and was transferred to an obscure base in New Mexico whose only claim to fame was that it had been raided twice by the famed revolutionary Pancho Villa. But if Willoughby thought he could hide from his German heritage in New Mexico, then he was wrong. Some of his superior officers must have thought it poetic justice when he was named commander of the Twenty-fourth Infantry, whose claim to fame was being one of only two black infantry units in the entire U.S. army.

By 1921—with the war long over—he was reassigned to San Juan, Puerto Rico, where he led the Sixty-fifth Infantry as company and battalion commander. He shifted gears in 1923, becoming an intelligence officer in South America, setting down a path that would carry him through both World War II and the Korean War. In the early 1930s, Willoughby taught intelligence and military history at the Command and General Staff School at Fort Leavenworth, Kansas. Then in 1936, he began four years as an instructor at the Infantry School at Fort Benning, Iowa, rising to the rank of lieutenant colonel.

An assignment overseas came next, and in mid-1940, Willoughby sailed for the Philippine capital of Manila as logistics officer at Army headquarters for the Pacific region. World War II saw many officers rise quickly in the ranks, and Willoughby rode the wave right into the new Philippine headquarters of Supreme Allied Commander Gen. Douglas MacArthur. In 1942, Willoughby received his first star as brigadier general, to go along with his new job as MacArthur's chief of intelligence. As the "G2," as the post is called, Willoughby oversaw the Southwest Pacific region, which included Australia, the Philippines, Borneo, New Guinea, and parts of Thailand and China.

He was on the Philippine island of Bataan for a reconnaissance mission when the Japanese invaded, and he received the Silver Star for leading a counterattack. He then earned the Army's second-highest decoration, the Distinguished Service Cross, when he joined a U.S./Australian unit in a jungle fight to capture an important village in the battle of Buna-Gona on New Guinea.

Willoughby was at MacArthur's side when the commander in chief fled the Philippines in 1942 on a PT boat. He also was on the deck of the *Missouri* battleship on September 2, 1945, when the Japanese signed the surrender papers, and he joined MacArthur in Tokyo during the occupation.

He received his second star and the rank of major general at the end of the war in 1945. Willoughby remained MacArthur's chief of intelligence for a decade, eventually leaving the military in mid-1951 during the Korean conflict, a few months after President Harry Truman relieved MacArthur of his command in Korea.

Nearly twenty-five years after his short stint with the U.S. Air Mail, no one questioned Willoughby's loyalty anymore. He did, however, take some criticism for intelligence failures around the loss of the Philippines in 1942, and then again in Korea. He wrongly maintained that China would not cross the Yalu River and enter the war on the side of North Korea, and he was roundly criticized by the U.S. press for that assertion.

He also caught flack for his friendship with the man he called the world's "second greatest general"—Generalissimo Francisco Franco, the authoritarian dictator of Spain. He visited personally with Franco, and lobbied the U.S. Congress in the early 1950s to give him $100 million in aid.

Throughout his years with MacArthur, Willoughby displayed a vehement dislike of Communists. Reporters in Tokyo who dug too hard for news during the occupation were labeled commies, and though Willoughby stood 6 feet 3 inches tall, MacArthur once referred to him in public as "my little Fascist." He became even more fervently anti-Communist and right wing during the Joseph McCarthy era in the 1950s. He was a friendly witness before the House Un-American Activities Committee in 1951, and he joined various Christian crusade and radical right organizations through the 1960s.

He retired to Naples, Florida, in 1968 and died in 1972 at the age of eighty. His distinguished career with the U.S. military lasted for forty-one years, from 1910 to 1951.

BELLEFONTE, PENNSYLVANIA

When scheduled night flight was extended from Cleveland to New York in mid-1925, Bellefonte, Pennsylvania, still occupied a strategic place on the transcontinental route.

The city had been preparing for the first night flight for months, hoping to recapture some of the glory and joie de vivre of the early days of "Wild" Bill Hopson and Slim Lewis. Not far from the original airmail field at the Beaver farm, the city had graded and constructed a new airfield that was better for night flying—bigger all around, greatly extending a pilot's margin for error in a night landing. When word spread that a new field was being built, a few of the nearby towns tried to entice the airmail away from Bellefonte, but none could compete with the $75,000 state-of-the-art terminal under construction in Bellefonte. The 90-acre site was ringed with forty-six lighted globes, with blue globes strategically placed to identify safe landing routes and red globes to identify danger like barns and electrical poles. Floodlights illuminated nearby woods and farms. A half-million candlepower beacon swept across the sky—pulling pilots in, instead of warning them away as lighthouses did for ships on the ocean.

It was a sight to see, the glow from the field bathing the air and visible from miles away. Thousands of people from all over Centre County turned out the first week of July to witness the dawn of night flying in Bellefonte. They were not disappointed when the first to set down was famed mail pilot Dean Smith, and music, fireworks, and speeches greeted him upon landing. He was on the ground only long enough to fill his airplane with fuel and his stomach with coffee, but the night's entertainment wasn't over with Smith's departure to Cleveland. Another westbound plane arrived around midnight, followed by the arrival of two eastbound planes around 3 A.M.

During the height of airmail operations in Bellefonte in 1925, as many as fifteen people worked there full-time. By 1926, though, powerful long-range aircraft were able to fly directly from New York to Cleveland, bypassing Bellefonte. The terminal was relegated to the status of emergency field only. All the other intermediary cities lost their regular service, too: Bryan, Iowa City, North Platte, Rawlins, and Rock Springs.

Today, the site of the Bellefonte airmail terminal, formerly the Beaver farm, is now the Bellefonte Area Senior High School. A single green, metal sign identifies what happened there eighty years ago.

ACKNOWLEDGMENTS

There were a number of people behind *Mavericks of the Sky* who made a difference, individuals like Jane Dystel, our agent, who helped bring this story to fruition and in the process made us the grateful beneficiaries of her professionalism and sense of fair play. Similarly, Jane's partner, Miriam Goderich, was also a great supporter.

Jim Miller, nephew of airmail pilot Max Miller, gave freely of his time and recollections. We owe thanks to Janet Phillips and Elinor Goettel for memories of their father Otto Praeger. Mort Turchin's legal expertise guided us through untrodden territory while Stan Hoffman's astute editorial observations we highly valued. Meg Ausman, historian of the United States Postal Service, remained ever helpful to us over the years, as did Nancy Pope and James O'Donnell of the National Postal Museum. We also owe a debt to Joyce Adgate of the Centre County Library and Historical Museum, Cathy Allen of the College Park Aviation Museum, and Bette Davidson Kalash for access to the photographs of the Jesse Davidson Aviation Archives.

Lastly, we would like to acknowledge the authors and historians William Leary and A. D. Jones whose scholarly works on airmail became the shoulders upon which this book now stands.

NOTES

CHAPTER 1: FLEET

1. The 12-cylinder Liberty: http://www.1903to2003.gov/essay/aerospace/earlyengines/aero4.htm.
2. Maj. Brindley died: The diary of Col. Thurman H. Bane, as reported in the pamphlet *Fifty Years of Air Mail, Honoring Our Air Mail Pioneers on Their Golden Anniversary, May 15, 1968,* by R. H. Fleet; Bernard L. Whelan, "Arch Freeman: the Birth of the Dayton-Wright Airplane Co.," www.earlyaviators.com/efreeman.htm; and "Maj. Brindley of Albany Met Tragic Death" (an unidentified news clipping, May 2, 1918), www.earlyaviators.com/ebrindle6.htm.
2. gates to McCook: Résumé, Maj. Reuben Fleet, "as reviewed by Major Reuben H. Fleet, 10/9/73," San Diego Aerospace Museum.
3. The Army bought the land: "Three Military Installations," Aeronautical Systems Center, http://www.ascho.wpafb.af.mil/centurygrowth/chap2.htm; and SAC Bases, "Wright Field, Patterson Field/Wright-Patterson AFB," http://www.strategic-air-command.com/bases/Wright-Patterson_AFB.htm.
4. The chastising went on: The diary of Col. Thurman H. Bane, as reported in the pamphlet *Fifty Years of Air Mail, Honoring Our Air Mail Pioneers on Their Golden Anniversary, May 15, 1968,* by R. H. Fleet.
7. A program was put in place: Résumé, Maj. Reuben Fleet, "as reviewed

by Major Reuben H. Fleet, 10/9/73," San Diego Aerospace Museum; "Biography—Major Reuben H. Fleet, dated Feb. 22, 1967," San Diego Aerospace Museum; transcript of interview by E. W. Robischon of Reuben Fleet, July 20, 1968, at Fleet's residence in San Diego; National Air and Space Museum, Smithsonian Institution, Reuben Fleet documents; and Joel Rumerman, "Consolidated Vultee Aircraft Corporation," www.centennialofflight.gov/essay/aerospace/consolidated_vultee/aero33.htm.

7. The Army had only seventy-three airplanes: "Rockwell Field," National Park Service, http://www.cr.nps.gov/nr/travel/aviation/rok.htm.

7. Fleet was transferred to the War Department: Résumé, Maj. Reuben Fleet, "as reviewed by Major Reuben H. Fleet, 10/9/73," San Diego Aerospace Museum.

8. Airpower would help the Allies: Pamela Feltus, "Henry 'Hap' Arnold," http://www.centennialofflight.gov/essay/Air_Power/Hap_Arnold/AP16.htm.

9. Both northbound and southbound runs: "Post Office Department, Second Assistant Postmaster General, Air Mail: 1918–1927," Government Operated, Records of the Post Office Dept., Bureau of Transportation, Domestic Mail Transportation Div., Air Transportation Branch, Contract Air Mail.

9. His orders had put four million: "Newton Baker," Learning Curve, National Archives, http://www.spartacus.schoolnet.co.uk/USAbakerN.htm.

10. the major could bloody well: Transcript of interview with Major Fleet, July 20, 1968.

11. The Wright-Martin Aircraft Company: *Morning Telegraph*, Monday, May 20, 1968, Belmont Racetrack Archives, Elmont, New York; William Wraga, "The Wright Brothers," http://www.curtisswright.com/history/1909-1919.asp; and Charles H. Hubbell, *History of U.S. Air Mail, 50th Anniversary, 1918–1968*, p. 14k, National Air and Space Museum, Smithsonian Institution.

13. Hitchcock had flown Fleet: "History of the Equestrian Sport of Polo," Two Friends Farms, LLC, www.sportpolo.com/History/default.htm; and Ralph Hickok, "Hitchcock, 'Tommy' (Thomas Jr.)," http://www.hickoksports.com/biograph/hitchcocktommy.shtml.

13. where he mastered Wall Street: Edward L. Bowen, *Thoroughbred Leg-*

ends, http://www.thoroughbredlegends.com/man_o_war/chapter_one. html/.

13. managed to snag the estimable hand: "Belmont Park, 1905–1968, New York Racing Association, Belmont Raceway Archives, Elmont, New York.

14. equine soldier remained: Ron Hale, "Man o'War: He Rewrote the Record Books," http://www.equinet.org/heroes/mow.html.

15. He'd sent to auction: http://www.bloodhorse.com/tb_champions/ excerpt.html.

15. Of course Maj. Fleet: Transcript of interview with Maj. Fleet, July 20, 1968.

15. But its 130 acres of flat: Press release, Office of Information, Post Office Department, March 28, 1918.

16. Certainly no aviator: James Edgerton, *Horizons Unlimited*, unpublished manuscript.

16. Crews of Army mechanics: Edith Dodd Culver, *Talespins* (Santa Fe, N. Mex.: Sunstone Press, 1986), p. 46.

17. Parcel post was helping merge: *The Postmaster's Advocate*, July 1914.

19. "Can you feature being a mailman . . .": Culver, *Talespins*, p. 42.

19. After enlisting in the Army: Ibid., p.46; and http://www.rcooper.ocatch. com/ealjohn2.htm#SEC6, The Early Birds of Aviation, Inc.

19. A downed plane could be easy pickings: Culver, *Talespins*, p. 47.

19. There never seemed to be a shortfall: James H. Bruns, *Mail on the Move* {Polo, Ill: Transportation Trails, 1992), p. 99.

19. Fleet's team had only eighteen hours: Edgerton, *Horizons Unlimited*.

20. "The tail came up with a rush . . .": Transcript of a radio talk delivered at the New York Air Show, Madison Square Garden, by James Edgerton.

21. "The major came near to taking . . .": Ibid.

21. Fleet would then follow: Letter from R. H. Fleet to Jesse Davidson, July 20, 1961, National Air and Space Museum, Smithsonian Instition.

22. red, white, and blue stripes: Culver, *Talespins*, p. 49.

24. "Perhaps three gallons . . .": Transcript of interview with Maj. Fleet, July 20, 1968.

25. the mechanic gives the propeller a quick downward pull: "Part II, Rules and Instructions for Government of Pilots, Mechanics and Riggers, Post Office Department, Office of the Second Assistant Postmaster

General, Division of Airpost Service," National Archives, Washington, D.C., 1918.

25. "It took me at least a dozen . . .": Letter from Fleet to Davidson, July 20, 1961, National Air and Space Museum, Smithsonian Institution.

27. "I could have reached out . . .": Culver, *Tailspins*, p. 49.

27. Penn had helped establish: "The Story of the Mail," U.S. Post Office Department Archives; and Tuomi J. Forrest, "William Penn, Visionary Proprietor," http://xroads.virginia.edu/~CAP/PENN/pnintro.html.

27. He issued an open invitation: Culver, *Talespins*, p. 49.

28. "We grouped all available autos . . .": Letter from Fleet to Davidson, July 20, 1961, National Air and Space Museum, Smithsonian Institution.

CHAPTER 2: BURLESON

29. "They wound down across the Mall . . .": Rolph Block, untitled article, *The Tribune*, May 16, 1918.

29. Newspaper reporters and cameramen hovered: Ibid.

30. The "ubiquitous, sneaking submarine": "The War and the United States Mail," *Postmaster's Advocate* 22 (May 1917).

30. "nailed the stars and stripes to the North Pole": Bradley Robinson, "Commander Robert E. Peary, USN," http://pearyhenson.org.

31. People understood how a great genius: Robert M. Poole, *Explorers House: National Geographic and the World It Made* (New York: Penguin Press, 2004), p. 73.

31. "He jumped down from his red sleigh . . .": "Flight of the Silver Dart," in *Great Adventures with National Geographic*, ed. Melville Bell Grosvenor, (Washington, D.C.: National Geographic Society, 1963), p. 456.

31. if properly nurtured by government: "Alexander Graham Bell Urges Aeroplane Mail Lines," *Aerial Age Weekly*, January 24, 1916, p. 446.

32. the war having shown the value: *Postmaster's Advocate* 20, no. 11, (May 1915).

32. Praeger saw no reason: *R.F.D. News* 16, no. 16 (April 20, 1918): 3.

32. He sat behind the wheel of an automobile: Interview by Barry Rosenberg with Otto Praeger's daughter Janet Phillips.

32. someone "who is doing things": "Synopsis of the Work of Albert Sidney Burleson as Postmaster General," Albert Sidney Burleson Archives, University of Texas at Austin.

32. "get down to terra firma": *R.F.D. News* 16, no. 16 (April 20, 1918): 3.

32. a black umbrella that he carried: "Albert S. Burleson Dies at 74; War-Time Postmaster General," *Herald Tribune*, November 25, 1937.

33. Wilson established the Federal Reserve System: "United States History: The Gilded Age (1890) to World War I," http://www.emayzine.com/lectures/Gilded~1.htm.

35. "Has anybody ever hit those trees . . .": Col. C. V. Glines, "The Somewhat Mixed Up Events of Our Very First Air Mail Flight," *American Legion Magazine*, May 1968.

35. "to cut down the tree six inches below the ground . . .": Recollections of Reuben Fleet written on personal letterhead stationery, June 26, 1961, from the Paul Culver Air Mail Collection at the Garber Center, National Air and Space Museum, Smithsonian Institution.

35. "Nothing short of right is right": "Biography—Major Reuben H. Fleet," February 22, 1967, San Diego Aerospace Museum.

36. "You know your business, Fleet . . .": Recollections of Reuben Fleet written on personal letterhead stationery, June 26, 1961, from the Paul Culver Air Mail Collection at the Garber Center, National Air and Space Museum, Smithsonian Institution.

36. "Never fear because Boyle is here!": Glines, "The Somewhat Mixed Up Events of Our Very First Air Mail Flight."

38. They were Ford trucks: Personal observations of original photographs.

38. with more than six thousand letters: "First Airplane Postal Line Opened," *Air Service Journal*, May 1918.

38. The sight of the notoriously terse postmaster: Block, untitled article, *The Tribune*, May 16, 1918.

38. "The aviator took them helplessly . . .": Ibid.

39. there is no cause for despair: Unpublished article on human interest stories related to Albert Burleson, Albert Sidney Burleson Archives, University of Texas at Austin.

40. "I had delegated Capt. B. B. Lipsner . . .": Recollections of Reuben Fleet written on personal letterhead stationery, June 26, 1961, from the Paul Culver Air Mail Collection at the Garber Center, National Air and Space Museum, Smithsonian Institution.

41. "The hum of the engine faded . . .": Block, untitled article, *The Tribune*, May 16, 1918.

CHAPTER 3: REGULARLY SCHEDULED SERVICE

44. "There she goes!": "New York-Philadelphia-Washington Aerial Mail Great Success," *Aerial Age Weekly*, May 27, 1918, p. 532.

44. A children's choir from Queens: "First Airplane Postal Line Opened," *Air Service Journal* (May 1918): 8.

44. People cheered and waved their hats: "First Air Mail in Washington in 200 Minutes," *New York Times*, May 16, 1918.

44. fully 144 pounds of U.S. government mail: "New York-Philadelphia-Washington Aerial Mail Great Success," *Aerial Age Weekly*, May 27, 1918, p. 532.

45. "I decided on a southern approach...": Edgerton, *Horizons Unlimited*.

45. Fleet, too, was on hand: Ibid.

45. successful delivery of nearly 750 pieces of mail: "Aero Mail a Success," *Washington Post*, May 16, 1918, p. 1.

45. "the beginning of an epoch...": Otto Praeger, "Burleson in Action," unpublished article.

46. "Beats the Railroads": "Aero Mail a Success," *Washington Post*, May 16, 1918.

46. That change in accounting: Otto Praeger, *Moss from a Rolling Stone*, unpublished manuscript.

47. His engine about to quit: "Fog Mishap Hinders New Airplane Mail," *New York Times*, May 17, 1918.

48. engine trouble and approaching darkness: Edgerton, *Horizons Unlimited*.

48. He is in the air at 6:33: Ibid.

48. coming to see the pilot break his neck: Ibid., with Edgerton citing "First Regular Air Mail Flight," by Lt. H. Latane Lewis II, *Popular Aviation*, December 1935.

48. the polo field awash in the headlights of parked cars: James Edgerton, radio talk to be delivered at the New York Air Show, Madison Square Garden, May 5, no year cited.

48. "I'm OK": Recollections of Reuben Fleet written on personal letterhead stationery, June 26, 1961, from the Paul Culver Air Mail Collection at the Garber Center, National Air and Space Museum, Smithsonian Institution.

49. Boyle's dodging skills prove first-rate: "Mail Flier Boyle Loses Way North," *Washington Post*, May 18, 1919.

49. "The request is denied": Recollections of Reuben Fleet written on personal letterhead stationery, June 26, 1961, from the Paul Culver Air Mail Collection at the Garber Center, National Air and Space Museum, Smithsonian Institution.

49. "Lieuts. Miller, Bonsal and Culver . . .": "Lieuts. Miller, Bonsal and Culver, Flying, Have No Accidents," *Washington Post*, May 19, 1918.

49. "Unused to the sight and roar . . .": Praeger, *Moss from a Rolling Stone*.

50. The legend of the Inverted Jenny was born: George Amick, "Mr. Robey's Memorable Week," *American Philatelist* (October 1983): 912–918; George Amick, *The Inverted Jenny: Mystery, Money, Mania* (Sidney, Ohio: Amos Press, 1986); and http://www.postalmuseum.si.edu/exhibits/2f1a_inverts.html.

50. "Dear Wally . . .": Letter dated May 15, 1918, Walter (Wally) Praeger from his brother Otto.

51. Emergency landing fields: "First Airplane Postal Line Opened," *Air Service Journal* (May 1918): 3.

51. Airmail arriving at Bustleton: Press release, Office of Information, Post Office Department, May 15, 1918.

52. "Nothing is more disagreeable . . .": Manfred Von Richtofen, "Richthofen: The Red Fighter Pilot," "If Fly in a Thunder Storm," Chapter 6 from *The War Times Journal*, an online edition of his 1917 book *Der Rote Kampfflieger*, published in 1918 under the name *The Red Battle Flyer*, http://www.richthofen.com/arcdocs/richt_06.htrr.

52. reflecting a mere 78 percent: Press release, Office of Information, Post Office Department, May 7, 1919.

53. it was the Army controlling the flying schedule: Edgerton, *Horizons Unlimited*.

53. "establishing a plaything": "Burleson of Texas, the War Postmaster General," papers from the Burleson Archives at the University of Texas at Austin.

54. Praeger admitted that the only airplane operations: Praeger, *Moss from a Rolling Stone*.

54. "But mark this . . .": Ibid.

CHAPTER 4: OTTO

55. Praeger's parents had come to America: "The Handbook of Texas Online," Terry G. Jordan, http://www.tsha.utexas.edu/handbook/online/articles/GG/png2.html.

55. with its fertile valley: "History of the Missions," National Park Service, http://hotx.com/missions/history.html.

56. His poor passengers lost a fortune: Praeger, *Moss from a Rolling Stone.*

56. Neither was he cut out to be a shopkeeper: Ibid.

56. Otto would hungrily devour: Ibid.

57. "I saw Dr. W. F. Carver kill 100 live pigeons . . .": Air Mail Pioneers, August-September 1965, Lester Bishop, "Reminiscence: Mr. Otto Praeger, Father of the Air Mail Service."

57. "worked with Dana on the *Sun*": Praeger, *Moss from a Rolling Stone.*

57. A few months' pay banging out stories: Ibid.

57. Author-to-be Mark Twain: Ibid.

58. Trouble was, nothing much was happening: Ibid.

58. "I know that I disappointed my editor . . .": Ibid.

58. But he did have that great "rattlesnake" story: "Praeger's Long Bicycle Ride," *New York Times,* June 13, 1893; and Praeger, *Moss from a Rolling Stone.*

59. "Could I have realized the proportion . . .": Praeger, *Moss from a Rolling Stone.*

60. "Why, it is going to be you": Ibid.

60. "The old political ring . . .": Ibid.

61. From his station in the press gallery: Ibid.

62. The next morning: Ibid.

62. Wilson carried the nation: David Leip, "Atlas of Presidential Elections," http://www.uselectionatlas.org/.

63. there were only 23 miles of train track in the entire United States: Bruns, *Mail on the Move,* p. 64.

63. "I view (the post office) . . .": Kelly B. Olds, "The Challenge to the U.S. Postal Monopoly, 1839–1851," *Cato Journal* 15, no. 1, http://www.cato.org/pubs/journal/cj15n1-1.html.

64. The man was a two-time congressman: "William Jennings Bryan," http://www.u-s-history.com/pages/h805.html.

64. "Cup of Joe": Information Services Branch of the State Library of

North Carolina, "Josephus Daniels," http://statelibrary.dcr.state.nc.us/ nc/bio/ncbiz/daniels.htm.

64. It was only natural: Ibid.

65. "Now, the way out . . .": Praeger, *Moss from a Rolling Stone.*

65. This Scot was born for the fight: "Opposition Did Not Worry Bur-leson," *Dallas Morning,* Col. Robert E. Cowart, private secretary of Postmaster General A. S. Burleson, undated.

65. a man who never sought praise or credit for himself: Interview with Otto Praeger's daughter Elinor Praeger Goettel, 2004.

66. The idea of lying or cheating: "O. Praeger, Washington Postmaster," *New York Times,* February 19, 1914.

66. oysters from Norfolk: Praeger, *Moss from a Rolling Stone*

66. he held the process in high regard: Ibid.

67. "Well, if it will solve the problem": Ibid.

67. they required no oats: "What It Means to Deliver the Mail by Auto," *Postmaster's Advocate* 22 (April 1917): 3.

67. During his term: William J. Henderson, James H. Bruns, and Carl Burcham, *An American Postal Portrait: A Photographic Legacy* (New York: The United States Postal Service, HarperResource, 2000).

67. He was not about to dip: "Burleson of Texas, the War Postmaster Gen-eral," Center for American History at the University of Texas at Austin.

67. When it came to delivering: *R.F.D. News* 15, no. 19 (May 12, 1917).

67. By October 1914, Burleson: United States Postal Service, "History of the Post Office," http://www.ceol.com/vvpo/history.html.

68. he saved the city $300 a day: Praeger, *Moss from a Rolling Stone.*

68. Praeger would find himself stepping into the postmaster general's inner circle: Ibid.

68. Enjoy the day: Ibid.

69. What he'd achieved: Interview with Otto Praeger's daughter Elinor Praeger Goettel, 2004.

69. u.s. mail—visible for all to see: Bruns, *Mail on the Move,* p. 113; and George Langley Conner, *A Brief Biography of Hon. Otto Praeger, Second Assistant Postmaster General 1915–1921,* unpublished manuscript, p. 5.

69. Everything needed to look up-to-date: Bruns, *Mail on the Move,* p. 159.

69. Praeger, however, was beginning to encounter isolated: Praeger, *Moss from a Rolling Stone.*

69. Its mail delivery contractors: Ibid.

69. Opposition to the plan: Ibid.

69. "It was not necessary . . .": Ibid.

70. By mid-1917: "What It Means to Deliver the Mail by Auto," *Postmaster's Advocate*, April 1917.

70. "I soon had them shifted . . .": Praeger, *Moss from a Rolling Stone*.

70. overworked civil servants were tearing their hair out: *R.F.D. News* 15, no. 19 (May 12, 1917).

70. To reduce breakdowns: "Special Parcel Post Auto Truck Soon to Operate," *R.F.D. News* 15, no. 45 (November 10, 1917).

70. It was hellish when it rained: Ibid.

CHAPTER 5: INTO THE EYE

72. They unearthed more than enough ships: "Aeroplane Mail Carried 15,300 Feet in the Air," *R.F.D. News* 16, no. 24 (June 15, 1918).

73. in the spirit of *Liberté, Fraternité, Égalité*: "Open Air Mail Service to Boston Tomorrow," *New York Times*, June 2, 1918.

73. Though both pilot and mechanic survived: A. D. Jones, *Aerial Mail Service: A Chronology of the Early United States Government Air Mail March–December, 1918* (Mineola, N.Y.: American Air Mail Society, 1993), p. 47.

73. He would scout the air path to Boston: "Aeroplane Mail," *R.F.D. News* 16, no. 24 (June 15, 1918); and Donald B. Holmes, *Air Mail: An Illustrated History, 1793–1981* (New York: Clarkson N. Potter, 1981), p. 98.

73. "Upon the eyes of these pilots . . .": An advertisement appearing in *Aerial Age Weekly*, June 17, 1918.

73. Webb descended onto the racetrack: "Aeroplane Mail," *R.F.D. News* 16, no. 24 (June 15, 1918).

74. This wasn't what he had bargained for: Werner Bamberger, "Aviator Recalls 1st Airmail Run," *New York Times*, May 13, 1968.

74. "Visibility was zero . . .": Ibid.

74. Then, following a brief stop at Mather Field: "Open Air Mail Service to Boston Tomorrow," *New York Times*, June 2, 1918.

75. Willoughby and Spaatz: Kenneth J. Campbell, "Major General Charles A. Willoughby: General MacArthur's G-2—A Biographic Sketch," *American Intelligence Journal* 18, no. 1/2 (1998): 87–91; http//intellit.Muskingum.edu/wwii_folder/wwiifepacwilloughby.html; and http://usaic.hua.army.mil/history/pdfs/mwillou.pdf, which

refers to C. L. Sulzberger, *A Long Row of Candles* (New York: Macmillan, 1969), p. 765.

75. They claimed that daily operation: Praeger, *Moss from a Rolling Stone*.

75. The chief routinely surrounded himself with the best minds: Bob Ball, "Harold E. Hartney," http://www.earlyaviators.com/ehartney.htm; and "Harold Hartney," http://www.theaerodrome.com/aces/usa/hartney.html.

75. Together, the group provided the experience: *Remarkable Record of One Month of Aero Mail Creates Demand for Extension* (report) by Augustus Post, secretary, Aerial League of America.

76. "the air was full of air pockets . . .": "Charles Forster Willard, 1883–1977," http://www.earlyaviators.com/ewillard.htm; and Holmes, *Air Mail*.

76. Paramount of all: *Remarkable Record of One Month* (report) by Augustus Post.

76. Raw data, that's what was needed: *Report on Aeroplane Mail Service, Washington-Philadelphia-New York Route, for Year of May 15, 1918 to May 18, 1919,* Post Office Department, Office of Second Assistant Postmaster General, May 15, 1919.

77. "I was trained, in fact brain-washed . . .": Transcript of a James Edgerton radio talk delivered at the New York Air Show, Madison Square Garden; and Edgerton, *Horizons Unlimited*.

77. A pilot spying such a mountain: Guy Murchie, *Song of the Sky* (Boston: Houghton Mifflin, 1954), pp. 181–186.

78. He knew that turning back: Edgerton, *Horizons Unlimited*.

78. Like Praeger, he understood: *Popular Aviation*, December 1935, p. 2, San Diego Aerospace Museum.

78. With that, Edgerton picked up the gauntlet: Edgerton's flight report to DC headquarters, May 22, 1918, National Air and Space Museum, General Documentation file.

78. Pulling back on the stick: Ibid.

79. Attacked by solid waves of air: Edgerton, *Horizons Unlimited*.

79. "like hammer blows": Edgerton's flight report to DC headquarters, May 22, 1918.

79. "I supplied what I hoped was intelligent direction . . .": Edgerton, *Horizons Unlimited*.

80. Trees had been torn from their roots: Article from *Popular Aviation*, December 1935.

80. The chief would be happy: Edgerton, *Horizons Unlimited*.

CHAPTER 6: WILLOUGHBY

81. Unknown, however: "Aeroplane Mail," *R.F.D. News* 16, no. 24 (June 15, 1918); and www.1903to2003.gov/essay/Evolution_of_Technology/NACA/Tech1.htm.

81. his handwriting wavering across the page: Flight records kept by Lt. Edgerton, 1918.

81. At that altitude: "Aeroplane Mail," *R.F.D. News* 16, no. 24 (June 15, 1918).

82. "In the future . . .": Memo from C. A. Willoughby to Lt. James Edgerton, June 29, 1918, National Archives, Washington, D.C.; and Edgerton, *Horizons Unlimited*, pp. 33–34.

82. "You can tell by the price a girl pays . . .": "Aeroplane Mail," *R.F.D. News* 16, no. 24 (June 15, 1918).

82. thought it wise to change the family name: "George V," http://www.spartacus.schoolnet.co.uk/MOgeorgeV.htm.

82. assumed the maiden name of his mother: "Charles Willoughby," www.spartacus.schoolnet.co.uk/JFKwilloughbyC.htm.

83. so he could land behind German lines: http://usaic.hua.army.mil/history/pdfs/mwillou.pdf.

83. A Benedict Arnold he wasn't: Letter from Willoughby to Burleson, July 28, 1918.

83. At the height of its work: Original report, *Part 3. Mail Censorship*, Otto Praeger's report on censorship to the War Department, September 13, 1940.

84. A peace plan from Pope Benedict XV: John R. Smestad Jr., "Europe 1914–1945: Attempts at Peace," http://www.loyno.edu/history/journal/1994-5/Smestad.htm#10; and Michael Duffy, "Primary Documents: Pope Benedict XV's Peace Note of 1 August 1917," http://www.firstworldwar.com/source/papalpeacenote.htm.

84. Publish a Socialist newspaper: "Socialist Paper Restored to Mail," *R.F.D. News* (June 11, 1921): 4.

84. Refrain from playing: *Part 3. Mail Censorship*, Otto Praeger's report on censorship to the War Department, September 13, 1940.

85. including one promising to blow up: Untitled article, Burleson Archives, University of Texas at Austin.

85. "Pilots are not to call Washington . . .": Memo #2 from A. C. Weidenbach, June 1, 1918, Burleson Archives, University of Texas at Austin.

86. affectionately called "the iron compass": Memo #3 from A. C. Weidenbach, June 6, 1918, Burleson Archives, University of Texas at Austin.

86. He had fought for his country: Original handwritten letters from Willoughby to Burleson, undated, Burleson Archives, University of Texas at Austin.

86. he could handle affairs himself: Edward V. Rickenbacker. *Rickenbacker: An Autobiography* (Englewood Cliffs, N. J.: Prentice-Hall, 1967), p. 81.

87. Even his favorite racecar: Ibid., p. 206.

87. "Airplane engines are always breaking down . . .": Ibid., p. 104.

87. got himself assigned as staff driver: Ibid., p. 108.

87. Rickenbacker would find himself in flight school: Ibid., p. 109.

88. Just ten days: Letter from Otto Praeger to Newton Baker, July 24, 1918.

89. The general estimated he needed: Captain Benjamin B. Lipsner, *The Airmail: Jennies to Jets* (Chicago: Wilcox & Follett Company, 1951), p. 60; and Dr. Steven E. Anders, "POL on the Red Ball Express," *Quartermaster Professional Bulletin*, Spring 1989, http://www.qmfound.com/pol_on_the_red_ball_express.htm.

89. If the Army could spare: Letter from Otto Praeger to the Adjutant General, War Department, Washington, D.C., July 8, 1918.

89. Lipsner submitted his resignation: Letter from B. B. Lipsner, Capt., A.S.S.S.C. U.S. Army (Temp.) to the Adjutant General of the Army (Through Channels). War Department, Office of the Director of Military Aeronautics, Washington, July 10, 1918.

89. He learned a few things: Lipsner, *The Airmail: Jennies to Jets*, p. 50.

90. Right from the start: Praeger, *Moss from a Rolling Stone*.

90. the U.S. Army folded its tents and pulled out: Charles. H. Hubbell, *History of U.S. Air Mail, 50th Anniversary, 1918–1968* (pamphlet), p. 14L.

CHAPTER 7: LIPSNER

92. "I was National's top salesman . . .": Lipsner, *The Airmail: Jennies to Jets*, p. 53.
92. One of the young men: Ibid.
93. He'd graduated from chauffeuring: James H. Bruns, *Turk Bird: The High-Flying Life and Times of Eddie Gardner* (Washington, D.C.: National Postal Museum, Smithsonian Institution), p. 19; and Bruns, *Mail on the Move*, p. 125.
93. he was Turk Bird: Bruns, *Turk Bird*, p. 19.
93. For five such performances: Lester Bishop, "Reminiscence with Bob Shank," *Air Mail Pioneers News*, January-February-March 1966.
94. folks thirsty for amusement: *This Fabulous Century 1920–1939* (Alexandria, Va.: Time-Life Books, 1969), p. 63.
94. Taking pity on their plight: Bishop, "Reminiscence with Bob Shank."
94. handled the business side of things: Harold F. Morehouse, "Marjorie Stinson, Early Wright Pilot–Instructor," in *Flying Pioneers Biographies* (Washington, D.C.: National Air and Space Museum, Smithsonian Institution).
95. "But then the war came along . . .": Bishop, "Reminiscence with Bob Shank."
95. Having garnered fully twelve hundred hours: Press release, Office of Information, Postal Department, August 6, 1918.
95. a $600-a-year airplane mechanic: A. D. Jones, *Max, I Didn't Get to Know Him Very Well* (Mineola, N.Y.: American Air Mail Society, 2004), p. 18.
96. "I have carefully considered . . .": Ibid., p. 13.
96. He tried carving out a life: Ibid., pp. 7–9.
96. Born in Oslo, Norway: Ibid., p. 4.
96. The full complement of fliers hired: William M. Leary, *Aerial Pioneers: The U.S. Air Mail Service, 1918–1927* (Washington, D.C.: Smithsonian Institution Press, 1985), p. 53.
96. Each man would vow: Letter from Praeger to the Chief of Maintenance and Equipment, March 16, 1920; and memorandum, "General Directions to Entire Personnel," p. 2.
97. The Curtiss JN-4H: Untitled report by Otto Praeger to the Postmaster General, May 15, 1919, covering the operation of the first year of the mail service.

97. They directed auto manufacturers: "The Aircraft Trade Review," *Aerial Age Weekly*, May 20, 1918.

97. Even the Army Signal Corps: *Aerial Age Weekly*, April, 15, 1918.

98. The group made similar pests: Press release, Office of Information, Post Office Department, August 6, 1918.

98. The 150-horsepoweer engines: http://www.hispano-suiza-sa.com/en/activites/societe/histoire/index.htm.

99. He was even wearing a smile on his face: *Aerial Age Weekly*, August 19, 1918.

99. Commercial aviation was at its "zero hour": Untitled memo by Otto Praeger, Records of the Post Office Department Bureau of Transportation, Domestic Mail Transportation Division, Contract Air Mail.

99. These JR-1Bs were the first: *The Tractor*, the employee publication of the Standard Aircraft Corp.; and Bruns, *Turk Bird*, p. 23.

99. It was only a matter of time: Untitled memo by Otto Praeger, Records of the Post Office Department Bureau of Transportation, Domestic Mail Transportation Division, Contract Air Mail.

99. "Transportation through the air . . .": Lipsner, *The Airmail: Jennies to Jets*, p. 83.

100. he'd never flown a Standard: Bruns, *Turk Bird*, p. 26.

101. "the spirit of adventure is curbed . . .": "Brief History of Capt. B. B. Lipsner," unattributed and unsourced; and Leary, *Aerial Pioneers*, pp. 53–54.

101. "As a pilot in the Air Mail Service . . .": Letter from the General Superintendent of the Air Mail Service to All Division Superintendents of the Air Mail Service, March 8, 1921.

101. Beginning today: Otto Praeger, *Organization and Operation of the Air Mail Service* (report).

102. The behemoth ship: "The Handley Page Bomber," http://www.geocities.com/roynagl/handleypage.htm.

102. The British had been flying swarms: Christopher Chant, *A Century of Triumph: The History of Aviation* (New York: Free Press, 2002), p. 111.

102. simple but brilliant slotted wing design: "The Handley Page Bomber," http://www.geocities.com/roynagl/handleypage.htm.

102. its twin motors: *Flying* 8 (1919–1920), Aero Club of America, New York.

CHAPTER 8: CIVIL SERVICE

104. Pilots quickly learned to sideslip: Edgerton, *Horizons Unlimited.*

105. "His trial and our error": Transcript from Edgerton's radio talk delivered at the New York Air Show Madison Square Garden.

105. Day after day, mail ships descended: Ibid.

105. Operations quieted down after 1912: "College Park Airport," http://www.cr.nps.gov/nr/travel/aviation/col.htm.

105. Proudly pinned to his leather jacket: A two-page, biographical sketch "Max Miller, Air Mail Pilot #1 of the Postal Aviation Service, Established August 12, 1918," p. 2.

106. If the bad guys didn't respect the badge: E. Hamilton Lee, *I Fly the Mail,* unpublished manuscript, United Airlines Archives, Chicago, Ill.

106. He had become *Civis Aerius Sum*: Jack Knight personnel file, United Airlines Archives. Knight's successor airmail pilots proudly took on the motto.

106. Pilot and ship arrived intact at 2:15 P.M.: A biographical sketch, "Max Miller," p. 2.

106. The southbound team: Ibid.

107. An "X" on the board: Bruns, *Turk Bird,* p. 29.

107. Surely if the captain were working: Lipsner, *The Airmail: Jennies to Jets,* p. 80.

107. There was good weather: Report entitled "Air Mail Service Consolidated Statement of Performance from May 15, 1918 to Dec. 31, 1921."

108. Praeger's highly touted aero mail service: Hubbell, *History of U.S. Air Mail, 50th Anniversary, 1918–1968,* p. 14M.

109. When Franklin proposed connecting Philadelphia and Boston: "The New York Post Office," *Scribners Monthly* 16, no. 1 (May 1878).

109. The New York–Washington route: Report of the Postmaster General, 1919, p. 17.

109. "There is no guess work about it": Edward Marshall, "Flying Across Sea Regarded as a Certainty," *Sunday Star,* June 19, 1919.

109. the Twentieth Century Limited: Otto Praeger, "Aerial Mail in the United States and Abroad," *Flying,* March 1919.

110 . Talk under the dome: Paul T. David, *The Economics of Air Mail Transportation* (Washington, D.C.: Brookings Institution, 1934), pp. 15, 16; and Praeger, *Moss from a Rolling Stone.*

110. Wasn't keeping America strong: Leary, *Aerial Pioneers*, p. 57, who cites a letter from Burleson to Baker, August 27, 1918, AF/CDF 311.125.

110. "There is a gain to commerce . . .": Ibid.

111. Mechanical difficulties . . .": Press release, Office of Information, Post Office Department, August 6, 1918.

112. "Here was a young man . . .": Lipsner, *The Airmail: Jennies to Jets*, p. 78.

112. and a French horn or saxophone: Ibid.

CHAPTER 9: PATHFINDERS

113. Max was particularly impatient: Max Miller, "In His Own Words— Blazing the Air Trail to Chicago," *Flying*, October 1918.

113. The National Climatic Data Center had made weather reports available: A. D. Jones, *Aerial Mail Service: A Chronology of the Early United States Government Air Mail March–December, 1918* (Mineola, N.Y.: American Air Mail Society, 1993), p. 70.

113. "Look me up when you get . . .": Capt. Benjamin B. Lipsner, as told to Leonard Finley Hilts, "How They Flew First Air Mail to Chicago," *Chicago Sunday Tribune*, September 2, 1951.

114. The mechanic would be there: "Chicago Air Mail Halts in Cleveland," *New York Times*, September 6, 1918.

114. "Forget it," Gardner said: Lipsner, *The Airmail: Jennies to Jets*, p. 115.

114. He put his Standard into a westerly heading: "Chicago Air Mail Halts in Cleveland," *New York Times*, September 6, 1918.

115. For the next two hours: Miller, "In His Own Words—Blazing the Air Trail to Chicago."

115. Mrs. Bennett, standing there: Jones, *Aerial Mail Service*, p. 78.

116. helping America catch up with the Europeans on aeronautics: Judy Rumerman, "The National Advisory Committee for Aeronautics (NACA), U.S. Centennial of Flight Commission, http://www.centennialofflight. gov/essay/Evolution_of_Technology/NACA/Tech1.htm.

116. Was he all right?: Jones, *Aerial Mail Service*, p. 78.

116. Just forty-five short minutes later: Miller, "In His Own Words—Blazing the Air Trail to Chicago."

116. Lipsner ordered him to get it fixed: Lipsner, "How They Flew First Air Mail to Chicago."

117. Stiff winds: Bruns, *Turk Bird*, p. 36, citing Eddie Gardner's log report, September 5, 1918.

117. "He just landed at Lock Haven . . .": Lipsner, "How They Flew First Air Mail to Chicago."

117. He had to go down: Bruns, *Turk Bird*, p.36, citing Eddie Gardner's log report, September 5, 1918.

117. Thanks to some local miners: Jones, *Aerial Mail Service*, p. 87.

117. Miller had left Lock Haven two and a half hours earlier: Bruns, *Turk Bird*, p.36, citing Eddie Gardner's log report, September 5, 1918.

118. "That sure gave me a good scare": Miller, "In His Own Words—Blazing the Air Trail to Chicago."

118. "There was such a mob of people . . .": Ibid.

118. ". . . What happened?": Lipsner, *The Airmail: Jennies to Jets*, p. 124.

118. his rival was still at Lock Haven: Lipsner, "How They Flew First Air Mail to Chicago."

119. with its cushy "prepared surface": Hubbell, *History of U.S. Air Mail*, p. 14M.

119. Despite the hour, the Cleveland Police: "Two Mail Planes Halted in First Trip to Chicago," *Chicago Daily Tribune*, September 6, 1918.

119. "They were the dumbest lot . . .": Jones, *Aerial Mail Service*, p. 86.

119. Once again he was faorced to land: Miller, "In His Own Words—Blazing the Air Trail to Chicago"; and "Chicago Air Mail Halts in Cleveland," *New York Times*, September 6, 1918.

120. his pesky radiator was checked out: Jones, *Aerial Mail Service*, p. 90.

120. the "very ace of mail fliers": Major L. B. Lent, general supervisor Air Mail Service, *Flying the Mail*, unpublished manuscript, San Diego Aerospace Museum.

120. and the richest, most expensive leather jacket: Bruns, *Turk Bird*, p. 64.

121. ". . . 'Where's Eddie?' . . .": Lipsner, *The Airmail: Jennies to Jets*, p. 126.

121. Finally, around seven o'clock: Miller, "In His Own Words—Blazing the Air Trail to Chicago"; and "Chicago Air Mail Halts in Cleveland," *New York Times*, September 6, 1918.

121. The news of his success: Lipsner, "How They Flew First Air Mail to Chicago."

121. a tie was only proper: Bruns, *Turk Bird*, p. 66.

121. The flamboyant Augustus Post: "Augustus Post, 1874–1952," http://www.earlyaviators.com/epostaug.htm.

121. "epoch making first trip": "First Air Mail from New York Takes 23 Hours," *Chicago Daily Tribune*, September 7, 1918.

122. "Something's got to be done about Eddie": Lipsner, "How They Flew First Air Mail to Chicago."

122. "I'll pay for another battle, if necessary . . .": Ibid.

122. They wisely decided to set down: Ibid.

123. "Airgonaut is blown 150 miles . . .": "Two Mail Planes Halted in First Trip to Chicago," *Chicago Daily Tribune*, September 6, 1918, San Diego Aerospace Museum, Max Miller file.

123. In reality, he knew the opposite to be true: Lipsner, *The Airmail: Jennies to Jets*, p. 136.

123. There were parties to attend: Ibid., p. 133; and "First Return Air Mail Will Start Tomorrow," *New York Times*, September 8, 1918.

123. "Finally, I had to step in": Lipsner, *The Airmail: Jennies to Jets*, p. 133.

124. a military bomber had been lent: "Brothers of the Air," *Chicago Sunday Tribune*, September 8, 1918.

124. Sensing the postmaster's nervousness: Lipsner, *The Airmail: Jennies to Jets*, p. 135.

124. "The signals were to be reversed . . .": Ibid.

124. "For a guy who was reluctant . . .": Ibid.

125. "I thought the guy would never quit . . .": Ibid.

125. "Sure, provided that radiator doesn't wrap . . .": Ibid.

125. He departed at 6:26 A.M.: Miller, "In His Own Words—Blazing the Air Trail to Chicago."

125. Three hours later: Ibid.

125. "What?" exclaimed Lipsner: Lipsner, *The Airmail: Jennies to Jets*, p. 138.

126. ". . . You better stay right there tonight": Ibid., p. 139.

126. "Perhaps he never fully forgave me . . .": Ibid.

127. ". . . You knew that when you joined . . .": Ibid., p. 140.

127. "Left Cleveland at 1:12 . . .": Bruns, *Turk Bird*, p. 42, citing Eddie Gardner's log report, September 11, 1918.

128. Gardner arrived in Lock Haven: Ibid.

128. "—lights, lights, lights": James H. Bruns, "The 1918 Race to Chicago," *EnRoute*, October-December 1992 and April-June 1993, http://www.postsalmuseum.si.edu/resources/6a2d_racetochicago.html.

128. Turk continued pushing his way: Bruns, *Turk Bird*, p. 42, citing Eddie Gardner's log report, September 11, 1918.

128. ". . . We were really in a predicament": Lipsner, *The Airmail: Jennies to Jets*, p. 146.

128. "My eyes were burned out . . .": Bruns, *Turk Bird*, p. 47.

129. "I was certain this was the finish": Ibid.

129. Gardner came to in a daze: Lipsner, *The Airmail: Jennies to Jets*, p. 147.

129. It was Radel, pinned under the airplane: Ibid., p. 148.

129. Radel's back had been burned: *Report on Aeroplane Mail Service Made by the Second Assistant Postmaster General to the Postmaster General*, May 15, 1919.

129. In keeping with policy: Ibid.

129. "You made a great flight . . .": Telegram from Otto Praeger, the National Postal Museum.

CHAPTER 10: BELLEFONTE

130. Lock Haven was still the odds-on favorite: "Airplane Mail Serviced Routed Over Centre County," *Democratic Watchman*, September 6, 1918.

131. Five Pennsylvania governors: "Centre County History, ABCs of Centre County," http://centrecountyhistory.org/ABCsB.html.

131. Its rushing waters: "Mail-Carrying Aeroplane Visited Bellefonte," *Democratic Watchman*, September 27, 1918.

131. A courier then dashed off: http://bellefonte.topcities.com/founding/, which cites *Democratic Watchman*, 1895.

131. Woodrow Wilson Airway: "Bellefonte a Station on Air Mail Service Route," *Democratic Watchman*, October 13, 1918.

132. It took five minutes: http://bellefonte.topcities.com/founding/, which cites *Democratic Watchman*, 1895.

132. "In crossing the Alleghenies . . .": Ibid.

133. one eye on the sky: "Aeromail Next Wednesday," *Democratic Watchman*, September 20, 1918.

133. A plane is coming your way!: "Mail-Carrying Aeroplane Visited Bellefonte," *Democratic Watchman*, September 27, 1918.

133. keeping it high and dry: Ibid.

135. There was hardly enough money: "Belgian-American Chamber of Commerce," in journal entitled *The Conquest of the Air*, November 15, 1923, published in Brussels, which reprinted the speech given by Colonel Jordan.

135. "enthusiastic women of wealth . . .": Leary, *Aerial Pioneers*, p. 58, which

cites "Memorandum for Jordan," unsigned but corrections are in Lipsner's handwriting.

135. The City of Chicago: Leary, *Aerial Pioneers*, p. 62, which cites U.S. House
of Representatives, Subcommittee of the Committee on the Post Office
and Post Roads, Hearings: Claims for Construction of Hangars and Maintenance of Flying Fields—Air Mail Service, 67th Cong., 4th sess. (Washington, D.C., 1923); and *New York Times*, October 23, 1918, pp. 73–74.

CHAPTER 11: STINSON

139. "From where I sat behind my desk . . .": Lipsner, *The Airmail: Jennies
to Jets*, p. 109.

139. She'd been the first woman: Biographical sketch entitled "Katherine
Stinson," by Marjorie Stinson, and Katherine Stinson biography dated
1962, by Marjorie Stinson, from the Stinson Family Papers at the
University of New Mexico; and Harold F. Morehouse, *Flying Pioneers
& Biographies*, National Air and Space Museum, Smithsonian Institu-
tion.

137. "Of course, the record I was trying to break. . . .": *The World*, December 16, 1917.

137. Her rations for this trip: "San Antonio Aviatrix Leaves on Long Flight
with United States Mail Early Thursday Morning, Averaging 71 Miles
an Hour," *San Antonio Light*, May 23, 1918.

137. "One handful is my breakfast . . .": "Miss Stinson Makes New Flying
Record," *New York Times*, May 24, 1918, p. 9.

137. The postal department was up to its neck: Ibid.

138. At this rate: Joe Kirker and Art Pesin, "The Flying School Girl," *Airpost Journal* (March 1991): 94.

138. The week of rain had soaked everything: Ibid.; and "Miss Stinson
Makes New Flying Record," *New York Times*, May 24, 1918.

138. She had earned a distance record: Katherine Stinson biography dated
1962, by Marjorie Stinson, from the Stinson Family Papers; and "Miss
Stinson Makes New Flying Record," *New York Times*, May 24, 1918.

138. "My flight today proves . . .": "Miss Stinson Makes New Flying Record."

138. Undaunted, the diminutive aviatrix: Kirker and Pesin, "The Flying
School Girl," p. 94.

139. considering them far too emotional: Connie Plantz, *Bessie Coleman*
(Berkeley Heights, N.J.: Enslow Publishers, 2001), p. 40.

139. With gentlemanly politeness: Lipsner, *The Airmail: Jennies to Jets*, p. 109.

139. Senator Morris Sheppard: Letter from Newton D. Baker, Secretary of War, to Senator Morris Sheppard, Washington, D.C., July 27, 1918, from the Stinson Family Papers.

139. "The Army and Navy authorities . . .": Ibid.

139. Even the Stinson flying school: Interview with Katherine Stinson (Mrs. Michael Otero) by Kenneth Leish, July 1960, from the Stinson Family Papers.

139. Until the war ended: Letter from J. R. Whitehead, Captain, Signal Res. Corps, the Joint Army and Navy Board on Aeronautic Cognizance, Washington, D.C., to the Honorable Morris Sheppard, Washington, D.C., June 10, 1918, from the Stinson Family Papers.

140. prepared to give Stinson: Letter from Burleson to John Raker, chairman, Committee on Women's Suffrage, House of Representatives, December 24, 1917, Burleson Archives, University of Texas at Austin.

140. "be of one mind . . .": Woodrow Wilson, *Selected Literary and Political Papers and Addresses of Woodrow Wilson*, vol. III (New York: Grosset & Dunlap, 1921, published in arrangement with Harper & Brothers and Houghton Mifflin Company, 1893), p. 212.

141. When it came to suffrage: Arthur S. Link, *Woodrow Wilson and the Progressive Era, 1910–1917* (New York: Harper Torchbooks, The University Library, 1954), p. 60.

141. "The Katherine Stinson incident . . .": Lipsner, *The Airmail: Jennies to Jets*, p. 173.

142. the double-stick Wright controls: Kirker and Pesin, "The Flying School Girl," p. 95.

143. Left with no recourse: Ibid., p. 94; and Lipsner, *The Airmail: Jennies to Jets*, p. 110.

143. She would fly the Washington: Lipsner, *The Airmail: Jennies to Jets*, p. 111.

144. Newton had his wounds tended by a local doctor: Letter of H. L. Hartung to the Assistant Postmaster General, February 18, 1922.

144. Then dutifully filling out: *Report on Aeroplane Mail Service, Washington-Philadelphia-New York Route for Year of May 15, 1918 to May 15, 1919, Office of the Second Assistant Postmaster General May 15, 1919*, National Archives, Washington, D.C., May 15, 1919.

145. One of their submarines: www.pgs.org/wgbh/influenza/peopleevents/pandeAMEX88.html.

145. ". . . We have been averaging . . .": "A Letter from Camp Devens, Massachusetts," www.pbs.org/wgbh/amex/influenza/sfeature/devens.html.

145. By the time the epidemic: *Encyclopedia Americana*, 1954, vol. 15, p. 124, "Influenza Pneumonia—1918," www.roangelo.net/schlectweg/influenz.html.

CHAPTER 12: THE STAR

146. So far, for the months: Edgerton, *Horizons Unlimited*.

146. "Daddy": "Dana C. DeHart, Aerial Mail Pilot, Has Been Flier Since 1911," *Aerial Age Weekly*, May 12, 1919.

146. "Aviator Dana C. DeHart . . .": "Douglas Fairbanks Rides the Air Mail," in *Saga of the U.S. Air Mail Service, 1918–1927*, compiled and edited by Dale Nielson (Miami, Fla.: Air Mail Pioneers, Inc., 1962), pp. 14, 15.

146. Katherine Stinson: "Miss Katherine Stinson's Successful Buffalo-Washington Flight on Behalf of the Red Cross Fund," *Flying*, July 1917.

147. Sacrifice was the price: J. W. Studebaker, *Our Country's Call to Serve: Through Public and Private Schools-Work-Save-Give* (New York: Scott, Foresman, 1918), p. 43, as it appeared in *Best War Time Recipes*, Royal Baking Powder Co., New York, 1918, at http://freepages.military.rootsweb.com/~worldwarone/WW1/HomeFront/BestWarTimeRecipes/BestWarTimeRecipes.html.

147. He felt confident he could raise: Lipsner, *The Airmail: Jennies to Jets*, p. 97.

147. The result would be a certified: "Douglas Fairbanks Rides the Air Mail," pp. 14, 15.

148. "At the other end of the line . . .": Lipsner, *The Airmail: Jennies to Jets*, p. 98.

148. As a civilian instructor: online article, The Early Birds, CHIRP, March 1976, no. 82, "Dana C. DeHart 1886–1975," http://www.earlyaviators.com/edehart.htm.

148. he mugged for the cameras: "Douglas Fairbanks Rides the Air Mail," pp. 14, 15.

150. inspecting one's ship: Letter from the General Superintendent of the Air Mail Service, March 8, 1921.

151. But the man never uttered: "Douglas Fairbanks Rides the Air Mail," pp. 14, 15.

151. "I could have gone to the office . . .": Ibid.

152. "Handled with care . . .": Ibid.

152. For his part in things: Lipsner, *The Airmail: Jennies to Jets*, p. 98.

CHAPTER 13: IT'S OVER

153. helping out Praeger: Oral history notes with Daisy Marie Ricker, taken by Cathy Allen, College Park Aviation Museum, 1984.

154. Reduced to a schoolboy dunce: Jones, *Max, I Didn't Get to Know Him Very Well*, p. 58.

154. "Max was just very nice.": Oral history notes with Daisy Marie Ricker, taken by Cathy Allen, College Park Aviation Museum, 1984.

154. His upper-middle-class upbringing: Oral history notes with Jim Miller, 2004.

154. he'd grown up in Britain: Ibid.

154. The affable aviator: Ibid.

155. but rather with the weaker: National Museum of the United States Air Force, "Curtiss V2–3 Engine," http://www.wpafb.af.mil/museum/engines/eng18.htm.

155. The military designed planes: Memo by Otto Praeger, January 6, 1919, National Archives.

155. All they need do: Letter from Benjamin Lipsner to the Honorable Postmaster General, May 22, 1930.

155. "This thing acted . . .": Lipsner, *The Airmail: Jennies to Jets*, p. 157.

155. "I thought I could fly anything . . .": Ibid.

156. To his relief: Ibid., p. 158.

156. "Congratulations not in order . . .": Ibid., p. 159.

157. their smiles concealed: www.pbs.org/wgbh/amex/influenza/timeline/index/html.

157. With the event looming: "Bellefonte First Station on Aerial Mail Route," *Democratic Watchman*, November 15, 1918; and "Work Begun on Aerial Mail Station," November 22, 1918.

157. Someone on the organizing committee: Edgerton, *Horizons Unlimited*.

157. To Hartz would fall: Ibid.

158. fly over the usually off-limits airs space: Ibid.

159. "As I flashed by . . .": Ibid.

159. Later Edgerton heard: Ibid.

159. With the signing: Paul T. David, *The Economics of Air Mail Transportation* (Washington, D.C.: Brookings Institution, 1934), pp. 14–15.

159. The Army was offering: Press release, Office of Information, Post Office Department, December 3, 1918.

159. Ten new pilots: Ibid.

160. To his mind: Lipsner, *The Airmail: Jennies to Jets*, p. 174.

160. The first half of November: "Air Mail Service Consolidated Statement of Performance from May 15, 1918 to Dec. 31, 1921," Post Office Department.

161. It was his name: Edgerton, *Horizon Unlimited*.

161. the man defined: Lipsner, *The Airmail: Jennies to Jets*, pp. 176–177.

161. If the dials somehow: Dean C. Smith, *By the Seat of My Pants, A Pilot's Progress from 1917 to 1930* (B.D. King Press, no publication date), www.bdkingpress.com.

162. "I looked Eddie up . . .": Lipsner, *The Airmail: Jennies to Jets*, p. 177.

162. "I was furious . . .": Ibid.

162. Turk Bird's firing: Bruns, *Turk Bird*, p. 19.

162. If some considered: Oral history notes with Daisy Marie Ricker, taken by Cathy Allen, College Park Aviation Museum, 1984.

163. "regardless of weather conditions": Letter from Captain B. B. Lipsner to Richard M. Thomas, December 2, 1918.

163. "It requires the two engines . . .": *Flying* 8 (1919–1920), Aero Club of America, New York.

163. The mechanical breakdowns: Memorandum from Otto Praeger, January 6, 1919, National Archives.

164. "I wish to resign . . .": "Head of Air Mail Quits Service," *New York Times*, December 7, 1918, p. 1.

165. "Your letter from beginning . . .": "Burleson Denies Air Mail Charges," *New York Times*, December 8, 1918, p. 5.

166. "The achievements . . .": Ibid.

166. "Being in full sympathy . . .": Letter of resignation to Otto Praeger dated December 6, 1918, reproduced in Jones, *Max, I Didn't Get to Know Him Very Well*, p. 55.

CHAPTER 14: COMPLICATIONS

167. Edgerton had been forced down only once: Press release, Office of Information, Post Office Department, December 3, 1918, from Garber Center, Otto Praeger and The Air Mail; and C. V. Glines, Primedia History Group, www.thehistorynet.com/aviationhistory/articles/0594_text.htm.

167. Edgerton was playing an important role: Edgerton, *Horizons Unlimited*.

168. He spent the night tossing: Ibid.

168. "Good," Burleson replied: Ibid.

168. Edgerton's first order of business; Leary, *Aerial Pioneers*, p. 79.

168. Though Edgerton determined the cause: "Fatalities in the Air Mail Service," Post Office Department, San Diego Aerospace Museum; and *Report on Aeroplane Mail Service Washington-Philadelphia-New York Route for Year of May 15, 1918 to May 15, 1919, Office of Second Assistant Postmaster General, May 15, 1919*, Washington, D.C., p. 5.

168. "regardless of weather conditions": Letter from Otto Praeger to Ira O. Biffle, dated December 17, 1918, National Archives, Washington, D.C.

168. Newspapers stuffed into a flying suit: Fred Boughner, *Airmail Antics* (Sidney, Ohio: Amos Press, 1988), p. 114.

169. "You crazy?": Ron Parsons, "E. Hamilton Lee, One of Original Government Air Mail Pilots Has Flown About Everything That Flies," *Daily Gazette*, July 27, 1974.

169. added his name to airmail's swelling ranks: Captain E. Hamilton Lee, *I Fly the Mail*, unpublished manuscript, United Airlines Archives.

169. Lee was able to climb back: Ham Lee, "My Flying Career," p. 3, United Airlines Archives.

170. his head bandaged: Letter from George Langley Conner to Mr. Buente, dated October 8, 1921, National Archives, Washington, D.C.

170. Keenly aware of his age: Letter from Robert F. Shank to Mr. J. E. Whitbeck, Superintendent, Eastern Division, Air Mail Service, Hempstead, New York, dated March 7, 1922.

170. Edgerton had taken him off the duty roster: Letter to Mr. G. L. Conner from H. H. Hart, dated October 3, 1921, National Archives, Washington, D.C.

170. To help Newton get the work out: Letter from Otto Praeger to M. A.

Newton, Woodland Hills Park Aviation Field, Cleveland, Ohio, dated December 21, 1918.

171. Time lost: one hour: "Airplane Mail Serviced Started Between New York and Chicago, via Bellefonte on Wednesday," *Democratic Watchman*, December 20, 1918; and National Postal Museum, "Pilot Stories: Smith, Leon D.," www.postalmuseum.si.edu/airmail/pilot/pilot_rest/pilot_rest_smithLD.html.

171. a white bull's-eye.: *Pilots' Directions New York-San Francisco Route, Distance, Landmarks, Compass Course, Emergency and Regular Landing Fields, With Service and Communication Facilities at Principal Points on Route* (Washington, D.C.: Government Printing Office, Post Office Department, Office of Assistant Postmaster General, Division of Air Mails, 1921).

172. the university was an isolated: "The Morrill Act & the Land-Grant Colleges," University of Kentucky Archives, http://www.uky.edu/CampusGuide/land-grant.html.

173. everyone waiting at the airfield: Thomas J. O'Sullivan and Karl B. Weber, edited by Joseph L. Eisendrath, *History of the United States Pioneer and Government-Operated Air Mail Service 1910–1928* (Philadelphia: American Air Mail Society, 1973), p. 112.

173. "It was high time to shut down . . .": Edgerton, *Horizons Unlimited*.

174. It was a retrenchment: "Airmail Creates an Industry: A Bold Venture and Public Failure," http://www.postalmuseum.si.edu/airmail/airmail/foundation/airmail_foundation_venture_long.html.

174. the de Havilland DH-4s: Memorandum for Postmaster General from Second Assistant Postmaster General, dated December 30, 1918, Garber Center, Otto Praeger and The Air Mail.

174. "We have an ample supply . . .": Ibid.

174. Praeger was convinced: Praeger, *Moss from a Rolling Stone*.

175. he had already seen the Army and Navy: Ibid.

175. Commercial flying is an entirely different proposition: *Annual Report of the Postmaster General, 1919*, National Archives, Washington, D.C.

175. The Army's first consideration would always be flight training: David, *Economics of Air Mail Transportation*, p. 17, citing the "Post Office Appropriation Bill, 1920, Hearings, Senate Committee on Post Offices and Post Roads, January 9, 1919, 70–111."

175. Lightweight construction was causing them to flip over: *Flying* 8 (1919–1920), National Air and Space Museum, Smithsonian Institution.

175. The assembly gave way: Memorandum for Postmaster General from Second Assistant Postmaster General, December 30, 1918, Garber Center, Otto Praeger and The Air Mail.

175. "The longerons, which are the vital portions . . .": Ibid.

176. Edgerton wasted no time: *Popular Aviation*, December 1935, San Diego Aerospace Museum, James Edgerton's personnel file.

176. Such ideas and others were debated: Questionnaire to the Second Assistant Postmaster General, from Ira O. Biffle, dated March 5, 1919, National Archives, Washington, D.C.

176. L-W-F Manufacturing Co. of Queens, New York City, was contracted: Judy Rumerman, "The First U.S. Aircraft Manufacturing Company," U.S. Centennial of Flight Commission, http://www.centennialofflight.gov/essay/Aerospace/earlyU.S/Aero1.htm.

176. Longerons needed to be reinforced: Office of Information, Post Office Department, February 18, 1919, National Archives, Washington, D.C.

176. Engineers stabilized: Edgerton, *Horizons Unlimited;* and a statement from Second Assistant Postmaster General Otto Praeger issued January 4, 1919, from "Airmail, U.S. Army" file at San Diego Aerospace Museum.

176. During a crash the fuel tank: *Report on Aeroplane Mail Service Washington-Philadelphia-New York Route for Year of May 15, 1918 to May 15, 1919, Office of Second Assistant Postmaster General, May 15, 1919*, National Archives, Washington, D.C.

176. "The Post Office Department cannot . . .": Report from Otto Praeger, Garber Center, Otto Praeger and The Air Mail.

177. "There we would sit in his private office . . .": Edgerton, *Horizons Unlimited*.

177. Why, the coat closet alone: *Postmaster's Advocate*, June 1914; and Praeger, *Moss from a Rolling Stone*.

177. he was in every fiber of his being a humble man: Telephone interview by Barry Rosenberg with Otto Praeger's daughter Elinor Praeger Goettel, 2004.

CHAPTER 15: LETTERS, WHAT LETTERS?

178. The failed service: "Airmail Creates an Industry: A Bold Venture and Public Failure," http://www.postalmuseum.si.edu/airmail/airmail/foundation/airmail_foundation_venture_long.html.

178. "When you consider . . .": Statement about the New York–Chicago airmail route from Second Assistant Postmaster General Otto Praeger, January 4, 1919, National Archives, Washington, D.C.

179. As an American: H. L. Mencken, *The American Language* (New York: Alfred A. Knopf, 1921, and Bartleby, New York, 2000), p. 332; online at www.bartleby.com/185/pages/page332.html.

179. Its fleet of aero mail ships: Otto Praeger, "Aerial Mail in the United States and Abroad," *Flying*, March 1919, p. 144.

179. To record a 50 percent: Ken McGregor, "Beam Dream," part of an anthology of stories in the book *Saga of the U.S. Air Mail Service*, compiled and edited by Dale Nielson (Miami, Fla.: Air Mail Pioneers, 1962), p. 16.

180. Those problems that couldn't: *Report on Aeroplane Mail Service Washington-Philadelphia-New York Route for Year of May 15, 1918 to May 15, 1919, Office of Second Assistant Postmaster General, May 15, 1919*, National Archives, Washington, D.C.

180. Where exactly: Press release, Office of Information, Post Office Department, November 8, 1919.

181. Airmail's number one pilot: Letter of recommendation from James C. Edgerton to reinstate Max Miller dated April 4, 1919, as reproduced in A. D. Jones's *Max*, p. 51.

181. As the keeper of his own image: Oral interview with Jim Miller, December 2004.

182. Both Miller and Fry: *US Air Mail Pioneers News*, March 1959, letter from Lester Bishop, Chula Vista, California.

182. they had become folk heroes: www.si.edu/postal/learnmore/gardner.html.

183. If a long silence followed: Donald Dale Jackson, "Slim Louis Slept Here," *Air & Space*, October/November 1991.

183. In Cleveland, Eddie Gardner: "Airmail Creates an Industry: NY–Chicago," http://www.postalmuseum.si.edu/airmail/airmail/foundation/airmail_foundation-nychicago.html.

183. Flying eastbound: *The Air Mail, 1918–1927* (report), The Post Office Department, Second Assistant Postmaster General; and Karl B. Weber, "History of the U.S. Government Operated Air Mail Service 1918–1928," as it appeared in *Airpost Journal* (December 1952): 91.

183. He was killed instantly: *US Air Mail Pioneers News*, March 1959, letter from Lester Bishop, Chula Vista, California.

183. Their coveted bank notes: Untitled article by Floyd Taylor in *New York World-Telegram*, 1918.

184. The banker couldn't imagine: "Asks About Mail Lost with Airplane," *New York Times,* June 26, 1919.

184. "new Burleson game": Ibid.

184. "We have suffered . . .": Ibid.

185. "damaged beyond recognition": "No Trace of Bank Letters," *New York Times*, August 1, 1919.

185. With the stroke of a pen: David, *Economics of Air Mail Transportation*, p. 22; and "Loss of Mail by Aeroplane Fire, Hearing, House Committee on Post Office and Post Roads, July 19, 1919," p. 6.

185. In a further effort: An announcement of June 22, 1919, by Otto Praeger, Second Assistant Postmaster General, as cited in *Air & Space*, no further information.

185. Once again, Burleson and Praeger: Edgerton, *Horizons Unlimited*.

186. Even a small, unseen tear: *Rules and Instructions for Government of Pilots, Mechanics and Riggers*, Office of the Second Assistant Postmaster General, National Archives, Washington, D.C.

186. When a rigger was good: From an untitled poem by Gil Robb Wilson, San Diego Aerospace Museum.

186. Mechanics were required: Letter from Otto Praeger to Mr. Louis Glotznor, applicant, May 24, 1919; and Tex Marshall, in Nielson's *Saga of the U.S. Air Mail Service*, p. viii.

187. The mail was transferred: National Postal Museum, "Airmail Creates an Industry: NY–Chicago," http://www.postalmuseum.si.edu/airmail/airmail/foundation/airmail_foundation_nychicago.html.

187. Total time: Ibid.

187. The more powerful DH-4s: News release, Office of Information, Post Office Department, July 1, 1919.

187. Even all six of the original Jennies: Press release, Office of Information, Post Office Department, April 21, 1919.

188. "I have endeavored . . .": "Pilot Stories; Maurice Newton," National Postal Museum, "Pilot Stories: Maurice Newton," http://www.postalmuseum.si.edu/airmail/pilot/pilot_old/pilot_four_newton.html.

188. the $66.66 per month: "Memorandum of Data Concerning Organization and Operation of the Air Mail Service," Post Office Department, February 21, 1920.

188. "I am convinced . . .": Letter to Mr. Buente from G. L. Conner, October 8, 1921.

CHAPTER 16: DEAR MR. PRAEGER

190. now that it is early summer: "Air Mail Service Consolidated Statement of Performance from May 15, 1918 to Dec. 31, 1921."

191. "Why the motor quit is at the present unknown. . .": Pilot Budwig's accident report dated April 7, 1919, National Archives, Washington, D.C.

191. It would all go into Budwig's record.: Correspondence to James Edgerton from P.L.F., manager, Belmont Park Postal Aviation Field, April 7, 1919.

192. without missing a beat: Lipsner, *The Airmail: Jennies to Jets*, p. 178.

192. Founded by several ex-military aviators: Dean Smith, *By the Seat of My Pants*, p. 91.

192. "he delivered his mail to a 'branch' post office": Bruns, *Mail on the Move*, p. 126.

192. Ham Lee set himself ablaze: Lee, *Blue Sky Goodbye*.

193. The California-born aviator: Donald Dale Jackson, "Slim Lewis Slept Here," *Air & Space* (October/November 1991): 37.

193. he kept a couple of uncashed: Bernard Kelly, "Slim Lewis, Flying Frontiersman," *Empire Magazine*, February 20, 1966.

193. "Sometimes, they fly a route . . .": Lee, *Blue Sky Goodbye*.

194. "Neither snow, nor rain . . .": "The Story of the Mail," p. 2, U.S. Post Office Department Archives, Washington, D.C.

194. William Mitchell Kendall's eloquent expression of service: Report on the history of the "James A. Farley Building, New York, NY 10199," as excerpted from *The New Yorker*, February 12, 1938, p. 14, New York City Postal Archives.

195. Chalk up too many mechanicals or too many weather delays: Letter from D. B. Colyer, acting superintendent to Postal Aviation Field, College Park, Maryland, dated April 8, 1920.

195. Charles Lamborn died: National Postal Museum, "Pilot Stories, Lamborn, Charles W.," http://www.postalmuseum.si.edu/airmail/pilot/pilot_rest/pilot_rest_lamborn.html.

195. "In bad weather . . .": Jack Knight's account of his 1919 mail trip between Cleveland and Bellefonte, United Airlines Archives.

196. "My altimeter registered . . .": Ibid.

197. A short time later, Knight: Ibid.

CHAPTER 17: STRIKE

198. overheat when flying low and slow: Lee, *Blue Sky Goodbye*.
198. But Stevens took one look: Letter from Walter H. Stevens to Otto Praeger, "Insubordination of Pilots Smith, Lee, Webster and Stevens in Refusing to Fly Curtiss R4 Planes," July 22, 1919.
199. "On three trips . . .": Ibid.
199. he offered to fly a Curtiss Jenny: Letter from E. Hamilton Lee to Otto Praeger, "Insubordination of Pilots Smith, Lee, Webster and Stevens in Refusing to Fly Curtiss R4 Planes," July 22, 1919.
200. Five of the aviators: Memorandum to Postmaster General from Otto Praeger, December 30, 1918, Garber Center, Otto Praeger and The Air Mail.
200. shoot down five or more planes: http://www.theaerodrome.com/aces/nations.html.
200. "The summary dismissal . . .": Telegram sent from Belmont Park, New York, dated July 23, 1919, by the pilots of the airmail.
200. twenty of the pilots were refusing: "Conference Averts Aerial Mail Strike," *R.F.D. News* 17, no. 31 (August 2, 1919).
201. And Smith should have been booted: Letter from Asst. Supt. R.M.S. to Otto Praeger, "Insubordination of Pilots Smith, Lee, Webster and Stevens in Refusing to Fly Curtiss R4 Planes," July 22, 1919, National Archives, Washington, D.C.
201. "You do not regard a man's life . . .": Letter from Leon D. Smith to Otto Praeger, "Insubordination of Pilots Smith, Lee, Webster and Stevens in Refusing to Fly Curtiss R4 Planes," July 22, 1919, National Archives, Washington, D.C.
201. Also they know . . .": Press release from Otto Praeger, Office of Information, Post Office Department, Washington, D.C., July 25, 1919.
201. Praeger continued on the offensive: Ibid.
202. He assured the newspaperman that such set-downs: "Refuses to Reinstate Fliers," *New York Times*, July 25, 1919.
202. colluded to disrupt: Lee, *Blue Sky Goodbye*.
202. "The department cannot leave . . .": "Conference Averts Aerial Mail Strike," *R.F.D. News*.
202. "There is not much indicting . . .": *Post Office Department Aerial Mail Service* (report), October 24, 1919.
202. England was initiating: Praeger's report given to the assembly meet-

ing of post office employees, November 8, 1919, National Archives, Washington, D.C.

202. between Paris and Bordeaux: "Aerial Mail Records Being Made in France," *Aerial Age Weekly*, May 12, 1919.

202. inaugurated between Berlin and Weimar: Ibid.

203. world's first pilots strike: "Conference Averts Aerial Mail Strike," *R.F.D. News*.

203. "Here then . . .": Unpublished article on human interest stories related to Albert Burleson, Albert Sidney Burleson Archives, University of Texas at Austin.

203. "The order means that . . .": Report of the conference held between officials of the Post Office Department and the representatives of the pilots at the office of the second assistant postmaster general, July 16, 1919.

204. "With the pretext . . .": Edgerton, *Horizons Unlimited*.

204. Praeger didn't mind: Ibid.

204. found his salary cut back: "The First Reorganization Orders to the Air Mail Service Pilots," as reproduced in Jones's *Max*, p. 67.

204. to make up the shortfall: "Statement of Appropriations and Expenditures for Operation and Maintenance of the Air Mail Service from May 15, 1918 to August 31, 1927."

204. and salaries would be adjusted: "Conference Averts Aerial Mail Strike," *R.F.D. News*.

205. "I have to fight Congress . . .": Lee, *Blue Sky Goodbye*.

205. "Now, if I have to fight . . .": Corrections by Ham Lee to *This Week* magazine, September 6, 1949, United Airlines Archives.

205. he'd be given a bye: "Air Strike Settled," *New York Times*, July 28, 1919.

205. "an error of judgment . . .": Letter to E. Hamilton Lee from Otto Praeger, re Reinstatement of Pilot Lee, dated July 27, 1919, United Airlines Archives.

205. "talked too much": "Air Mail Pioneer Windy Smith Dies," *Air Mail Pioneers* 5, no. 5 (March 1960).

205. Praeger hadn't forgotten: Ibid.

CHAPTER 18: WIILSON

207. Albert Burleson was known as the "magician": Edgerton, *Horizons Unlimited*.

207. its wheels running along party lines: *R.F.D. News* 16, no. 38 (September 21, 1918).

207. Burleson saw no reason not to employ: Letter from Burleson to Joseph R. Wilson, from the collections in the Center for American History at the University of Texas at Austin.

208. Gen. Burleson, who served: L. W. Kemp, "The Handbook of Texas Online," Texas State Historical Association, http://www.tsha.utexas.edu/handbook/online/articles/view/SS/qes4.html.

209. in the Fourteen Points Wilson: "President Woodrow Wilson's 14 Points," classbrain.com as sourced the U.S. Dept. of State, citing Arthur S. Link et al., eds., *The Papers of Woodrow Wilson*, vol. 45 (1984), p. 536, http://www.classbrain.com/artteenst/publish/article_65.shtml.

209. The guardian of that morality: http://www.pbs.org/wgbh/amex/wilson/filmmore/fm_14 points.html.

209. His head throbbing,: PBS, "Woodrow Wilson: A Passionate Man," written by Carl Byker and David Mrazek.

210. "Please, get Doctor Grayson . . .": "President Wilson Suffers a Stroke, 1919," www.eyewitnesstohistory.com.

210. No one came in or out: Ibid.

211. "Which way," quipped Wilson: PBS, "Woodrow Wilson: A Passionate Man."

211. Wilson muddled through his remaining year in office: Ibid.

211. "the first woman President.": Ibis Communications, Inc., "President Wilson Suffers a Stroke, 1919," www.eyewitnesstohistory.com.

211. Increasingly, airmail was being labeled: William I. Votaw, *What a Life*, unpublished manuscript, Garber Center.

211. "Frisco or bust.": Lent, *Flying the Mail*.

212. On the DH-4's maiden trip: Ibid.; and http://www.postalmuseum.si.edu/airmail/historicplanes/postal/historicplanes.html.

212. there were reports that Maj. Belmont's: Chuck Albury, "The Mail Flies Again," *St. Petersburg Times*, June 5, 1966.

212. using the occasion to denounce: Lent, *Flying the Mail*.

213. It had taken a letter to Praeger: Letter from C. A. Parker to Second Assistant Postmaster General, dated October 18, 1920.

213. In October 1919, Turk Bird flew his last run: "Pilot Stories: Eddie

Gardner," http://www.postalmuseum.si.edu/airmail/pilot/pilot_rest/
pilot_rest_gardner.html.

213. The two would set up a little flying operation in Atlantic City: Nancy
Pope, "Pilot Stories: No Old, Bold Pilots," http://www.postalmuseum.
si.edu/airmail.

213. Daisy knew: Interview with Daisy Marie Ricker by Cathy Wallace
Allen, 1984.

214. In hindsight, it seems inexplicable: David, *Economics of Air Mail Transport*, p. 25.

214. ". . . They were usually rewarded with a spectacular splash . . .": Dean
Smith, *By the Seat of My Pants*, p. 111.

215. ". . . All this was going on at about 5:00 a.m. . . .": Lent, *Flying the
Mail*.

215. Like always, Slim made it: Ibid.

215. Praeger estimated he needed close to $3 million: Praeger's report given
to the assembly meeting of post office employees on November 8,
1919, National Archives, Washington, D.C.

216. All told, twenty-five planes crashed.: Lent, *Flying the Mail*; and Leary,
Aerial Pioneers, p. 102.

216. Never—ever—could railroads be made safe: Air Mail Service Data,
National Archives.

CHAPTER 19: A KILLER YEAR

217. he urged Daisy to stay inside: Interview with Daisy Miller by Cathy
Allen, College Park Aviation Museum, College Park, Maryland.

217. "Postmodernism": William Van Dusen Wishard, "Between Two
Ages; The Meaning of Our Times," September 22, 1998, http://www.
commonwealthnorth.org/transcripts/wishard.html.

218. Prohibition might be giving rise: Catherine H. Poholek, "Thirteen
Years That Damaged America Prohibition in the 1920s," http://www.
geocities.com/Athens/Troy/4399/.

219. Praeger conducted his money transfers: Lent, *Flying the Mail*.

219. A complete inventory of the airmail: "Statement Showing Appropriations and Expenditures for Operations and Maintenance of the Air
Mail Service from May 15, 1918 to and including August 31, 1927,"
overview, the Second Assistant Postmaster General.

219. it was prepared to do the same as it went west: Government-Operated

Air Mail Service Memoranda, 1918–1927, Records of the Post Office Department, Bureau of Transportation, Domestic Air Mail Transportation, National Archives; and Lent, *Flying the Mail*.

219. in preparation for the inauguration of the Chicago–Omaha line.: Votaw, *What a Life*.

219. McCandless had decided to fly on ahead: Ibid.

220. They would come to recognize the little town: "Pilots' Directions New York-San Francisco Route, Post Office Department, Office of Assistant Postmaster General," www.airmailpioneers.org/flightinfo/directions.htm.

220. Just west of Cheyenne, Wyoming: "Flying West," http://www.historic wings.com/features99airmail/splash-intro.html.

220. Should a man go down there: Votaw, *What a Life*.

220. fly the "secret pass": Letter to D. B. Coyler, Chief of Flying, from H. W. Cook, pilot, Cheyenne, Wyoming, dated November 1, 1920.

221. "It elated us to conquer time and space.": Edgerton, *Horizons Unlimited*.

221. Mrs. Sherlock was furious: National Postal Museum, "Pilot Stories: Sherlock, Harry C.," http://www.postalmuseum.si.edu/airmail/pilot/pilot_rest/pilot_rest_sherlock.html.

221. "Our acquaintance with him was rather brief": Ibid.

222. "Their deaths haunted my thoughts . . .": Edgerton, *Horizons Unlimited*.

222. To Edgerton, radio was the answer: Ibid.

222. if weather patterns could be tracked: Ibid.

222. Armed with some findings: Ibid.

223. Praeger would soon be leaving: Praeger, *Moss from a Rolling Stone*.

223. "When I return in a month . . .": Edgerton, *Horizons Unlimited*.

223. "You have just $20,000 to pay the bill": Ibid.

223. Charles Stanton, a former second lieutenant in the Army Signal Corps: Michael Sean Margolius and David Schwartz, "Smithsonian Institution, Charles Ingram Stanton, Sr. Collection," http://www.nasm.si.edu/research/arch/findaids/stanton/stanton_sec_3.html.

223. But he did pass an exam: Edgerton, *Horizons Unlimited*.

223. "Confidence blinded me to the impossible": Ibid.

224. A thorough rummaging: Ibid.

224. "We were the best beggars . . .": Lent, *Flying the Mail*.

224. the mayor was more than willing: Edgerton, *Horizons Unlimited*.

224. To save money: Ibid.

225. "I will never forget the little man . . .": Ibid.

225. The planes were built: *Annual Report of the Postmaster General, 1921,* National Archives, Washington, D.C.

225. The plane looked even better: Lent, *Flying the Mail.*

226. Gen. Mitchell, by comparison: Ibid.

226. "It seems as if our hopes . . .": Ibid.

227. Just one week later: Press release, Office of Information, U.S. Post Office Department, Washington, D.C., September 3, 1920.

227. If a flier failed to show up: The staff of *FAA Aviation News,* "1920 FSS 1970 Pioneers of Flight Safety," National Air and Space Museum, Smithsonian Institution, Air Mail General Documentation file.

227. ". . . They hung around . . .": Tex Marshall, in Nielson's *Saga of the U.S. Air Mail Service,* p. viii.

228. The plane was fortunately cleared: A. J. Poetz, "Reminiscence," San Diego Aerospace Museum.

228. ". . . She gave one reproachful moo . . .": Smith, *By the Seat of My Pants,* p. 135.

228. "Flying low.": Ibid., p. 136.

228. Walter Stevens: Poetz, "Reminiscence"; and H. W. Thomas, "Western Division of Air Mail Has Made Record," *Salt Lake Tribune,* June 17, 1923.

228. one of them was struck: Leary, *Aerial Pioneers,* p. 99.

229. Lent's investigations: Lent, *Flying the Mail.*

229. "Our previous thoughts of a fire-safe plane . . .": Ibid.

229. sending him irrevocably to his death: Online article, "Pilot Stories, Robinson, Frederick A.," http://www.postalmuseum.si.edu/airmail/pilot/pilot_rest/pilot_rest_robinson.html.

230. ". . . The larger part of the mail cargo . . .": "Pilot Stories: Murphy, Irving M.," http://www.postalmuseum.si.edu/airmail/pilot/pilot_rest/pilot_rest_murphy.html.

230. Murphy was terribly burned: "How Good Is Your Memory," *Centre Democrat,* September 12, 1935.

CHAPTER 20: KNIGHT

232. The ten-time congressman: *Biographical Directory of the United States Congress, 1771–Present,* "Steenerson, Halvor," http://www.infoplease.com/biography/us/congress/steenerson-halvor.html.

232. a man with a "bitter hatred": Lent, *Flying the Mail*.
232. funds earmarked for railroad operations: David, *The Economics of Air Mail Transportation*, p. 25.
232. As a result, airmail was slower: Ibid., p. 26.
232. "During the period between April 1 . . .": Ibid., p. 30.
233. Steenerson was attacking: Leary, *Aerial Pioneers*, p. 139.
235. "Bill was a terrific pilot . . .": Smith, *By the Seat of My Pants*, p. 136.
235. Lewis, a pilot with the airmail for only a month: "Fall Kills Pilot in Air Mail Race," *New York Times*, February 23, 1921; and National Postal Museum, "Pilot Stories, Lewis, William E.," http://www.postal museum.si.edu/airmail/pilot/pilot_rest/pilot_rest_lewisW.html.
236. "My broken nose was paining me . . .": Votaw, *What a Life*.
236. Smith followed the luminescence: Ibid.
236. "I felt as if I had a thousand friends . . .": Lee, *I Fly the Mail*.
236. "We didn't even suggest he carry on . . .": Votaw, *What a Life*.
237. Already the crowd was beginning to disperse: Ibid.
237. "We can't let it bust up here,": Ibid.
237. They tore the maps off the wall: Ibid.
237. "Leave the lights on for an hour. . . .": Ibid.
237. With no beacons: Ibid.
238. Practiced and practiced: A. M. Anderson and R. E. Johnson, *Pilot Jack Knight* (Chicago: Wheeler Publishing Company, 1950), p. 54.
238. Edgerton, too, knew that Jack: Edgerton, *Horizons Unlimited*.
238. Guided by his compass heading: Votaw, *What a Life*.
238. "I stuck my face over the side of the cowl . . .": Lee, *I Fly the Mail*, p. 8.
239. ". . . But my faithful old Liberty . . .": Votaw, *What a Life*.
239. ". . . Then I lost my horizon . . .": Ibid.
239. What Jack didn't know: Transcript from Jack Knight's radio talk on WLS, November 24, 1937, p. 4.
239. "By the time I had placed two railroad flares . . .": Unidentified first-person account, though it is obviously the night watchman, undated, from Jack Knight files at United Airlines Archives, Chicago.
240. ". . . But as the day grew brighter . . .": Lee, *I Fly the Mail*; and script for Jack Knight, WCAU, May 17, 1940.
240. Total time for the railroad: Weber, "History of the U.S. Government Operated Air Mail Service, 1918–1928."

240. "Accept my hearty congratulations . . .": Telegram, Otto Praeger to pilot James Knight, February 23, 1921.

240. "Any one of the airmail pilots . . .": Script for Jack Knight, WCAU, May 17, 1940.

240. Praeger threw a farewell dinner: Burleson Papers, cited in Leary, *Aerial Pioneers*, p. 143.

241. "the effective, the merely spectacular . . .": Praeger, *Moss from a Rolling Stone*.

241. ". . . I thank you most earnestly": Letter from Otto Praeger to Albert Burleson, January 28, 1921, provided by Elinor Praeger Goettel.

EPILOGUE

242. "My Dear Mr. Hopson . . .": Letter from Otto Praeger to William Hopson, March 5, 1921.

243. The new philosophy: E. H. Shaughnessy, *Aviation* 12 (January 23, 1922): 96–99.

243. Gone were the two: "Air Mail Changes," *Aviation* 10 (June 20, 1921): 784; and "Aerial Mail Service (Government-Operated) Chronology," no attribution.

244. For the time being: "Aerial Mail Service (Government-Operated) Chronology."

244. Shaughnessy realized: *Post Office Department, Second Assistant Postmaster General, Division of Air Mail Service, Air Mail: 1918–1927, Government Operated* (report); and Weber, "History of the U.S. Government Operated Air Mail Service, 1918–1928," p. 132.

244. "The Department, true to its traditions . . .": Ibid., p. 133.

245. Sadly, Shaughnessy: "The Knickerbocker Snowstorm of January 27–28, 1922," http://www.weatherbook.com/knickerbocker.htm.

245. His father-in-law: F. Robert van der Lindin, *Airlines and Air Mail, The Post Office and the Birth of the Commercial Aviation Industry* (Lexington: University Press of Kentucky, 2002), p. 7.

245. Completing the safety equipment: "History of the United States Air Mail Service, U.S. Post Office Department," June 20, 1935, Postal Archives.

245. Postmaster General Hays resigned: "Hays, Will H.," *The Columbia Encyclopedia*, sixth ed., 2001–05, http://www.bartleby.com/65/ha/Hays-Wil.html.

246. Airmail continued unabated: From "Aerial Mail Service (Government-Operated) Chronology."

246. the only other two-time winners: "The Collier Trophy," http://www.aerofiles.com/collier-trophy.html.

246. Flying day and night: "History of the United States Air Mail Service, U.S. Postal Department"; and Linden, *Airlines and Air Mail*, p. 8.

246. "They are continually on the lips . . .": Otto Praeger, "Couriers of the Air: Uncle Sam's Mail-Bearing Eagles and Their Cross-Continent Flights," *The Mentor*, June 1925, p. 25.

247. Named for Pennsylvania: "Airmail: The Air Mail Act of 1925 through 1929, U.S. Centennial of Flight Commission," http://www.centennialofflight.gov/essay/Government_Role/1925-29_airmail/POL5.htm.

247. new aviators like Charles Lindbergh: Linden, *Airlines and Air Mail*, p. 23.

247. Automaker Henry Ford: Ibid., p. 21.

248. Over the coming decades: Asif Siddiqi, "United Airlines," U.S. Centennial of Flight Commission, http://www.centennialofflight.gov/essay/Commercial_Aviation/UnitedAirlines/Tran16.htm.

248. AIRMAIL BY THE NUMBERS (1918–1927): Air Mail Statistics, Government Operated Chart, and Rich Freeman, "Walter Folger Brown: The Postmaster General Who Built the U.S. Airline Industry," U.S. Centennial of Flight Commission, http://www.centennialofflight.gov/essay/Commercial_Aviation/Brown/Tran3.htm.

249. Praeger and his youngest boy: George Langley Conner, *A Brief Biography of Hon. Otto Praeger, Second Assistant Postmaster General 1915–1921*, unpublished manuscript.

250. ". . . 'There goes the Coast Artillery.' ": Praeger, *Moss from a Rolling Stone*.

250. Praeger was recommended: Interview by Barry Rosenberg with Praeger's daughter Janet Phillips, 2004.

250. Hugh McCormick Smith: Praeger, *Moss from a Rolling Stone;* and "Scientific Crew of *Albatross*," http://www.nmnh.si.edu/vert/fishes/albatross/people.html.

251. "The captain demanded . . .": Praeger, *Moss from a Rolling Stone*.

251. Majesty King Prajadhipok: "Prajadhipok," http://en.wikipedia.org/wiki/Prajadhipok.

251. From north to south: Praeger, *Moss from a Rolling Stone*.

251. His new job: Personal letter from Otto Praeger to Wayne Coy of the Federal Security Agency, who was involved in his interview process to rejoin the government, April 22, 1941.

252. regulate American ocean commerce: "Maritime Administration (MARAD)," http://www.nvr.navy.mil/marad.htm.

252. Despite their financial struggles: Written history of Praeger's retirement years, Elinor Praeger Goettel.

252. The children were raised: Interview by Barry Rosenberg with Praeger's daughters Janet Phillips and Elinor Goettel.

252. "I see by this clipping . . .": Letter from Otto Praeger to A. S. Burleson, September 22, 1936.

253. "He was gone several months . . .": Written history of Praeger's retirement years, Elinor Praeger Goettel.

253. He was finally hired: "National Youth Administration," from the Eleanor Roosevelt Papers collection at George Washington University in Washington, D.C., http://www.gwu.edu/%7Eerpapers/about eleanor/q-and-a/glossary/nya.htm.

254. "In spite of his advanced years . . .": Record of personal interview, conducted by T. M. Brewer with Otto Praeger, March 10, 1942.

254. The new people coming: Written history of Praeger's retirement years, Elinor Praeger Goettel.

254. "To you, perhaps more . . .": Letter from Second Assistant Postmaster General Harllee Branch to Otto Praeger, May 15, 1938, and reprinted in a press release from the Post Office Department Information Service on the same date.

255. "The success of the air mail . . .": Radio transcript, radio station KFSD, May 18, 1938, interview of Mr. Otto Praeger, Major Reuben H. Fleet, and Mr. Ed Havens, in regard to early airmail, by Tom Bomar, Manager Aviation Department, San Diego Chamber of Commerce.

255. Otto Praeger's obituary: "Otto Praeger, 77, Air Mail's 'Father,'" *New York Times*, February 6, 1948.

255. When Burleson's post office: Untitled article, Burleson Archives, Center for American History, University of Texas at Austin.

255. the number of parcels delivered: "Burleson of Texas, The War Postmaster General," no byline, Burleson Archives, Center for American History, University of Texas at Austin.

256. He also struck a blow: Untitled article, Burleson Archives, Center for American History, University of Texas at Austin.

256. In January of 1921: "Burleson, Albert Sidney (1863–1937)," "The Handbook of Texas Online," http://www.tsha.utexas.edu/handbook/online/articles/view/BB/fbu38.html.

256. "The outstanding personal attributes . . .": Otto Praeger, unpublished six-page manuscript, *Burleson in Action*, undated, Praeger Family Papers.

257. Shouts of *eureka*: "Tried to Quit, Royalty Prevents," no attribution, Burleson Archives, Center for American History, University of Texas at Austin.

257. She had the political bug: Laura Burleson Negley Papers, 1880–1973, University of Texas, San Antonio Archives.

257. "As you say . . .": Letter from Albert Burleson to Josephus Daniels, February 19, 1926.

258. "The title of 'Father of the Air Mail' . . .": Praeger, *Moss from a Rolling Stone*.

258. "These are the men . . .": Otto Praeger, unpublished six-page manuscript, *Burleson in Action*, undated, Praeger Family Papers.

259. He was survived: "Burleson, Albert Sidney (1863–1937)," "The Handbook of Texas Online," http://www.tsha.utexas.edu/handbook/online/articles/view/BB/fbu38.html.

259. He held that position: Résumé, Maj. Reuben Fleet, "as reviewed by Major Reuben H. Fleet, 10/9/73."

260. Fleet invested $15,000: A loose page torn out of a calendar from the San Diego Aerospace Museum; and online biography, National Aviation Hall of Fame, www.nationalaviation.org/website/index.

260. He used his money: Online biography, National Aviation Hall of Fame, www.nationalaviation.org/website/index.

260. He knew everyone: Résumé, Maj. Reuben Fleet, "as reviewed by Major Reuben H. Fleet, 10/9/73."

260. Golem succumbed: "Fleet Secretary Injured in Crash," *Buffalo Evening News*, September 14, 1929; and letter from Consolidated Aircraft Corp. assistant general manager to Lt. Commander H. B. Sallada.

260. It was a massive relocation: "Biography—Major Reuben H. Fleet," February 22, 1967, from San Diego Aerospace Museum.

261. the B-24 Liberator: Michael L. Bowler, "Reuben Fleet: The Industrial Autocrat Who Transformed San Diego," San Diego Aerospace Museum.

261. Consolidated booked: "Biography—Major Reuben H. Fleet," February 22, 1967.

261. "Rosie the riveter": "Reuben H. Fleet (1887–1975)," San Diego Historical Society, http://www.sandiegohistory.org/bio/fleet/fleet.htm.

261. "Nothing Short of Right Is Right": "Biography—Major Reuben H. Fleet," February 22, 1967.

262. "The greatest alimony . . .": From San Diego Aerospace Museum files.

262. The settlement was for: Transcript of interview with Mrs. Dorothy Fleet, April 9, 1974.

262. He served as chairman: "Biography—Major Reuben H. Fleet," February 22, 1967.

263. "Airmail Pilot No. 1": Letter of Reuben Fleet's son Preston M. "Sandy" Fleet to Martin Harwit, executive director, National Air and Space Museum, May 23, 1994.

263. Herbert Hoover: Edgerton, *Horizons Unlimited*.

263. appointed a member of the Reorganization Committee: "U.S. Air Service," 17 (July 1933): 24, National Air and Space Museum.

264. he was named executive assistant: "Commerce Offices Put in Two Groups," *Washington Post*, June 17, 1933.

264. Following the outbreak: Bruce Morris, "Air Mail Pioneer Col. Edgerton, 77," *Miami Herald*, October 29, 1973.

264. He retired in 1945: Ibid.; and Richard Slusser, "James Edgerton, 77, Dies; Flew First Air Mail to D.C.," *Washington Star*, October 28, 1973.

264. After leaving government: Kevin Allen, "History, Benjamin B. Lipsner," National Postal Museum.

264. as "Father of the Regular Air Mail Service": Ibid.

265. "You can readily understand . . .": Letter from Benjamin Lipsner to Postmaster General Will Hayes, December 9, 1921; and Memorandum for Colonel Shaughnessy, December 13, 1921, from C. F. Egge, General Superintendent.

265. "The Air Mail Service was established . . .": Letter from Benjamin B. Lipsner to Postmaster General Walter Folger Brown, May 22, 1930, National Archives.

265. End of story: Memorandum from Second Assistant to the Postmaster General, May 28, 1930.

265. "I am unable to locate . . .": Letter from the Second Assistant Postmaster General to the Postmaster General, May 28, 1930.

266. "I continued to keep my eyes . . .": Lipsner, *The Airmail: Jennies to Jets*, pp. 190–191.

266. donated his archives: Kevin Allen, "History, Benjamin B. Lipsner," National Postal Museum.

267. Knight was the most senior pilot: Letter from Postmaster General Harry New to James H. Knight, October 7, 1927.

267. "kiwi, a funny kind of bird . . .": Capt. Jack Knight, as told to James Bassett Jr., "18,000 Hours under the Stars," *Los Angeles Times Sunday Magazine*, January 2, 1938.

268. "aviation confidence": Press release, "On the ground after twenty years," by Jack Knight, issued by United Airlines, December 1937.

268. The corporation also cornered: "Brother, Can You Spare a Billion? The Story of Jesse H. Jones," http://www.pbs.org/jessejones/jesse_ww2_3.htm.

268. "I am still going higher": Bruns, *Turk Bird*, p. 87.

268. Using connections he had made: Ibid.

269. The very stunts: Ibid., p. 89.

269. "Gardner went into a tailspin . . .": Ibid., p. 95.

269. Gardner survived the impact: Ibid., p. 96.

269. Any pilot other than: "Pilot Stories—William Hopson," http://www.postalmuseum.si.edu/airmail/pilot/pilot_old/pilot_flying_hopson_long.html.

270. Hopson was thrown: "Pilot Hopson Killed Flying the Night Mail," *Democratic Watchman*, October 26, 1928.

270. The post office launched: Ibid.

271. driving an ambulance: Interview with Katherine Stinson (Mrs. Michael Otero) by Kenneth Leish, July 1960, Stinson Family Papers.

271. reach deep into the country: "Women Aviator Seeks Mail Job," *Stars & Stripes*, January 10, 1919.

271. "I hope . . .": Letter from Mr. Judson Sayre to Katherine Stinson, January 7, 1919, Stinson Family Papers.

271. In their vows: "Aviatrix Is Now Home Designer in New Mexico," Santa Fe, New Mexico, Associated Press clipping,, no further information, Stinson Family Papers.

271. In her later years: Interview with Katherine Stinson (Mrs. Michael Otero) by Kenneth Leish, July 1960, Stinson Family Papers.

272. "I had hoped . . .": Joy Gallagher, "Early Flights Recalled By Pioneer Woman Pilot," *ABG Journal*, December 17, 1953.

273. he was named commander of the Twenty-fourth Infantry: http://usaic.hua.army.mil/history/pdfs/mwillou.pdf.

273. rising to the rank of lieutenant colonel: Ibid.

273. He then earned: online articles: Frank Kluckhohn, "Heidelberg to Madrid—The Story of General Willoughby," *The Reporter* (New York journal), August 19, 1952; http://www.maebrussell.com/Articles%20and%20Notes/charles%20Willoughby.html; and "Battle of Buna-Gona," http://en.wikipedia.org/wiki/Battle_of_Buna-Gona.

274. was roundly criticized: Kluckhohn, "Heidelberg to Madrid—The Story of General Willoughby."

274. He visited personally: http://usaic.hua.army.mil/history/pdfs/mwillou.pdf, originally from Elliott R. Thorpe, *The Intimate Account of an Intelligence Office in the Pacific, 1939–49* (Boston: Bambit, 1969), p. 95; http://home.st.net.au/~dunn/sigint/willoughby.htm, Peter Dunn, "Major-General Charles A. Willoughby, Chief of Intelligence G-2, GHQ, SWPA," 2003; and Kluckhohn, "Heidelberg to Madrid—The Story of General Willoughby."

274. He was a friendly witness: Kenneth J. Campbell, "Major General Charles A. Willoughby: General MacArthur's G-2—A Biographic Sketch," *American Intelligence Journal* 18, no. 1/2 (1998): 87–91, http://intellit.Muskingum.edu/wwii_folder/wwiifepacwilloughby.html.

274. His distinguished career: "Charles Willoughby," www.spartacus.schoolnet.co.uk/JFKwilloughbyC.htm, citing Dick Russell, *The Man Who Knew Too Much* (New York: Carroll & Graf, 1992).

275. Another westbound plane arrived around midnight: "Service Inaugurated Wednesday Night. Bellefonte Only Station Between New York and Cleveland," *Democratic Watchman*, July 3, 1925.

275. During the height: Ibid.

INDEX

Aviation Section of, 6, 97, 99
Rickenbacker rejected by, 87
Arnold, Henry "Hap," 7–8
Atlantic City, N.J., 51, 213
Atlantic Ocean, 1, 22, 45, 48, 109,
137
German U-boats in, 30, 72, 145
Lindbergh's solo crossing of, 247
automobiles, 22, 26, 31, 32, 62, 89,
98
bucket-seat roadster, 92
horses vs., 69–70
manufacture of, 97
racing, 87, 92, 93
road conditions and, 70–71
traffic jams with, 12
auto-trucks, 31–32, 37–38, 45, 63,
64, 67–71, 163
Army surplus, 70–71, 163
maintenance of, 70
aviation:
civil, 139, 178, 186
clubs in support of, 45, 72, 100,
115, 121, 148
commercial, 31, 99, 110, 178,
247
cross-country, 180
joint Army/Navy board in charge
of, 139
military, 3, 7, 52, 72–73, 175
private investment in, 247–48
U.S. spending on, 7, 8–9, 32, 100,
108, 140, 162, 180, 204–5, 217,
240, 247, 248
in World War I, 1, 2, 5–6, 8, 34,
52, 157

B-17 bombers, 261
B-36 bombers, 262
Baker, Newton, 6, 9, 35–36, 49, 72,
88, 89, 110, 139
Bald Eagle Creek, 130, 131

Baltimore, Md., 17, 67, 70, 82, 106,
169
Bane, Thurman, 2, 4
Baruch, Bernard Mannes, 151–52
Beaver, James Addams, 134
Beaver, Tom, 133, 134
Beaver Farm, 133–34, 171–72, 276
Bell, Alexander Graham, 30–31
Bellefonte, Pa., 130–35, 157, 162,
170–73, 182, 193, 197, 229–31,
269, 275–76
Brockerhoff Hotel in, 134, 173
Grange Fair in, 131–32, 157, 172
Belmont, August, 13, 14, 179
Belmont, August, II, 13–15
Army assignment of, 14
fleet and, 13, 74
racing and horse-breeding inter-
ests of, 13–15, 141, 212
wealth and prominence of, 13–14
Belmont Park Race Track, 76, 141
grandstand at, 43
horse-racing of, 212
as northern terminus of airmail
service, 12–13, 15, 16, 20, 21,
28, 43–44, 47, 51, 74, 107, 111,
125, 126, 128, 129, 151, 161,
163, 170, 187, 199–200, 212
Benedict XV, Pope, 84
Bennett, Mrs., 115–16
bicycles, 11, 45–46, 62, 63, 68
Biffle, Ira O., 168, 187, 248, 269
Bishop, Lester, 181–82
Black Death, 145
Bleriot, Louis, 93, 98, 170
Boeing, William, 259, 267
Boeing Air Transport, 267
Bolling Field, 157–58, 167–68, 223
Bonsal, Stephen, 19, 21, 47–48, 49,
85
Boonstra, Harry, 248
Boston, Mass., 36–37, 51, 67, 109